JUSTICE, THE STATE AND INTERNATIONAL RELATIONS

Justice, the State and International Relations

Leo McCarthy

First published in Great Britain 1998 by
MACMILLAN PRESS LTD
Houndmills, Basingstoke, Hampshire RG21 6XS and London
Companies and representatives throughout the world

A catalogue record for this book is available from the British Library.

ISBN 0–333–71668–X

 First published in the United States of America 1998 by
ST. MARTIN'S PRESS, INC.,
Scholarly and Reference Division,
175 Fifth Avenue, New York, N.Y. 10010

ISBN 0–312–21019–1

Library of Congress Cataloging-in-Publication Data
McCarthy, Leo Francis.
Justice, the state, and international relations /
Leo McCarthy.
p. cm.
Includes bibliographical references and index.
ISBN 0–312–21019–1 (cloth)
1. International relations.   2. Justice.   I. Title.
JZ1242.M38 1998
327.1'01—dc21   97–38379
                                                       CIP

This book is printed on paper suitable for recycling and made from fully managed and
sustained forest sources.

10   9   8   7   6   5   4   3   2   1
07 06 05 04 03 02 01 00 99 98

Printed in Great Britain by
The Ipswich Book Company Ltd
Ipswich, Suffolk

For Ellen and Michael Joseph McCarthy

Contents

Acknowledgements

Some of the people mentioned below read this book in whole or part during one of its many gestations, and it and I both benefited greatly from their comments, criticisms, and suggestions. Others have not seen the book in preparation, but have greatly influenced my thinking about political theory and international relations. My especial thanks are due, in no particular order, to Gavin Williams, Peter Pulzer, Richard Little, Sam Nohlutshungu, Chris Binns, the late John Vincent, Michael George, Daryl Howlett, Richard Gunn, Richard Bellamy, David McLellan, and Lisa Dominguez. I apologise to anyone left out who ought to have been included. Thanks also to my father, Michael McCarthy, a most excellent and patient (most of the time) proof-reader, commentator and English stylist. Thanks to everyone at Macmillan.

Without the help of these people, this book would be the worse. In fact, it would probably never have been written.

L.M.

List of Abbreviations

ASEAN	Association of South East Asian Nations
CFA	Communauté du Franc Africaine
COMECON	Council for Mutual Economic Aid
ECOSOC	Economic & Social Agency (UN)
EU	European Union
GATT	General Agreement on Tarifs and Trade
GNP	Gross National Product
IBRD	International Bank for Reconstruction and Development
IMF	International Monetary Fund
NATO	North Atlantic Treaty Organisations
OAS	Organisation of American States
OAU	Organisation of African Unity
OECD	Organisation of Economic Co-operation and Development
OPEC	Organisation of Petroleum Exporting Countries
UDI	Unilateral Declaration of Independence
UNCTAD	United Nations Conference on Trade and Development
UNESCO	United Nations Economic Social and Cultural Organisation
UNIFIL	United Nations Interventionary Force in Lebanon

Introduction

If any sense is to be made of any particular issue of international justice, whether it be the political self-determination of nationalities or other ethnic groups, the desirability of linking foreign policy to the human rights records of target states, or the sort of international resource transfers that the Brandt Report and other campaigns for a New International Economic Order once called for, we need some overall conception of principles of international justice, and of the role of the state in implementing those principles. We need to know which sorts of justice are best understood and secured within the state, and which point towards a global context for their satisfaction.

It has long seemed evident to me that the 'realist' conception of the role of the state in securing justice, and of the supposedly limited significance and effectiveness of justice-claims beyond it, is in important senses both arbitrary and inconsistent. Since the realist view of international relations more or less continues to inform the foreign policy of the Western powers (and by no means theirs only), its normative presuppositions seem an especially worthy target of criticism.

But whatever the imperfections of the institution of the state as a means of securing justice, it remains the case that the tradition of 'cosmopolitan' international theory, the greatest exponent of which was Immanuel Kant, does not lead us to a viable alternative to the system of sovereign states. This is particularly true of the more modern variants of this tradition. We shall see that the cosmopolitan tradition's depreciation of the state as a vehicle or constituency of justice is open to charges of utopianism, but more serious than this is the fact that it proceeds from a false analogy of the role of the state in domestic society with the role to be played by conjectured global political institutions. Since the spirit that created the major texts of cosmopolitan theory persists in contemporary demands for the reform of the international system via extension of the power of the United Nations, the European Union or other supranational organisations, the cosmopolitan theory of international justice appears as appropriate a target for some searching criticism as is realist theory.

By reason, then, of their historical pedigree, the range of literature represented in them, and their continued contemporary relevance, the realist and cosmopolitan traditions of international theory are the

1

ones with which we shall be principally concerned, in the earlier part of this book at least. But what of other, recent theories of justice, the state and international relations?

In the last twenty years or so, there has been a remarkable revival of interest in the traditional concerns of 'grand' political philosophy. Of particular note has been new, pathbreaking work in the areas of justice, rights and the forms of civil association.[1] It is not surprising that these developments in 'domestic' political theory should have been applied to international questions, often in fruitful and interesting ways.[2]

In the end, however, these modern approaches to the conceptualisation of the role of the state in respect of justice, and of the interstate and global dimensions of justice beyond, have also appeared unpersuasive. The international applications of concepts and doctrines whose origins lie within the traditional, 'internal' theory of the state have often been impressive in their originality and sophistication. But these efforts at the level of international political theory often set out to do more than is possible. They bring along a greater burden of explanation than can successfully be borne. The problem is that exclusive characterisations of the relationship between the state and the values of international justice cannot account for the richness, and the often paradoxical nature, of the subject matter. Something else is needed.

If in this book we turn to older traditions of the state and international justice which modern theories have so far failed to eclipse, it is to show how and why the realist and cosmopolitan traditions have been no more able to supply a satisfactory theoretical framework than have their modern successors. We shall see that the classical 'natural law' or 'society of states' understanding of international relations, an unfashionably teleological conception of the state and justice in international relations against which almost all modern theorists have turned their backs, continues to provide yet the richest source of understanding of questions of international ethics.

This is not to deny that there are substantial difficulties with natural law theory, not least the more famous epistemological ones.[3] There is little in the classical natural law tradition that reveals much about the basic conditions of the legitimacy of the modern state's authority over the individual; still less about the relationship between the justice-claims of individuals and those of collectivities, societies as well as states; and least of all about the specific content of the obligations of justice existing between states.

Despite these omissions, the premises of natural law theory go far in supplying the defects in other traditions and theories; in exactly what ways remains to be seen. In thinking about these questions, something of importance becomes clear. If developments in modern political philosophy have proven insufficient in themselves to provide a satisfying overview of our subject, they could be used in a most valuable way to supply the deficiencies of natural law theory in its classical formulation. Of particular value have been developments in the philosophical theory of human rights and of the more recent, and precise, conceptions of basic right;[4] in the theory of self-determination and the ethical status of the rights and obligations of collectivities; and in the theory of distributive justice. There is now an extensive modern literature on the theory of international law and jurisprudence which permits us to focus more exactly on the contemporary relevance of the old distinction between the Natural Law and the *jus gentium*, or positive Law of Nations, and to judge how far modern international law has the capacity to serve as a vehicle for the promotion of an international society and international justice.

In what follows we shall draw heavily on some of the most promising of these areas of literature to supplement the basic conceptions of the natural law tradition, and to offer a more expansive and at the same time more exact view of the role of the state in the context of international justice than that tradition alone provides. We shall certainly not hesitate to mix the old and the new in the theory of international relations.

Some strong claims will be made, then, for natural law theory. For all its descent from favour, it retains not only a moral profundity, but an immediacy of application to the urgent issues of international justice in which we are all in one way or another concerned, and which other, more modern and 'advanced' conceptions of international justice do not possess, however attractive they initially appear. And there is another great value to the natural law tradition: this lies in its capacity to confront the unavoidable and permanent tension that exists between ideal political theory and the contingent and imperfect value of actual political institutions, together with the anticipated costs of reforming or abolishing them. The failure to count the moral and material costs of system transformation is the main weakness of the cosmopolitan tradition; but this failure vitiates much other international theory also.

1 Justice in International Relations

The question with which we are concerned is how far the state is necessary or sufficient or even relevant as a constituency of human justice.

If answers to this question are considered as forming a continuum, at one end all questions of justice are seen as having meaning only within the state. The state is co-extensive with the special relations and obligations existing between members of a particular society, and as giving unique legal sanction to those relations; or the state is the political expression of national self-determination; or it represents in some other way the rights and interests of its people. At the other end of the continuum, questions of human rights, distributive justice and even self-determination have an independent value irrespective of whether they arise within the state or are considered globally.

Most views of the relationship between justice and the state fall between these two extremes, and avoid an 'all or nothing' conception of the state as the guarantor of justice and rights, whilst offering a more circumspect account of how far human rights or economic justice transcend the limits of the state and the special relations existing within it. We shall examine three traditions of political thought, which differently describe the relationship of the state to various forms of justice.

The realist tradition stresses the state as the principal or unique constituency of justice. International relations, including international law, are viewed as an unsuitable environment for the realisation of individual justice or human rights. Even interstate principles of justice such as self-determination and non-intervention play only a limited role in regulating states' conduct. Global or 'humanity-wide' conceptions of justice are seen as wholly out of place. The anarchic nature of international relations leaves ethical considerations with only a marginal significance.[1]

The cosmopolitan tradition, conversely, maintains that the independent sovereign state is an obstacle to justice correctly conceived. Principles of justice that international relations do support, and for the satisfaction of which nations and others groups contend, are viewed as too weak to carry universal moral weight. Individual justice and rights

4

are stressed, but these are conceived in an egalitarian sense as elements of a greater, global conception of the human good. Inasmuch as the state furthers the interests of its particular section of the human race to the exclusion of the interests of others, its moral claims are seen as illegitimate. The international environment is characterised as becoming more hospitable towards a cosmopolitan conception of justice; or it is maintained, following Kant, that 'universal right' requires that this should become the case.

The 'natural law' or 'society of states' tradition has its modern origins in the work of theorists such as Grotius and Pufendorf.[2] The state is accepted as the immediate dominant political unit, but the self-subsistent moral personality which much of political realism and the positivist tradition of international law after Vattel ascribe to it, is rejected. The moral personality of the state depends ultimately on the moral personalities of the people who compose it. Natural law is equally binding, and binding in the same form, on states as upon individuals.

The state is the means by which justice for individuals and groups is primarily realised, but the global conception of justice is retained, in the sense that the particular justice of the state is itself only a partial fulfilment of the natural law which binds all of humanity. According to the natural law tradition, the reality of international relations does not support the cosmopolitan conception of justice, nor does it justify the moral scepticism which the Hobbesian or realist vision of the international 'state of nature' engenders. The idea of an international society is compatible with the coexistence of Hobbesian and cosmopolitan elements, but it must proceed from a demonstration of the possibility of ethical principles in international relations, and argue for the state as a practically necessary, though not self-sufficient or enclosed, constituency of justice.

1.1 THE IDEA OF JUSTICE

'Just' is used both as a term of general moral approbation – a just policy is one which is morally correct – and to describe a particular apportioning of benefits and burdens, rights and duties. In this latter sense, justice connotes 'fairness'.[3] In the apportioning of such benefits and rights, the subjects of justice should be treated similarly in those respects in which they are alike, and dissimilarly in those respects in which they differ. The main stipulation, the import of the concept of justice, is that differences in characteristics between these subjects should be relevant to the differences in treatment they receive. Conversely, those characteristics in which they resemble one another should be relevant to their receiving equal treatment.[4] This is the formal criterion of justice. Is it easier to reach agreement on the formal criterion of justice than it is on the substantive criteria: what differences are to be counted as justifying unequal treatment? Aristotle's is the classic statement of this problem:

> [A] just act necessarily involves at least two terms: two persons for whom it is in fact just, and two shares in which its justice is exhibited. And there will be the same equality between the shares as between the persons, because the shares will be in the same ratio to one another as the persons; for if the persons are not equal, they will not have equal shares, and it is when equals have or are assigned unequal shares, or people who are not equal, equal shares, that quarrels and complaints break out. ... This is also clear from the principle of assignment according to merit. Everyone agrees that justice in distribution must be in accordance with merit in some sense, but they do not all mean the same kind of merit: the democratic view is that the criterion is free birth; the oligarchic that it is wealth or a good family; the aristocratic that it is excellence.... So justice is a sort of proportion....[5]

This is partly an empirical question, so far as different attributed characteristics are said to be psychological, cultural, racial, or whatever in nature. Indeed, there is seemingly no end to human ingenuity in proffering 'factual' arguments to sustain discriminatory treatment. As H.L.A. Hart has noted,

> so deeply embedded in modern man is the principle that *prima facie* human beings are entitled to be treated alike that almost universally where the laws do discriminate by reference to such matters as colour and race, lip service at least is still widely paid to this principle.[6]

Strictly, the belief in the equality (in some sense) of human beings represents more than an application of the purely formal criterion of justice. It is, at least in part, a culturally conditioned belief.[7] An entirely formalistic approach to justice in the treatment of persons seems impossible to imagine. The range of possible reasons acceptable as relevant for determining the differential treatment of persons is circumscribed, in a general sense, by the moral understanding of a society. Now, it is conceivable that there should be a society which entirely disavowed the principle that human beings have any prima facie right to equal treatment. But even in the Greek justification of slavery, that some men were naturally the instruments of others, a reason was offered for unequal treatment. To argue that such a reason is bogus, and based on false (but potentially verifiable) assumptions about human nature, is to miss the point. These arguments are intended to constitute relevant reasons for the institution of slavery.

Whilst all forms of justice are distributive in the most general sense, in that they specify the assignation of rights and duties, benefits and costs, distributive justice in Aristotle's meaning conveys both more and less than the term in its modern usage. Distributive justice 'is that which is shown in the distribution of honour or money or such other assets as are divisible among the members of the community.'[8] So distributive justice is concerned with status and recognition, as well as with the division of tangible benefits in a society. The idea of rights as criteria for distributive justice is, however, absent.

Here, it is intended to use the term 'distributive justice' in both a broader, and a narrower sense than this. The terms of the contemporary international debate inevitably concern the international redistribution of economic resources. Arguments for distributive justice, at least in the variant of it referred to generally as 'social justice', usually presuppose that the wider social interest is, at least under certain circumstances, more important than the narrower, 'contractual' rights to income or wealth on the part of individuals.

It is evident that there is a latent conflict between distributive and 'reciprocal' justice. The latter implies that obligations between parties should be fulfilled, irrespective of whether the wider good is served by the rights and obligations into which those parties have entered. Reciprocal justice also requires equal respect, for people as well as for states (the principle of sovereign equality). The principle of non-intervention is a principle of reciprocal justice. The significance of this is seen in the question whether states can make legitimate claims in their own right as the moral analogues of persons, or only as claims derivative of the rights and interests of their citizens. The claims of distributive and reciprocal justice are quite distinct. Whilst the strength of a state's claim to a greater share of global economic resources is doubtless enhanced by the existence of a high degree of domestic social justice, its claim for recognition of its sovereign rights as a state by other states is not intended as a claim whose legitimacy depends in any way on this.

This tension exists alongside another which Aristotle makes. 'Arithmetic' justice is expressed in the claim to be respected as an equal within a particular community. 'Proportionate' justice, if it is to be compatible at all with such equality, will itself incorporate a distributive element. For example, all states recognised by the United Nations are entitled to membership and votes in the General Assembly. The cost of funding this organisation, however, is met according to the means of its members: a form of proportionate justice not incompatible with respect for sovereign equality.

Canons of Distributive Justice

David Miller has elucidated the conceptual distinctiveness of, and possible conflict between, the three canons of rights, deserts and needs.[9] In domestic society, the three criteria of justice testify to this concern for the individual: the principle of rights by guaranteeing security of expectation and freedom of choice, the principle of desert by recognising the distinctive value of each person's actions and qualities, the principle of need by providing the prerequisites for individual plans of life.[10]

It seems easier to translate justice-claims based on rights or needs from the level of the individual to that of the state than to translate such claims when they depend upon the notion of desert. One of the supposed benefits of rewarding desert or merit in society is the effect of such reward on promoting future initiative and hard work on the part of the individual rewarded, or others who might emulate him. Whilst the welfare of most persons depends predominantly upon the policies of the state within which they live, global interests in trade, peace, or ecological protection require international co-operation. Can the rewarding of 'merit' displayed by states heighten this co-operation?

The experience of the 1970s suggested that attempts to tie the purported benefits of détente to improvements in Soviet domestic behaviour met with questionable success. The Final Act of the Helsinki Conference on Security and Co-operation in Europe of 1975 implicitly recognised the post-World War II territorial settlement in Europe. The quid pro quo was that the Soviets explicitly undertook to respect a wide catalogue of human rights in the seventh of the 'Principles Guiding Relations Between Participating States'. Once again, the belief that a mixture of incentives and outright cajoling could alter Soviet behaviour in this respect was belied by the facts. Helsinki monitoring groups in the Soviet Union and its satellites continued to be persecuted, whilst the Principles concerning non-intervention in the affairs of participating states were stressed by the Soviets, in response to allegations that their commitment to human rights had been merely propitiatory.

When the Soviet Union participated in international organisations, and in the conventions of international law, it asserted, in common with all states, its equal sovereign status. It is unsurprising that the Soviet Union maintained that states were the sole subjects of international law, and that sovereignty was a sufficient condition of full international personality. States, according to its view, did not come to have rights according to the morality of their domestic and external conduct. The American stress on civil and political rights, in contrast to the Soviets' professed emphasis on economic and social, collective, and non-interference rights, was thus perceived by the Soviet Union as insidious. American propagandist use of the issue of Soviet abuse of human rights suggested that Soviet commitments in this area, albeit expressed within the 'soft law' of international conventions, should be a test of the political legitimacy of the Soviet state. This amounted in the eyes of the Soviet leadership to an encroachment on sovereignty, an illegitimate interference in Soviet internal affairs. Other measures such as the 1974 Jackson–Vannik amendment, seeking to tie Soviet 'most favoured nation' status with Soviet policy on Jewish emigration, seemed to confirm this American policy.

There are other reasons to be sceptical about the idea of desert or merit in international relations. One is that it simply pushes the analogy of states and individuals too far, further than it is pushed by rights and needs. The usefulness of rewarding merit assumes certain facts of human psychology, including the desire for approbation and esteem. It is difficult to see how these facts are helpful at the level of the state. It assumes a degree of what might best be termed 'intimacy' in moral evaluation which, whilst it might conform to the facts of interpersonal psychology, seems inappropriate at the state level. Whatever moral personality we consider states to have must be derivative. States are not analogous to persons; first-order moral properties can only be ascribed to sentient beings.

The language of desert is certainly used, sometimes obliquely and sometimes directly, in international relations. The former Soviet leadership was never likely to let the rest of the world forget the role of the Soviet Union in the defeat of Nazi Germany. The United States' leaders were shocked and bemused whenever anyone failed to grasp the vital role of American policy in extending the scope of freedom and justice globally. The former South African apartheid government long berated the West for forgetting its heroic role as last bastion against godless communism. But such claims of 'merit' are made by governments to add a little extra moral weight to the imperative of respecting reciprocal rights of sovereignty, and not as the basis for independent claims.

Rights and needs remain as possible canons of international distributive justice. Legal rights are explicitly relational; they exist in so far as an individual is subject to legal provisions enacted by a competent legal authority. But moral rights, too, are often thought of as being relational. H.L.A. Hart considers that a right 'entails having a moral justification for limiting the freedom of another person and for determining how he should act'.[11] He distinguishes 'special rights' from 'general rights'. The former 'arise out of special transactions between individuals or out of some special relationship in which they stand to each other'.[12] They include promises, rights of interference previously accorded to another agent, and rights which arise from a 'mutuality of restrictions'. The latter are rights which arise within society, and form the grounding of political obligation:

> when a number of persons conduct any joint enterprise according to rules and thus restrict their liberty, those who have submitted to these restrictions when required have a right to a similar submission from those who have benefited from their submission...[T]he moral obligation to obey the rules in such circumstances is due to the co-operating members of the society, and they have the correlative moral right to obedience.[13]

General rights are prohibitions against interference, which do not depend upon some relationship between the holder of those rights and others, nor upon the character of the activity to which the rights refer. Rights of freedom of association, religious belief, and so on, are examples of general rights. They express the equal right of individuals to freedom, where principles creating special rights are not in effect. Whilst special rights created by promises may have as their objects the acquisition and transfer of physical resources, they do not include rights to welfare and subsistence, for example, which do not arise from some particular transaction or relationship between individuals.[14] Nor do these latter, 'positive' rights fall under the category of general rights. The recognition of individual freedom imposes constraints on interference, but not upon the provision of any resources, material or otherwise, upon which the exercise of that freedom depends.[15]

Need is the remaining canon of distributive justice. There are some unavoidable difficulties in distinguishing wants and needs. Both physical goods and personal opportunities once considered luxuries may become so commonplace in society that the sense of deprivation felt by people when they are unavailable is acute. The social context of needs must therefore be taken into account. So, too, must the features of individual and social psychology by virtue of which a sense of want so subjectively powerful that it becomes difficult for the individual to distinguish it from need can be artificially generated to suit the economic purposes of a consumer society. But a stricter understanding of the difference between wants and needs is still required. 'Needs' defined extensively would include the prerequisites in the way of resources and opportunities for people to pursue a 'plan of life' or to maintain a degree of self-respect. These claims can be understood at the level of the community as well as of the individual. Needs defined narrowly include whatever is necessary to basic subsistence, and to any possibility of future progress in economic or social terms.[16] The 'basic needs' approach of the World Bank, intended as a response to the assertion of rights to development or 'solidarity rights' by the Group of 77 states in the mid-seventies, embodies this definition.

If needs are to be taken as simply equivalent to the content of positive rights, this has at least not yet been shown. The existence of needs gives rise to rights, but not in such a way that the two concepts collapse into one another. The provision of needs may be constrained by shortage of resources and by the state of development of technology – the treatment of serious illnesses in the Middle Ages, for example. The need is actual whilst the right to have one's needs catered for is only potential. The right itself is ultimately grounded in a deeper right to equality of treatment and respect.[17] Indeed, it will be seen that such equality of respect necessitates the ascription to people of 'positive rights', as well as of those rights which Hart distinguishes as 'special' and 'general', and which are strictly negative in their content.

There is also a difference in epistemological status between rights and needs. Rights are qualities ascribed to people in recognition of their moral autonomy and capacity for rational action. Needs are contingent, empirical states of affairs. They are the prerequisites of agency. People may be said to have a right to have certain kinds of needs satisfied, but the two concepts must still be distinguished.

An important sense in which positive and negative rights differ is that the latter are always binding, whereas the former are only contingently so. Rights to reciprocal fulfilment of contract, or to immunity from coercive interference, are limited only by the existence of other rights. As imperative principles governing action they have a universal form. Positive rights, however, only become concrete when the means of their fulfilment are available. This is a necessary truth, because 'ought' must imply 'can', and it in no way derogates from the binding status of positive rights. The inability to satisfy needs as a result of the non-availability of resources is quite different from the neglect of those needs in consequence of a particular pattern of distribution of such resources.

The type of rights to which human need gives rise has been aptly termed 'basic rights'.[18] These are different from the rights Hart identifies as based on 'mutual limitations', the quasi-contractual rights of civil society. The comprehensive specification of rights is certainly more exhaustive than the provision of certain types of primary need; but basic rights are most important because on their satisfaction depends the possibility of defending all other rights. Since the idea of a right involves a correlative obligation on someone else's part, the existence of basic rights places responsibilities upon people outside the societies in which needs arise, and irrespective of the historical or causal relationship in which they stand as regards the plight of the needy.

The concept of basic rights will be centrally important to our theory of the state and international justice. We shall have to show what the content of those rights is, and how the pattern of distribution of correlative obligations falls on other states and societies.

Justice-claims are made by, or on behalf of, individuals, social groups, nations, states, or a putative 'community of mankind'. These different sorts of claims may come into conflict.[19] Above all, the conception of human rights (and their correlative obligations) as universal attributes of all persons threatens the logic of state sovereignty, indeed the central role of the state in mediating the moral claims of individuals and groups.

Justice and Law

If the idea of justice presupposes a common moral tradition, how far does such a moral tradition extend beyond the frontiers of the state? One way of measuring this is by reference to international law. We shall see in Chapter 4 how far it is analogous to domestic law, and how far it can be seen to reflect the emergence of a 'global justice constituency'. At this stage, a few comments on the relationship between justice and law are in order.

The classical natural law theorists distinguished between the actual, positive law of nations and the immanent, idealised natural law, maintaining that the latter was the higher. Yet Grotius, for example, saw clearly that the real relations between states, given their rival interests, could only give rise to a form of law less perfect than natural law.[20]

This regressive derivation of law from a series of deductive axioms has, of course, been largely rejected in the modern era in favour of sociological explanations of law. In Durkheim's work, for example, law reflects social relationships based upon the social division of labour. Simple, homogeneous society, with close ties of community, kinship and mutual dependency manifested a form of social solidarity which he describes as 'organic'. Modern, heterogeneous societies engender more flexible, voluntary forms of co-operation, based on a high degree of division and specialisation of labour, and manifest 'mechanical' solidarity.[21] These types of solidarity also express distinct relations between the individual as a moral agent, and the ethos of the wider society, the *conscience collective*. Law mirrors the transition from one form of society to another, specifically in shifting from prohibitive and punitive rules, to laws of contract (civil law).

For Marx, law is the manifestation of social relations determined by the organisation of production within a society. It exists, according to Marx, to serve the interests, and to defend the rights and property, of the dominant class in society. It belongs, along with religion, philosophy, political and economic thought, and culture generally, to the realm of the superstructure, determined by the relations of production in a society.[22]

These conceptions of law all agree that it proceeds from, and reflects, a particular order. It relates to specific relations between states, or between groups and individuals within states. It also expresses, to a lesser or greater degree, a particular conception of justice within a society. The efficacy of law in a society and the degree of social cohesion present in that society are partly determined by how well law does express this conception; that is, how just laws are seen to be. It is not contradictory to hold both that it is possible to have an a priori and non-relativistic understanding of justice, and that our particular conceptions of justice have a social and cultural origin.

Unless an especially alien entire system of law is imposed upon a society from outside, say through conquest, a durable legal system must come to reflect important social conceptions of justice.

In practice, law does more than this; it contributes to order generally, as well as upholding a particular order, by providing an authoritative means for determining questions of justice. Justice as a legal concept is of its nature less contestable than justice as a moral concept. Law provides, in principle, procedural criteria for deciding questions of justice.

1.2 SCEPTICISM ABOUT JUSTICE IN INTERNATIONAL RELATIONS

It is one thing to produce an abstract outline of the concept of justice; it is another to show that it is of any practical application to international relations, a sphere considered by many writers to be fundamentally inhospitable to any claims of justice. Powerful traditions of scepticism about international justice have come down to us in the literature of international politics from Thucydides to the modern realists, via Machiavelli, Hobbes, Rousseau and Hegel. We shall have to meet the force of these objections in order to make any progress, and for that reason much of this book is concerned with the refutation, or at least moderation, of the claims of international moral sceptics. But their case is at times a powerful one, and it serves to bring our subject more sharply into focus if we now rehearse some of the main arguments against almost any idea of international justice.

One form of scepticism is that the state as a sovereign entity and as an autonomous distributive sphere is an insurmountable obstacle in the way of international or global justice. For example, demands for distributive justice may be made generically, on behalf of the 'Third World'. Collective action in pursuit of such demands may be undertaken by a group of states bound together by economic interest (although the demands of the Group of 77 made through the UN Commission for Trade and Development (UNCTAD) for a New International Economic Order have been, at best, marginally successful), but the identity of states is not submerged in these collective demands. States are party to trade agreements, to bilateral or multilateral aid packages, to arrangements seeking to defend or contain the operations of multinational corporations. Most importantly, the leaders of states claim that external attempts to affect the distribution of resources within their territory – for example, the tying of aid to agreements by recipient governments to sponsor particular projects, or to produce benefits for particular sectors of society – amount to violations of their sovereignty.

Conversely, donor governments may claim that aid, or beneficial trade agreements, are not rights of the recipients, but sovereign acts on the part of the donors. By appealing to the same principle of freedom of action, the political expression of state sovereignty, they may seek to justify the tying of aid to purchases by the recipient states of the donor country's goods. The respective claims to sovereignty clash with one another, and with the claims for international distributive justice. Yet states insist that respect for state sovereignty remains also a requirement of international justice. This conflict may become especially acute when international resource transfers are linked to the adoption of particular development strategies.

Claims for distributive justice are partly collective claims, and are related to the familiar contention that the concession of the right of self-determination only has meaning if the material conditions for at least a basic communal life are met. But they also come under the rubric of claims for 'human justice', in that the provision of subsistence, shelter, and so on must proceed from a recognition of those rights and duties ascribed to individual persons. However these claims are meant, the leaders of states insist on their unique competence to determine how resources should be distributed domestically.

When what Hedley Bull calls 'a conspiracy of silence entered into by governments about the rights and duties of their respective citizens'[23] is on occasion broken, this does not mean that governments enter into any commitment to have the internal or external legitimacy of their own authority, or of the nature of their states, judged according to their observation of human rights. The documents which enshrine principles of human justice and the recognition of the whole range of individual rights – the Universal Declaration of Human Rights, the European Convention for the Protection of Human Rights and Fundamental Freedoms, the International Covenants on Civil and Political Rights, and on Economic and Social Rights – have states as their exclusive signatories. Whilst the first two are binding upon members of the United Nations and the Council of Europe respectively, the last two Conventions are ratified by states generally on a strictly voluntary basis.

Human rights have largely remained within the orbit of the state; yet there are countervailing tendencies, suggesting the international recognition of human rights and duties against the sovereignty of nation-states. Developments such as the Nuremberg War Crimes Tribunal, the jurisdiction of the European Court of Human Rights in cases in which domestic law violates, in its view, those rights specified in the European Convention which established the Court, the investigations at The Hague into the conduct of alleged war criminals in former Yugoslavia, and the international influence of Amnesty International, represent rivals to the sole voice of the state on questions of individual justice and human rights.

Governments that insist on the general inviolability of sovereignty may defend violations of it in certain circumstances. The Organisation of African Unity repeatedly called for the cultural, economic and political isolation of South Africa, and demanded that its members should not recognise the latter as a fellow sovereign state. But if military intervention by the neighbours of apartheid South Africa had been at all feasible, perhaps then intervention would have found acceptance among most of the states of black Africa.

Distributive justice is to be distinguished from 'reciprocal justice' which requires equality of treatment based on some particular relationship that exists between parties, irrespective of the common good. The claim by governments to sovereign equality in a world of great disparities in wealth and power between states is such a demand.

Claims of state sovereignty can be interpreted as taking an absolute priority over the demands of distributive justice. This primacy of the 'national interest' is a key tenet of the realist tradition of international relations. Conversely, distributive justice may be taken to override sovereignty. Such an approach may be found in the tradition of international political thought that might be called 'cosmopolitan' or 'universalist'.

Sovereignty, at least in the sense that it involves unconditional rights of disposal over resources by the state, or by sub-national organisations or individuals acting with the authority of the state, may be accommodated with principles of international distributive justice through a process of mutual limitation. Two versions of how such a limitation or accommodation may be effected are distinguishable. One version justifies the continued existence of the state; what the other says about the state is more ambiguous.

The first version accepts the sovereign and independent qualities of the state, but maintains that states are nevertheless morally bound to aid each other – although not necessarily at the risk of jeopardising their own continued, independent existence. The coexistence of legitimate state sovereignty and definite moral obligations between states implies, as we shall argue later, the existence of an international society with at least a minimum consensus on principles governing international conduct. It corresponds broadly to the perspective developed by the founders of the 'natural law' tradition – Suarez, Grotius, Pufendorf – of a society of states, bound in their relations with one another not only by actual laws proceeding from their respective sovereign wills but by 'natural law'. By this is meant, roughly, principles of conduct necessary for a socially co-operative existence and the preservation, through the community, of life, property, and so on.

This tradition of thought has concerned itself with all forms of mutual co-operation and assistance, in peace and in war, between states, rather than with the narrower question of distributive justice in the sense of resource transfers or economic aid. The different perspectives within this tradition on the relationship of sovereignty and the necessary obligation of states towards one another are nevertheless illuminating for this analysis. They go to the very heart of the question of the justification of the state as the mediator of human relationships at the global level: the question of the justification of state sovereignty. It will appear later that this question is intimately bound up with that of international distributive justice.

The second version of the accommodation of sovereignty and international justice insists that the moral character of the state and the legitimacy of its claims against other states, for example the right to remain free from external intervention, depend on the variously specified relations existing between a state and its citizens, or more simply on the conditions of social justice within it.

On this view, ably defended by Charles Beitz,[24] attempts to justify the internal aspect of sovereignty by the use of such devices as the 'social contract' are specious; such fictions tell us nothing about actual state–society relations obtaining within a state.[25] Only by virtue of just domestic principles can the internal coercive order of the state be judged, from a normative point of view, to be qualitatively different from the external coercion of outside intervention, economic dependence, and so on. Only individuals possess moral autonomy, that is, constitute ends in themselves. Therefore, the moral autonomy of a state and the legitimacy of its claims vis-à-vis other states must always be contingent upon its internal respect for persons. Social justice is treated as an index of that respect.

When it comes to the definition of those principles of social justice, their scope cannot be limited to the sphere of the nation-state. States have become increasingly interdependent in economic terms. The growth of trade, the extreme sensitivity of national economies to fluctuations in demand, output, prices in other economies, the 'internationalisation' of production achieved by multinational corporations: all these developments suggest production to be an international co-operative process. If the distribution of benefits and burdens accruing from this process occurs on a global scale, then the state ceases to be the appropriate sphere of distributive justice, and international distributive principles come into operation, at least as regards that increment of the global economic product attributable to co-operation between states.

In this perspective, not only is the sovereignty of a state, in the sense of its moral, as opposed to its legal, international personality, contingent upon principles of domestic justice, but the right of the state to exercise that sovereignty in the disposition of national wealth is limited by principles of international justice. This theory of political sovereignty seeks to provide a way to relate human justice, at the level of the observance of individual rights and at the level of social justice domestically, to the claims of the state for just treatment by other states, in accordance with its claims to be acting in defence of those rights internationally. It seeks to justify the existence of state sovereignty, but only by reference to global principles of justice.

But the justification of the state purely in terms of domestic social justice and international distributive principles is a precarious one. There may be no possible justification of the state at all on these grounds; the state may assume the marginal role to which it is confined by the cosmopolitan tradition.

Order and Justice as Conflicting Values in International Relations

Realists believe that international order is the necessary precondition of all other desirable goals, including justice. The overwhelming need to preserve order in the international system, whilst it has always been felt, became most acute with the growth of the modern states system in Europe after the Peace of Westphalia in 1648.

The balance of power has served to create conditions of minimum stability within a system of states lacking any higher authority or sanctions-enforcing body. The medieval unity of Christendom was gone, and the Reformation had eclipsed the common spiritual authority. Although the Hobbesian state of nature might be less terrible for states than for individual men, this only meant that the lack of an overarching sovereign authority over states was less calamitous than it would be in a society of men without such authority. Order was still the absolute prerequisite of co-operative existence between states. If the Leviathan state were to be an effective magisterial power within a state, it must preserve its sovereignty externally.

Although order may be the primary good for the states system as a whole, states must seek to increase national power as a means of safeguarding their security and of furthering their economic or territorial ambitions, thus constantly threatening international order. Security cannot be ensured by co-operation among states, so the sceptical argument goes, in the absence of any higher authority to enforce compliance with any such arrangements. Therefore, by reciprocal logic, other states must seek to augment their national power as a means of self-protection. Security becomes essentially a 'zero-sum' competition. It is for this reason that the need for a mechanism to preserve order arises.

The balance of power has served to prevent the acquisition of power by one state, or by an alliance of states, such as to threaten hegemony in the states system within which it is active, thereby threatening the continued independent existence of rival powers. But whilst the balance of power has preserved both the sovereign states system from either anarchy or hegemony, and preserved as a consequence sovereignty as the general principle of that system, in no way does it guarantee the sovereignty of any particular state.

Whilst the balance of power could thereby preserve the independence and sovereignty of small states, the guarantee of sovereignty in any particular instance was of secondary importance to the preservation of order. The balance of power guarantees sovereignty almost as an afterthought. If rivalry between the great European powers has safeguarded the sovereignty of the various small principalities of Europe, it has also led to the extinguishing of sovereignty, as it did in the Partitions of Poland in 1772, 1793 and 1795–6.

Sceptics about international justice see order as the necessary condition of social life.[26] The defence of those rights with which justice is concerned depends upon the maintenance of order, and order rests ultimately upon the coercive order of the state. Domestic sovereignty, in the forms of government and law, is the guarantor of that order which is a necessary, but not sufficient, condition of justice. In addition, those social goods to which rights and duties are attached are enjoyed (where they are enjoyed at all) by individuals within states. Individuals are only marginally recognised as subjects of international law; it is to the state they must turn for protection of their rights.

It is argued that there is a disjunction between political and ideological influence in the United Nations and the responsibility for the maintenance of international order which must lie principally with the militarily and economically strongest states. This responsibility was recognised in the UN Charter, but the role of the General Assembly is said by its conservative and realist critics to have exceeded what was originally intended, and to have usurped the pivotal role of the major states.

It still remains the case that the formal equality of states as members of the United Nations in no way alters the facts of great inequalities of power among them. UN forces are provided largely by the more powerful states. Although any police action must be authorised by the Security Council, there is a clear danger that powerful states will employ Security Council Resolutions to add an aspect of international legitimacy to projects of intervention which would have been undertaken anyway out of pure self-interest. Conversely, powerful states may refuse to commit military forces where it might prima facie seem that the most major issues of justice and rights are at stake. We might compare the Gulf War of 1991 with the United States' attitude to intervention in Bosnia. In any case, the absolute right of veto of any of the five Permanent Members of the Council – the UK, USA, Russia, France and China – contrasts sharply with the principle of one state–one vote in the General Assembly, in which, of course, developing and Non-Aligned states have a majority.

Perhaps inevitably, the major Western powers, especially the United States, have shown impatience towards the General Assembly and the UN agencies, particularly UNESCO. At one time the former Soviet Union felt, with some justification, that the United States and its allies sought to use the General Assembly as a vehicle for anti-Sovietism. And with the increase in the 1950s and 1960s of Third World, Communist and Non-Aligned members of the United Nations, it became the turn of the Western powers to feel resentment and lack of confidence in an institution for whose funding they remained largely responsible, and whose military capacity they largely provided.

It is the usual response of governments meeting any sort of concerted opposition to their policies to retreat into the hard shell of sovereignty, and to object to the 'interference' of opposing states or transnational organisations. Certainly, criticisms of the Western powers, and the resentment among them which this has engendered, is not new, nor is this response. In the early years of the United Nations' existence, the United States fell foul of it over its intervention in Guatemala, as did Britain over its refusal to supply the Committee on Information with political details about its colonies, whilst France walked out of the General Assembly in 1955 after the latter attempted discussion of Algeria. Britain and France both claimed that these were matters of national sovereignty. The United States claimed that the Organisation of American States (which, of course, it dominates) was the appropriate body in which to raise questions of US–Guatemalan relations.

These examples suggest that the dictates of order and justice may be incompatible, and that the divergent interests of states will lead them to assign different priority between the two.[27] The realist perspective suggests that the concept of international justice is actively subversive of international order. In a world where there is such little agreement on principles, it is argued, to proceed as though this were not so is dangerous. By assuming a greater compatibility between international order and international justice than exists, the risk is run of undermining even those minimum conditions of both that do exist.

The preference of states (or, more accurately, of dominant elites within them) that benefit from the preservation of order at the expense of change is in itself no demonstration that order has an intrinsically higher value than justice. 'Order' implies, at least, pattern, regularity, predictability, a degree of stability, the absence of which qualities in a society precludes the possibility of organised social life. It also implies a substantive content of order; things are not merely arranged, they are arranged in a certain way. Rights and obligations are respected, resources are distributed, interests are attacked or defended, in particular ways. Any particular qualitative order can therefore be described as just or unjust. And any order (in the first, abstract, sense) that is more than purely coercive must enshrine at least some just principles if it is to be durable. Another way of putting this is that the particular order obtaining must be sufficiently just to sustain order generally. Only on this condition will states or persons respect or value international order. At the same time, the willingness of a state to disrupt international order to achieve an objective to which it attaches a higher value need not imply repudiation by that state of order generally. Some degree of order, in the first sense, is likely to be a condition of its enjoying its success.

The Absence of Shared Moral Values

A third source of scepticism about international justice is the supposed lack of shared moral and political values between states that is
seen to vitiate attempts to create a more just or harmonious international system.[28] Indices of the existence of an international society
would include respect for international law, common diplomatic practices, or binding principles of the conduct of trade and economic
exchange, and these are held to be absent, or at best uncertain in
practice.

Political values are seen to be defined in increasingly nationalistic
terms.[29] In the age of mass popular political ideologies – democratic
and totalitarian – the particular social and political values and institutions of a nation become identified with universal values, national
interests with the interests of humanity as a whole. In his book *Politics
Among Nations*, Hans Morgenthau identifies in this trend the undermining of both the concept and the reality of international society,
proceeding from the time of the French Revolution. The persistence
of international conflict, the impossibility of reconciling differing
interests by reference to a commonly accepted set of principles, and
the futility of trying to promote justice or rights outside the confines
of a particular national society are regular themes of this critique.

The idea of an international society in which strict ethical principles
bind states in their relations first fell into disrepute long ago.

Vattel argued in the eighteenth century that relations between states
were governed only by 'voluntary law'; no mutual obligations extended beyond the point where the safety or the vital interests of the
state itself were threatened.[30] These relations were constituted instead
by reciprocal acts of sovereign will. States were, in their relations with
each other, analogous to persons, most importantly in the sense that
they constituted moral ends in themselves. They, and not individuals,
were the exclusive subjects of international society.

This doctrine, developed by the positivist tradition of international
law and which continues to influence the realist school, presaged the
end of the idea of an ethical international community. Ian Brownlie
has argued, in the case of British treaty making, that even until
the mid-nineteenth century, arrangements could be made with a
wide variety of political entities:

First, there was no regional or cultural limitation on recognition of
personality in international relations. Secondly, there was no

emphasis placed upon the formal criteria of 'statehood'. The legal doctrine of the time reflected this state of affairs. It followed that the existence, the sovereignty, of a state did not depend upon the recognition of other powers.[31]

However, legal doctrine from the second half of the nineteenth century was far less liberal:

> Personality in the new doctrine depended upon recognition by the European States and recognition was not dependent upon any objective criteria. Statehood became a more important concept, and was associated with political thinking about 'nations', but in the law of nations the matter of definition was of no real significance: recognition, as the political stamp of approval, appeared to take care of the problem of definition.[32]

The era of the supremacy of the European states system produced stringent if rather inexact criteria for admission to full statehood. This recognition depended upon there being a political system within a fixed territory, and more generally upon the ability of a candidate for recognition of statehood being able to perform the obligations of statehood, according to a European prescription of what was involved in this.

If states were the only subjects of international relations, and of international law, then the rights of nations existed only in so far as they had attained statehood. In the sixteenth century, however, Franciscus de Vitoria had argued that Spanish settlers were bound by principles of natural law in their dealings with South American Indians, despite the fact that the latter were clearly not organised as states in the European sense of the term.[33] He denied specifically that the settlers could, by appealing to papal authority, make war on the Indians in order to convert them to Christianity. Grotius, too, whilst distinguishing between natural law and the actual law binding states in their relations with one another – the 'Law of Nations' – had made individual men the ultimate subjects of natural law, and consequently of the international system.[34] All this seemed a very far cry from the conception of international society prevalent during the ascendancy of the European states system.

The classification by international lawyers of peoples as 'civilised', 'barbarian' and 'savage' persisted into the late nineteenth century.[35] Beyond the European states system lay those nations of the periphery, China, Persia or the Ottoman Empire, accorded honorary membership of the club of states so far as trade or military interest required recognition. Even then, the lack of a common culture or of common institutions between these states and the main European states system was such as to preclude any sense of shared membership of an international society. In any case, this represented the limit of the states system, beyond which lay only 'savage' peoples, having none of those rights to statehood, or even nationhood, claimed by Europeans. These parts of the globe – Africa, South and South-East Asia, Australasia, South America – were to be colonised for the benefit of civilised nations. Obligations to these peoples arose only from Christian piety, and not from any recognition of their potential claims to statehood, or of the need to 'prepare' them for it. Indeed, the rights of individuals in what was once called the Third World were affirmed, with the gradual abolition of slavery, up to a century before their collective rights to statehood, or at least to a degree of self-determination and political independence, began to be acknowledged. The idea that there existed even a fledgling international society outside the charmed circle of European (and more latterly North American) states, in which political principles had either application or relevance, developed only slowly.

Diplomats from the 'civilised' European states shared common outlooks, values, codes of honour, and backgrounds; predominantly, of course, aristocratic. The minute observation of protocol and ceremony reflected and reinforced commonality of ethics and mores. This cosmopolitan approach to international relations re-created an element of homogeneity in an international society in which the sense of belonging to the larger whole of Christendom was gone, replaced by religious cleavages across the frontiers of the new states.[36] But if the rulers of states dealt with each other on the basis of shared values and commonly understood rules, political power was still the goal of their mutual competition. Common standards for the conduct of diplomacy hardly amount to agreement between states on questions of morality or political principles. Such a consensus on values as there was in European international society could not withstand the threat of revolutionary doctrine spreading across Europe after 1789, or the growth of rampant nationalism, or the growth of mass revolutionary movements.

The full development of international society was completed by the independence of the former colonies of the European powers. Self-determination as a right displaced the formal criteria for international recognition of states. Colonial principles of dependent status and responsibility were rejected. In the process, the principle of sovereignty became ever more closely associated with territoriality; specifically, with territorial integrity. France, for example, was forced into the subterfuge that Algeria was actually a part of metropolitan France. France, like Britain and, later, Portugal, lost her empire because of economic and military inability to maintain it rather than through a revolution in moral perspective. This last example shows, at least, how rapidly a great European power could lose confidence in its ability to appeal to principles of sovereign right previously well understood among the European powers.

A Political Philosophy of International Relations?

There is a further objection in the way of the development of any theory of international justice. This is the assumption, until recently quite generally held, that the theory and practice of international relations, and the principles and concepts of political philosophy, were mutually exclusive and incompatible. Again, the dominance of the realist perspective in international theory and practice largely explains this circumstance and the long-time absence of any substantial body of literature on the political philosophy of international relations.

The features of international anarchy that realism identifies as the determinants of international ethics have excluded the concepts of political philosophy from international relations theory. The transfiguration of the natural law tradition of the 'society of states' into what has been termed the 'morality of states',[37] that is, the direct analogy of states and persons in terms of their rights and other moral capacities, has also encouraged such an exclusion.

The central concepts of political philosophy – justice, rights, liberty, equality, democracy – have been developed within the context and confines of the state. In turn, questions about the legitimacy of state power, questions which have always been at the centre of political philosophy, have been articulated in terms of these concepts. The ethical problems of international relations, however, extend beyond the compass of the state.[38]

Self-determination as an ethical issue does address itself to contractarian problems concerning the nature of state authority, and also to the rights of communities, and possibly also of individuals. At this level, its dimensions can be comprehended by 'traditional' political philosophy. But when self-determination is introduced as a principle of justice which binds the relations of states, and which requires states to allow secession of part of their territories, or to grant political independence to their colonies, issues of authority and legitimacy are raised that are not entirely resolvable in terms of the relations of states to their peoples.

Again, intervention, which we may understand as the use of coercion (ranging from diplomatic or economic sanctions to military invasion) by a state or group of states against another with the intention of changing the domestic policy or political constitution of a state against the will of its leaders, presents problems for political philosophy. Intervention, especially when defended on humanitarian grounds, certainly raises questions about the legitimacy of the state, but these questions are sometimes posed outside the state; they are not resolved in terms of its relation to civil society.

Above all, moral questions of direct concern to individuals, such as human rights or social justice, have been seen as concerning exclusively the relations of the state to the individual or group. The idea that human rights and distributive justice are legitimate subjects for international, and even global concern, is a relatively recent one in international relations and in international law.

In 'domestic' political theory (except for anarchism), the concepts 'state' and 'society' have usually entailed each other. Realism denies the existence of an international society, where 'society' is understood to imply states co-existing in mutually recognised interdependence, according to common and binding rules and with a significant degree of shared moral and cultural understanding. In the dominant realist perspective the absence of an international society and the impossibility of a world state are concomitants.

One of our central concerns is to show that questions about justice and rights, which address the legitimacy of state authority, are not possible only within the state. The concepts of international justice raise still more important questions, such as the question of what is essential about the state in securing justice and rights, and whether this might be done better by some alternative institution. Understanding the moral relationship between the state and its citizens is necessary to the understanding of the moral relations between states, and to the rights and needs of people in other states – as well as to those of people effectively excluded from the states system, such as refugees. So, far from the concepts of political philosophy being irrelevant to the terms of international relations discourse, it will be seen that the moral justification of the state in respect of its own citizens is itself impossible to resolve without both an adequate theory of human rights in and beyond the state, and a theory of distributive justice as a counterpart to distribution within the state.

But if the concepts of political philosophy are at best partial and restricted when separated from their international dimension, the prospects for international justice still depend upon there being a practical recognition of their applicability in world politics. Alongside the development of a theory of the state and international justice, it will be important for us to show that the normative elements of a society are sufficiently evident in the relations of states for it to be possible to speak in practical terms of an international society as a context for justice-claims.

1.3 CONTENDING VIEWS OF JUSTICE AND THE STATE

The realist belief that justice-claims have no inherent meaning outside the state, and that the state in providing the unique validating context for such claims comes thereby to acquire moral autonomy, or to constitute, in Hegel's terms, a self-subsistent ethical order, will be found to be untenable.

The cosmopolitan tradition, in contrast, points to the state, or at least to the sort of states characteristic of the contemporary international system, as an obstacle to human justice. We shall see in Chapter 3 that this tradition misunderstands the role of modern states in securing both justice and order, and further underestimates the value of a system of independent states in offering possible refuge against gross injustice in any particular state. It will be seen also that an unjustifiable 'social contract' analogy is drawn between the legitimisation of the authority of the state in its relationship to its citizens and the projected legitimisation of a global authority. The problem of unequal representation of classes and other organised interests within the modern state is expected by many cosmopolitan theorists to be overcome in the case of a global authority or federation. However, no good reasons are offered as to why this should be possible, and a critical ambiguity as to what an authority rivalling or superseding that of the state would look like, and how it would be able to achieve a higher degree of justice, is present in cosmopolitan theories.

One view is that the source of the moral autonomy of the state lies in the extent of its promotion of domestic social justice.[39] All other claims of states, such as to a 'fairer share' of global resources, are to be judged according to how far their satisfaction would promote social justice. This form of 'moral cosmopolitanism' does not require the political structures advocated by other cosmopolitan theories, but it does make the justification of the state as a discrete political institution a contingent one. Being a member of a state confers no special (moral) privileges. Obligations of justice exist outside the state with the same imperative force as those within it.

Three objections to this position can be noted here. First is that the argument from social justice seems to suggest a varying degree of moral autonomy of states, and this seems strikingly at odds with the recognition of sovereignty as an indivisible principle that is the central norm of international relations. Second, we must distinguish between domestic social justice as a legitimating criterion of the external claims of states, and social justice and rights in their positive sense as values secured (where they are secured) through the legal and political institutions of states. The preservation of those institutions as a necessary (though certainly not sufficient) condition of justice and rights may also justify the principle of non-intervention as an international norm. It might still be possible to specify circumstances in which states lost the moral right to non-interference, but it seems more plausible to think that this would be as a result of their coming positively to menace the rights of their citizens, and not simply according to some sliding scale of social justice existing within them. Last, to posit individuals as moral agents bearing certain rights intrinsically does not imply that social justice is no more than the aggregate of individuated rights. As we shall see, certain collective rights that defy the essentially pragmatic or utilitarian approach to social justice common to many cosmopolitan theories may point to a justification of political independence along quite different lines.

Another view makes the sovereignty of the state, and the continued existence of a system of such states, the primary international norms. The state is seen as the focus of other moral and political demands and aspirations: democratic institutions, modernisation and economic development, the securing of human rights, national and cultural autonomy, the avoidance of global structures of domination, and so on.[40]

How is the authority of the state to be justified? It may be pointed out that contractarian rights-based theories of the state serve neither to explain the historical origins of actual states, nor the true role of states in the positive stipulation (and denial) of human rights. The claims of rights and of sovereignty appear to be, at least potentially, opposed to one another – most especially in time of war.

The reconciliation of this antagonism is, according to this view, impossible from within the perspective that makes human rights prior to the state, or that which views the state as the progenitor of all rights. Instead, a 'constitutive theory' of rights is offered.[41] This has its roots in Hegelian political theory, and argues that rights must be understood as specific relations between individuals, and their content and inner nature specified in relation to the practices and institutions through which these relations are mediated. Rights and institutions are said to imply each other. Purely 'egoistic' rights characterise civil society as considered in separation from the state: the rights of one man appear as irksome constraints on the freedom of another. Such rights are transcended in the political form of the state (for Hegel, the conjunction of human freedom and reason). Indeed, it is as members of a state, as participants in the matrix of mutual obligations and restraints embodied in the state, that individuals come to be 'constituted' as such, and come to recognise themselves and one another as bearers of rights. Crucially, both the individual's sense of his own individuality and his capacity to bear rights are constituted within definite practices and institutions. The apparently divergent logics of sovereignty and of rights are thus reconciled when they are viewed as existing in a dialectical relationship. It is, on such a view, not only mistaken but incoherent to ask which comes first.

Problems arise with this view also. The idea that the content of demands for different sorts of international justice point towards the preservation of the sovereign state as a *conditio sine qua non* must be understood differently in its legal-political and normative contexts. Individuals and groups look first to the state to satisfy their rights and other demands, but the discourse of human rights and global distributive justice overtly challenges the state's moral competence to determine the content of those claims without reference to universal principles taking precedence over the particular interests of the state and its citizens. Certain claims of international justice that seem most specifically focused on the state – such as self-determination and non-intervention – may be misleading in this focus. The demands for autonomy expressed in claims for self-determination may be satisfied by less than full political independence, whilst the case for non-intervention is often defended with reference to the rights of autonomy of communities, and not simply as a corollary of de facto sovereignty.

The constitutive conception of individuality is said to offer a synthesis between the logics of sovereignty and rights, but it remains as murky as ever in its modern formulation. Political and civil rights indeed form a vital measure of the individual's self-understanding, in so far as this in turn derives from his position within society. But to say that it is the participation of an individual that alone constitutes his authentic individuality seems obscure and implausible. So, too, does the notion that it is his participation within the state that is the source of the individual's ethical reality. Perhaps the rights that the individual enjoys as a member of a state are 'superior' in some way to the egoistic and antagonistic rights of civil society; but if the constitutive approach is to amount to anything more than an overcomplicated way of saying that the state is the condition of individual rights, in other words is morally prior to the individual, then the intrinsic moral capacity of the individual to be a bearer of rights, even of the special kind of rights secured by the state, must be established. Individuals are no more disqualified as moral agents in the absence of the state than they are deprived of individuality or self-awareness.

On another view, international society and the law which gives normative expression to it lack the aspect of 'purposive association' which is (or may be) a characteristic of states, and are better regarded as forms of 'practical association'.[42] In other words, whilst the state may be considered as an association for the promotion of common ends, including the securing of substantive rights in accordance with some overall scheme of social justice, equality or other objective, international society is better described in terms of institutions and rules providing for a degree of coexistence between states, and for the reconciliation of conflicts encountered in the promotion of societies' diverse ends. The possibility of a common moral discourse suggests, on this view, the possibility of disagreement as well as agreement; it does not require any degree of consensus on substantive moral goals. Morality is concerned with limits on the pursuit of ends, rather than with the specification of the ends themselves. This is seen to be especially true of morality as applied to the affairs of international society, characterised as it is by the greatest diversity of values and beliefs.

International law is, on this view, a framework 'of restraint and coexistence among those pursuing divergent purposes', embodying 'certain common standards of conduct'.[43] Any prospect of either international law or international morality acting as a measure (or promoter) of common standards or goals in a world of profound cultural, political and ideological diversity and conflict is held to be a naive one. Whilst international moral discourse may provide a source of criticism and even reform of elements of international law, both the law and the moral precepts of international society are seen to constitute 'authoritative practices' regulating the mutual accommodation between states of their goals and the means they use to pursue them. Where these two authoritative practices conflict, there is no simple way to determine which gives way. Legal right and moral right are seen as two quite distinct things.

This conception has the merit of demonstrating that the idea of international society does not depend for its validity on the existence of a high degree of ideological, political or cultural consensus. The central function of international law is indeed to regulate the relations of states in such areas as diplomatic exchanges, air and sea navigation, access to natural resources in international waters and the regulation of international trade where no such consensus need be assumed to exist. However, it does not show that no degree of consensus on substantive, as opposed to purely procedural, common purposes need exist for international society to be properly so described, nor that no such consensus exists.

We can to some extent distinguish the state from the international political order as a sphere of purposive action, or action directed towards common goals. The exclusivity, and usual effectiveness, of the state's authority are important in this, whilst the greater ideological and cultural diversity of international society is compounded by the absence of any central authority. For this reason, agreement on procedural and co-operative principles is likely to be easier to obtain than is agreement on substantive ones. But this distinction should not be overstated. The practical/purposive distinction is not equivalent to one of agreement/non-agreement. Political action may be purposive without specific agreement – let alone consensus – both within the state and in international society. This is true of much taxation and public expenditure; internationally it is true where states are constrained to obey laws and the moral precepts embodied in those laws in a way that cannot meaningfully be considered as 'voluntary', particularly when those laws predate the state itself. At the same time, particular states and international society as a whole may wholly fail to reflect in their actions values and beliefs widely held by governments – and by individuals.

It is generally correct to say that international law is both less equivocal and more practically effective in regulating, say, international shipping than in defining principles of non-intervention or self-determination, let alone in deciding on particular cases of the violation of either principle. But such principles do have a place in international law (as we shall see in Chapter 4). The problem lies in making a distinction between procedural rules of international society and rules for the pursuit of common substantive goals. The principle of non-intervention is on one level a procedural one – it preserves, though not unfailingly, order among states lacking a common superior. But it is also a substantive normative principle; its defenders maintain that it is a good thing, a desirable state of affairs, that people within sovereign states be left to choose their own social and political arrangements. It might be retorted that non-intervention is not valued as a substantive goal, but only because it allows people to pursue substantive goals dependent upon it. But all principles – legal, moral and social – are 'procedural' in an ultimate but trivial sense. Respect for rights enables people to pursue their self-chosen projects – and to stay alive. This freedom from intrusion helps people pursue their happiness. If nothing short of consensus on why it should be desirable that people be happy were to count as demonstrating substantive agreement, then the issue ends in absurdity.

It is difficult to imagine what a common international discourse would consist of without some agreement about common substantive ends. To agree on what a human right is involves acceptance of the need to uphold the conditions for its fulfilment. To recognise human rights at all is to recognise them as moral imperatives, for they would be conceptually incoherent without this imperative form.

The sway of moral criticism over international law may well be limited, and so also may be the role of international law as a vehicle for international justice. But the characterisation of international society in either its moral or its legal dimensions as a sphere of purely prudential co-operation without agreement on any substantive values is premature. Law, like morality, is concerned with ends as well as limits.

1.4   THE NATURAL LAW TRADITION AND INTERNATIONAL RELATIONS

Each of these approaches to the state and international justice assumes the inadequacy or the irrelevance of the natural law or 'society of states' tradition. Realism rejects the idea of evaluative standards of states' behaviour independent of the customs and practices of diplomacy, as well as the idea that individuals or sub-state groups are the ultimate bearers of rights and duties in international relations. The cosmopolitan view abhors the moral diffidence of the naturalist view; it wants in the end to deny any ethical significance to the state. Cosmopolitan theorists, in general, reject as inadequate the proviso that the claims of states are only to be understood as being derivative of the rights and interests of their peoples. Not only are such claims held generally to be without foundation, but the parochialism of the view that a section of humanity should have any special rights by virtue of being born in one state and not another is condemned as inimical to the true rights and interests of humanity.

As for the three modern views discussed, one insists that the natural law tradition has led to a specious 'morality of states'; another that rights and justice-claims have their origin only within the practices of civil society as mediated by the state; while the last holds that the qualitative difference between the practices characteristic of domestic and international society render ineffectual the claims of natural law theory to address both spheres.

The natural law tradition of international thought, though long ignored by modern writers, continues to provide a richer and more comprehensive theory of the state and international justice than do rival perspectives. Its great post-renaissance re-flourishing is found in the works of Suarez, Gentili, Vitoria and others in the sixteenth and seventeenth centuries, reaching its mature expression in the works of Grotius and Pufendorf. Though this Christian tradition of thought conceived the Law of Nature as being ultimately of divine ordination, it was widely accepted from the time of Aquinas onward that human reason could also discover the necessary principles of secure social existence.[44]

Many characteristics of human beings, and of the ultimate good that their natures require them to pursue, were adduced in support of natural law theory. Amongst these were the vulnerability to attack and the consequent permanent insecurity of all individuals; their relative equality, such that none was so much more powerful than all others as to be effectively protected from attack by them in combination; and the need to reconcile the great diversity of human ends and purposes. The great benefits to be had from social co-operation and orderly coexistence were seen to require respectively a climate of secure expectations provided by the principle of *pacta sunt servanda* and a means of adjudicating the justice of resort to arms when no peaceful means of settlement were available. Thus natural law doctrine developed in intimate connection with 'just war' doctrine. Indeed, in the works of Grotius in particular, the latter became the vehicle for the former.

Most importantly, the primacy of natural law over the 'Law of Nations' or positive international law was maintained by the naturalist theorists. Whilst the reality and efficacy of positive law in a world society of independent sovereign powers was recognised, the moral priority of natural law was asserted as a standard for the evaluation and amendment of the Law of Nations, or international law. This was especially significant in the reconstruction of the Law of Nations from the fragmentary remnants in post-Reformation Europe. Ideas that owe much to the insights of the natural law tradition continue to play an important role of criticism and amendment in contemporary international law.

The natural law tradition has in general refused to make any rigid distinction between the spheres of international law and international politics. This fact, along with the asserted priority of natural over positive international law, has been the target of critics of the natural law tradition, who see its supposed ambiguity in these matters as a source of international stability. The refusal to confine matters of international 'justiciability' (to use C.W. Jenk's phrase)[45] to the realm of 'non-political' disputes between states has been and remains significant. In the natural law tradition, individuals and not states are seen as the ultimate bearers of rights and duties. In consequence of this, states have in their actions towards one another no exemption from the rules that apply to individuals:

> princes and peoples were bound by rules in their dealings with one another primarily because princes and peoples were men and thus subject to natural law.[46]

There are both prescriptive and descriptive elements to the natural law tradition. In order to substantiate the 'society of states' conception of international relations to which it subscribes, it will be necessary to identify significant elements of solidarity and common moral understanding in international relations. Natural law theory depends for its effectiveness on a high degree of practical correspondence between its world-view and the 'real world' of international politics, and not merely on its coherence as a body of ethical doctrine. It will be necessary to show that the contemporary international system does manifest sufficient characteristics of an international society to sustain the continued relevance of natural law doctrine.

Among the most valuable aspects of the natural law tradition is the constant recognition of the political and cultural diversity and pluralism of the international system, and the complexity of issues of justice, rights and legitimacy. It avoids the rigidity of the monothematic theories referred to above, yet seeks to promote common values and understanding as ground on which to build, without falling into the moral solipsism of the realist school or the precipitate and unworldly rejection of the state by cosmopolitan thinkers. If the strictly religious or metaphysical grounds of natural law are no longer accepted in their literal form, its precepts continue to combine utilitarian, rationalist and intuitive elements without becoming vacuous.

Perhaps most importantly, the natural law tradition rejects the claims of states to any sort of ethical self-subsistence, recognising that human beings are the only ends in themselves. From this it must follow that their needs and rights constitute the only grounds of the legitimacy of all claims of justice and rights made by or on behalf of states.

Simple and Complex Theories of the State and International Justice

If realism attaches too great and too exclusive a normative significance to the state, cosmopolitan theory fails to confront the practical significance of the state in securing justice. We are left with the contradictory logics of state sovereignty on one side, and justice and rights on the other. We noted that the effort to reconcile these logics through a complex dialectic of relations between individuals, civil society and the state is, in the end, obscurantist and question-begging. Nor is it persuasive to argue that the facts of sovereignty preclude any substantive agreement on questions of rights and justice internationally, and confine such agreement exclusively within the state. It will later be argued at length that it is unwarranted to characterise international society as lacking in any agreement on substantive moral values, or to view international law as solely concerned with regulating peaceful coexistence.

Evidently, some reconciliation of the facts of sovereignty with the moral imperatives of justice and rights is necessary for any general account of the state and international justice. We need to show why it is that justice and rights, which are concepts with a universal and autonomous nature, are most effectively upheld by the state, an institution which is inherently restrictive, imperfect and transitory in its nature. Before an outline conception of the state and international justice is proposed, some major difficulties in developing such a conception should be noted.

No fully coherent or self-sufficient overall theory of justice, the state and international relations is likely to be possible for the evident reason that no equivalent domestic theory of justice, or of its relationship to the legitimacy of the state's authority, is available either. There is no solid base of theoretical agreement from which to build upwards or outwards. No 'tidy' general theory is available because the determinants of the legitimacy of the state from within point to its moral duties outside its own sphere. In other words, the concepts used in the theory of the state, and particularly from our point of view the concept of justice, point to the denial of the universality of the state, and delimit the sphere from which it may legitimately exclude others.

Even if it were possible to obtain a really adequate 'domestic' justificatory theory of the state, it would be further necessary to show on what grounds the state can simply exclude the rights and needs of others outside its boundaries from moral concern.

If rights and obligations are immanent in the nature of individuals as moral agents, then the idea that rights are *essentially* relational concepts, understandable only in terms of specific social practices and finding their transcendent, non-egoistic form in the state, must ultimately be rejected. Consequently, so too must be the contention that it is only with the acceptance of the restrictions on individual freedom enforced by the state that rights as such come into being. It may still, of course, be held that such restrictions are essential for the securing of the content of those rights. The idea that rights obtain their binding moral force within the structure of relations constitutive of civil society, with the corollary that the individual cannot be said to possess any rights against civil society, is an epistemological and psychological affront to the common understanding of rights as injunctions against treating people in certain ways, as is the contention that the state is itself the originator of rights. These considerations also compound the difficulties of conceiving the state as an exclusive moral order.

Another point must be stressed: it is one thing to propose a justificatory theory of the state's authority with respect to those within it; it is quite another to posit an exclusive or necessary relationship between a particular community and a particular state. We shall later reject the claims that the idea of nationhood confers a right to unified statehood (that is, the claim that a 'cultural' nation must be allowed to constitute itself as a 'political' nation), and that there is a presumptive cultural, historical or political 'fit' between states and societies which provides a strong normative defence of state autonomy and the principle of non-intervention. Above all, the idea of the state as a self-subsistent ethical entity will be shown to be unacceptable. It is not denied that the state is a necessary sphere of certain, very important rights; specifically, those rights sometimes called 'special rights', and which assume for their nature a legal order in which specific forms of contract, immunities, and so on are guaranteed. But rights more generally both pre-exist and survive the state, and these rights are possessed by those excluded from any particular state (or from statehood itself). These general, immanent rights are best understood as human rights as such; they are separate from, and rivals to, the particularist and restrictive rights secured by the state, and which presuppose the legal and political institutions of the state. Any adequate theory of the legitimacy of the state must refer to rights in both these senses.

Natural Law and the Complex Instrumentality of the State

Rather than vainly chase an elusive 'unitary' theory of justice, the state and international relations, in this book we propose to defend what might best be called a 'complex instrumental' theory of the state and international justice, a theory that draws on the philosophical and political insights of the natural law tradition as its fundamental basis.

The theory is 'complex' in as much as the adequacy of any mono-thematic account of the state and international justice is explicitly denied. The internal and external justification of the state, and of the legitimacy of its claims, depends on its relation to individuals and groups outside as well as within the state, and not merely on the state's fulfilling one set of criteria in respect of its citizens, such as the securing of domestic social justice, or on its supposedly constituting a unique sphere of ethical relationships.

Contractarian, natural law and other theories of legitimacy have succeeded in varying degrees in shedding light on the limits of the legitimate conduct of the state towards its citizens, and on the obligations the state must discharge towards them. But the key terms here are 'state' and 'citizens'; these terms connote specific and restrictive relationships. Their logic is to exclude non-citizens from the state's area of moral concern, and to support the exclusive claims it makes as agent of its citizens' rights and interests. Theories of legitimacy from the perspective of within the state are important, to be sure, but their tendency is often to make of the state an absolute. The state passes from something to be justified to the necessary embodiment of its own justification.

The state may be said to be 'instrumentalist' in its nature because the practical efficacy of the state in securing the manifold forms of justice and rights for its members, and in meeting the obligations of its community towards other political communities in terms of international justice, is the only source of the state's ethical significance. It has no self-subsistent or teleological value as an institution, nor any moral warrant for its authority, beyond its instrumental role.

But the state is a necessary vehicle for securing justice, and is likely to remain so in any foreseeable future developments of the international political system. This practical necessity of the state requires us to make no assumptions about its 'inner ethical nature'; this necessity is only contingent. It exists because of the lack of workable alternative institutions. Because of this necessity, the instrumental theory of the state and international justice is also a prescriptive one. So far as the state secures justice, rights and other values, including not least the specific claims and rights associated with civil relations intrinsic to its particular society, there is lent to the state and to its protection a definite ethical value.

Elements of a Theory of the State and Justice

A complex instrumental version of the state in relation to international justice such as that offered here seeks to deal *inter alia* with a number of lacunae in traditional natural law doctrine, and to specify further elements that make it more congruent with the political theory of modernity. These include accounts of justice and rights that entail a 'positive' element, that is, the recognition of entitlements to a minimum provision of economic and social resources, as well as the older, negative rights of security of property and person, and the range of civil and political liberties. Such an account of rights provides a specifiable content to the obligations existing between states and societies, and most importantly it provides substance to the natural law conception of the individual as the ultimate member of international society, and bearer of rights and obligations in that society.

The moral status of independent states derives from their role in protecting the rights and interests of their citizens. What is explicitly rejected is the later degeneration of the natural law tradition found in the writings of Wolff and Vattel, in which the so-called 'necessary' as opposed to 'voluntary' component in natural law is taken to concern exclusively the self-regarding interests of the state in its teleological project of 'perfecting' the society within, or below, it.[47]

In this conception, to repeat, states' claims are seen as derivative of individual and group claims; though we must be clear that the valid claims of groups are not merely the aggregates of the valid claims of individuals. At the same time, we must distinguish between those rights and justice-claims the satisfaction of which point beyond the state, and those specific forms of rights and justice which arise within a given political community and are uniquely possible and meaningful only within it.

The idea of agency, to be developed later, provides the philosophical underpinning of the first type of rights and claims; the second type assumes a legal system in which both the specific contractual rights and duties of civil society, and the broader principles of political obligation, are upheld. In other words, we must make clear the difference between those social and contractual rights of which the legal order of the state is the necessary condition and which have an autonomous validity, and moral rights in the broadest sense, especially as the latter circumscribe the validity of the state as a normative order. The existence of the state makes possible a certain class of rights, in so far as their existence is inconceivable without the state, whilst the state is itself transcended by the more inclusive set of rights commonly termed 'human rights', rights which create correlative obligations beyond the state.

The ambivalent relationship of the state to human rights compounds the conflict between the given reality of the state and the prescriptions of ideal theory. This alone seems to preclude any monistic theory of the legitimacy of the state couched in terms of rights or of 'social justice' understood in relation only to domestic society. The nature of the external obligations of political communities, especially in relation to international distributive justice, must be defined by balancing the two forms of rights and justice-claims so far as they are in conflict.

In summary, then, these are the main features of the complex instrumental theory of the state and international justice:

1. The appropriate normative conception of international relations is found, generally, within the tradition of natural law, whatever that tradition's metaphysical defects. Whilst states are the immediate, people are the ultimate members of international society. The idea of the *civitas maxima* developed in this tradition does not point to the

state as an obstacle to justice, but rather to the universality of right, and away from the idea that states are ethically self-subsistent. The difficulties in the natural law prescription of individual's rights are to be met by the idea of agency as the ground of rights.

2. No a priori defence of the state as an absolute value from either a domestic or international point of view is possible. The value of the state itself is derivative; it lies in the realisation of other values.

3. Individual and collective rights are the bedrock of the legitimacy of a state's internal standing and external claims. However, neither natural rights in their classical formulation nor more recent legal-positivist theories of rights are in themselves satisfactory. To defend (and reconcile) a broader spectrum of rights, a theory of rights based on human agency, and requiring the satisfaction of (at least) basic subsistence as a means of guaranteeing the conditions of that agency, is necessary.

4. Collective rights exist only because individual rights exist. To deny this would be to suppose that no individual could have valid claims against society or, by extension, against the state, and this is incompatible with the view that the individual is the only moral end in itself. Individuals are the subjects of collective rights; such rights are, however, *sui generis* in their form. This is another way of saying that collective rights are a sort of shorthand for the aggregate of rights held by individuals qua members of communities. The content of those rights includes individuals' identity and welfare as such. There exists between individual and collective rights a relationship of both complementarity and conflict; no 'one-dimensional' theory of the state in relation to the values of international justice can capture the complexity of the state's role in upholding both sorts of rights.

5. In the light of 1 and 2, however great the practical significance of the state in securing values, the nature of those values points beyond the uniqueness of the state as a sphere of justice. This is especially true of human rights and distributive justice, in respect of which the state is 'porous' as a sphere of justice. At the same time, those rights unique to civil society within the legal and political framework of the state have a validity which is distinct and separate from the universality of human rights asserted against and on behalf of states and societies.

6. The conflict between claims of sovereignty and of justice and rights must be distinguished at its empirical and normative levels. Ideal theory is important as a test and a measure of empirical reality, but its prescriptive uses must take account of that reality. It would be

absurd to postpone political theory until the world became perfect, but the valuation given to the political institutions that currently exist must depend in large part on the practicality and likely costs of alternatives.

2 Political Realism and the Primacy of the State

The realist tradition of international politics stresses the primacy of questions of security and power in the relations between states, and the dangers of allowing what it regards as utopian ideas about reform of international politics to intrude into the rational calculation of state interests. Realist thinkers are, to varying degrees, sceptical about claims for justice and rights, especially when debate about these is introduced into the conduct of diplomacy. Such claims are viewed as attempts to camouflage much more traditional state interests with spurious moral authority.

2.1 JUSTICE, RECIPROCITY AND INTERNATIONAL MORAL SCEPTICISM

The idea that international relations cannot support ethical principles finds its modern origins in the thought of Machiavelli and Hobbes.

Hobbes conceives international relations as analogous to the state of nature which he identifies as existing between individuals before the advent of the state:

> it is manifest, that during the time men live without a common Power to keep them all in awe, they are in that condition which is called Warre; and such a warre, as is of every man, against every man.[1]

In this condition, Hobbes tells us,

> there is no place for Industry; because the fruit thereof is uncertain: and consequently no Culture of the Earth; no navigation, nor use of the commodities that may be imported thereby, but of all, continuall feare, and danger of violent death; and the life of man, solitary, poore, nasty, brutish, and short.[2]

This is so because of the prerequisites of human survival in a world of scarce resources, and in which men are of relatively equal strength, and therefore of equal vulnerability. One man's means of defence becomes the means of offence towards another. Man's competitive egoism further compounds the already intractable problem of security. Each has a natural right to the means of self-preservation; that is all. The problem is that, 'as long as this naturall Right of every man to every thing endureth, there can be no security to any man'.[3] There is, however, a secondary law of nature,

> That a man be willing, when others are so too, as farre-forth, as for Peace, and defence of himself as he shall think it necessary, to lay down this right to all things; and be contented with so much liberty against other men, as he would allow other men against himselfe.[4]

Justice and Reciprocity

According to Hobbes, no man can bind himself to the restriction of his natural right unless there is a guarantee of reciprocal limitation by others. In the state of nature no such guarantee is possible. No man can be obliged to act justly towards others without this guarantee, since to do so would be to expose himself to destruction.[5] The problem is that for men to enter into a social contract or 'Convention' guaranteeing their reciprocal obligations, they would want some initial guarantee that all will abide by the terms of the contract. But such a guarantee is impossible in the absence of the sovereign that the contract brings into being. This is the famous paradox of Hobbes' state of nature.

The conditions of reciprocity which Hobbes thinks are indispensable to the idea of justice can never arise of themselves, because it will always be in the interest of each that others be bound by the contract, that is, that they should surrender their natural right, whilst he alone remains unbound by it. Hobbes argues that the problem of the 'free-rider' is readily solved by his Leviathan. Once the sovereign comes into being, his exercise of authority must no longer be considered to derive from the Covenant.[6] Disagreements about the legitimacy of the sovereign authority are disastrous, for

> there is in this case, no Judge to decide the controversie: it returns therefore to the sword again, and every man recovereth the right of Protecting himselfe with his own strength.[7]

In the state of nature between nations no Leviathan is possible. Therefore, the secondary law of nature, the binding force of which is ultimately prudential, does not apply. There is no escape from international anarchy:

But though there had never been any time, wherein particular men were in a condition of warre one against another; yet in all times, Kings, and Persons of Soveraigne authority, because of their Independency, are in continuall jealousies, and in the state and posture of Gladiators; having their weapons pointing, and their eyes fixed upon one another; that is, their Forts, Garrisons and Guns upon the Frontiers of their Kingdomes; and continuall Spyes upon their neighbours; which is a posture of Warre. But because they uphold thereby, the Industry of their Subjects; there does not follow from it, that misery, which accompanies the Liberty of particular men.[8]

The Limitations of the Hobbesian Image of International Relations

If international relations really do look like Hobbes' state of nature, then it appears that discussion of international justice is pointless. But there are problems both with the image, and with what Hobbes says about the nature of justice.

The latency of war and the acuteness of international security problems are evident, not least in the former Soviet Union and the Balkans. But in relations between the United Kingdom (and most other European countries) and the United States, or between the United States and Canada or Mexico, the 'state of war' is hardly apparent. Moreover, despite Hobbes' belief in the universality of war in the international state of nature, the advent of nuclear, chemical and bacteriological weapons has made war amongst the major powers irrational in Hobbes' own sense.[9] His first law of nature enshrines the right to self-preservation, to be achieved through peaceful means if possible. The threat of uncontrollable escalation makes self-preservation by any other means than peaceful ones highly problematic. There ceases to be any alternative, in Hobbes' own terms, to co-operation to prevent war. Reason dictates that states pursue what he believed only the Leviathan could achieve. Whether reason will be followed is another matter.

Unlike Hobbes' characterisation of the situation existing between individuals, there are forms of state defence that are not in themselves offensive. The defence policy of Switzerland is an example of this. This illustrates a weakness in the case for war as an inevitably recurring symptom of international anarchy. The egoism of the state is not like the egoism of the individual. As Marshall Cohen notes,[10] the international 'personality' of a state is revealed to other states in the economic, legal, and diplomatic contexts in which they interact. This contrasts with the anonymity of the alien 'other' in Hobbes' state of nature. The 'established reputation' of a state becomes the basis for settled expectations about its future behaviour and intentions.[11] Though the conflicts of the Cold War show how easily governments adopt a 'worst case' analysis of the likely behaviour of their opponents, states have means of assessing one another's aggressive or pacific intentions that are denied to individuals in the state of nature.

Hobbes does not, however, equate the 'state of war' with actual war, although the threat of the latter is always present. His characterisation of international relations is generally one of cut-throat competition. But the vast structure of international organisations belies the idea that no constructive co-operation between states is possible, though it remains true that the parochialism of the national interest determines the extent of co-operation through international agencies. We might say that the egoism of the state, like that of the individual in the state of nature, is the limiting constraint on the sort of co-operation which would be in the interests of all.

Nevertheless, international relations are not in the condition of arid backwardness of the state of nature. One reason is that many of the goals of state policy are unachievable by resorting to war. Increased economic interdependence, in the form of trade, resource access and, especially, the need to maintain a truly internationalised system of production based upon the activities of the multinational corporation – all these require intense co-ordination and co-operation between states. International politics are becoming largely 'domesticated'. As states concern themselves more and more with the provision of economic welfare in their societies, so they become more dependent upon global economic conditions, created by negotiation in international forums, bilateral arrangements with trading partners, and so on, to achieve those domestic goals.[12] The 'high' politics of regime security are replaced, at least to a degree, by the 'low' politics of international economic co-operation.

As a consequence of this, the developing world has obtained certain economic concessions from the Western states. The limited response of the OECD states to the demands of successive UNCTAD meetings, in the form of various international commodity agreements, a limited General System of Preferences within the General Agreement on Tariffs and Trade (GATT), or limited moves towards stabilisation of export earnings, hardly amount to a major shift of global power. The dependence of the industrialised world on mineral supplies, and

Western investment in developing countries have at times been exaggerated, but still create some leverage for the fulfilment of certain demands. The point is that the 'traditional' forms of state power – military, political, diplomatic – are no longer necessarily sufficient to ensure economic security. At the same time, the voting strength of developing states in international organisations strengthens their economic bargaining power. As Hobbes' notion of security in terms of absence of physical threat gives way to security defined increasingly in economic terms, so a disjunction between economic and military/political power begins to emerge, however slowly.

For Hobbesian realists, what order that exists in international relations is preserved by hierarchy and inequality among states. The trends we have just noted threaten a simple hierarchy of power, and suggest the emergence of a more complex distribution of power which changes across different issue areas. But a Hobbesian response to what we have just said is readily forthcoming. Limited concessions are not in themselves evidence of a move towards greater international justice, when the interdependence from which they arise is itself an interdependence of systemic inequality. The fact that concessions, where they occur, can be described as 'forced' seems further evidence of the contradiction between state policy as representative of the 'national interest' and the sorts of international co-operation to which principles of international justice refer.

That the degree of international justice requires much improvement is not at issue. What is at issue are the Hobbesian belief in the incoherence of justice as a possible quality of relations between states and the consequent belief that neither principles of international co-operation nor international law can serve as a vehicle for justice outside the state.

The State of Nature and International Law

Hobbesian scepticism about international law provides an illustration of a more general scepticism about co-operative principles of international relations.

In the absence of any sovereign above states to enforce it, international law is rejected as being binding upon states in any absolute sense; their adherence to it reflects only their immediate perceived interest. In holding this view, Hobbes is a forerunner of the equally unequivocal Hegel[13] though Hobbes' position has a very different logic. But does the lack of a Leviathan mean that international law is not really law at all? There are a number of reasons to think that states are constrained by the customs and conventions of international law irrespective of whether their immediate purposes are suited thereby.

One such reason is that governments usually feel constrained to claim that their actions are in fact in accord with international law. The right of self-defence, and self-help generally, is unlimited in Hobbes' state of nature. In Article 51 of the United Nations Charter, however, the 'inherent right of individual or collective self-defence' is specified only 'if an armed attack occurs'. The onus is very strongly upon the state embarking upon military intervention to show that it was the initial victim of attack. Thus Tanzania justified its intervention in Uganda on the grounds that the Amin regime's army had repeatedly attacked across Tanzania's borders. More spuriously, the United States exploited the Gulf of Tonkin 'incident' as a pretext to attack North Vietnamese positions.

In general, international law recognises collective intervention as valid where unilateral intervention, even in response to a prior intervention, is not. Such collective intervention is itself only explicitly sanctioned when organised under the aegis of the Security Council according to Chapter Seven of the UN Charter. Unilateral intervention in reply to 'counter-intervention' is usually considered by governments to be a safer plea internationally than the defence of even vital strategic interests, when these fall short of a direct response to armed attack upon a state's territory.

States acknowledge the generally binding nature of international law even when they claim exemption from its requirements on particular occasions, or when they feel justified in taking action not explicitly sanctioned by international law. When the United States refused to accept the decision of the International Court of Justice on the legality of its mining of Nicaraguan waters, it did not thereby challenge the general competence of the Court, or of other international tribunals. Nor does the United States deny their competence to adjudicate on any or all of its actions in the future. Nor did Britain repudiate international maritime law in declaring an exclusion zone for the duration of the Falklands conflict.

Of course, such a selective acceptance of the binding nature of law would not be possible within the state, and this is a key difference between domestic and international law. The Hobbesian sceptic replies to this that the very fact that states are selective in which international legal decisions they accept shows that appeals to international law are made only when these accord with national self-interest. Such appeals cannot constrain a state to act against its self-interest. The uses states make of international law are akin to the tribute vice pays to virtue in hypocrisy. But if it is contended that respect for international law amounts to no more than the fact that states generally perceive it in their interest to obey that law, then it is unclear that such a reason is any different in the case of individuals in society choosing to obey laws. The desire to avoid the penalties for violating the law might reasonably be assumed to enter into calculations of self-interest. It will be seen that there are significant penalties for states refusing to accept international legal norms, though these are admittedly neither as direct nor as automatic as for individuals.[14]

Yet there remains a disanalogy between the authority of domestic and international law. It is possible for states to challenge international law without the structure of that law disintegrating. Indeed, international law survives without the need of a Leviathan by virtue of this fact.

Ethical Principles in the State of Nature

If international conflict and anarchy are not endemic in the way that Hobbes took them to be, then the meaning attached by Hobbes to moral principles in general, and to justice in particular, is open to question. Charles Beitz has argued persuasively that Hobbes' scepticism about international morality collapses into scepticism about morality generally.[15] The idea that ethical judgements require an enforcing agency for their validity, and not merely for their efficacy, is at best counterintuitive. In fact, the absence of an agency to rectify wrongs may lend a special emotive power to ethical judgements. It is similarly counterintuitive to suggest that contractual legitimacy is the entire basis of justice. The erosion of such a belief has discredited, for example, the international legal doctrine that treaties negotiated under duress remain valid.

One major difference between the situation of a people without a sovereign and that of states without a common higher authority is that states are much more unequal in their power than men. This inequality means that vulnerability is not a universal condition – one of Hobbes' principal definitions of the state of nature – but it gives rise to the balance of power system, as we saw earlier.[16] Powerful states threaten to impose hegemony, and coalitions are formed against them, whilst the weak must seek powerful patrons. The operation of the balance of power has historically violated most or all precepts of international justice. Collective rights, for example of national self-determination, have been extinguished by the operation of the balance of power, and yet have also been preserved. The latter has been true of the minor European principalities, of Belgium before 1940, Austria after 1950, and Cuba after 1961.

The Paradoxical Defence of the State

It is this core of inescapable truth in the Hobbesian argument that motivated at least the post-Kantian cosmopolitan theorists to argue that the sovereign state is in itself an obstacle to moral progress. The very means by which the states system preserves itself seem to undermine prospects for a more just world order. To make a moral defence of the state against the critique of cosmopolitanism involves the recognition of the fact that a form of political organisation that is defensible in terms of individual and collective justice has historically depended on the periodic suppression of the justice-claims of people in other states, and of those excluded from the states system, such as the native peoples of colonies. A further aspect of the paradox of any ethical defence of the state is that states with a high degree of social justice and equality have historically been no more immune from the depredations of the Great Powers than the most morally regressive.

So the rejection of Hobbes' moral scepticism does not avoid the ambiguities involved in defending the state as a discrete political institution. The resolution of these ambiguities depends upon the relative weight to be attached to justice and order respectively.

The Force of International Moral Principles

Others have questioned the binding force of moral principles in international relations, without embracing the thoroughgoing scepticism of Hobbes. David Hume (in an unusually Machiavellian mode) does not characterise international relations as a state of nature, but still holds that the need for just conduct does not apply with the same force in relations between states as it does between individuals. Laws of justice are essential to the preservation of society, which individual men and women find essential:

> [We] may observe, that though the intercourse of different states be advantageous, and even sometimes necessary, yet it is not so

necessary nor advantageous as that among individuals, without which it is utterly impossible for human nature ever to subsist. Since, therefore, the natural obligation to justice, among different states, is not so strong as among individuals, the moral obligation, which arises from it, must partake of its weakness; and we must necessarily give a greater indulgence to a prince or minister, who deceives an other; than to a private gentleman, who breaks his word of honour.[17]

If a state does sustain within itself important values, including social justice and human rights, then it is worth defending. Yet the means necessary for that defence are often morally ambiguous. War always is. The just war doctrines of discrimination and proportionality in the conduct of war, indeed the doctrine from the time of Erasmus that the moral importance and the moral certainty of the goals pursued in war should constrain the violence of the means used, have always been problematic. Some writers have doubted whether the corpus of just war doctrine is now able to play any role in the limitation of violence in war.[18] In an era of war made absolute by technology and by the global conflict of ideologies, the importance of winning has never appeared greater.

Yet in spite of the risks of uncontrolled escalation, no state is prepared to renounce in advance any recourse to violence under whatever circumstances. To all but the most principled of pacifists, attaching value to a system of social life or to a set of strongly held beliefs implies a willingness to defend them. The risks of using force in an anarchic environment must be taken into any moral assessment a state undertakes before using force to defend itself. If a state should decide never to defend itself because of these risks, then the potential aggressor always achieves his objectives, by virtue of moral blackmail. The unwillingness to defend values where this defence threatens other values itself threatens to ensure what is intended to be avoided; that might always makes right.[19]

We might also reflect that Hume's low estimate of the importance of principles of international justice is dangerously myopic. Questions of international distributive justice aside, the denial of collective political rights, including that of self-determination within particular states, threatens regional stability. Problems of regional hegemony and security worsen. Nuclear proliferators and potential proliferators are often predictable rivals: Argentina and Brazil, Iraq and its neighbours, India and Pakistan, perhaps Australia and the Pacific Rim states. In a world of nuclear-equipped 'Paranoids, Pygmies and

Pariahs', to use Richard Betts' phrase,[20] 'moral blindness may bind us all to the final wheel of fire' (to borrow an equally graphic phrase from Marshall Cohen).[21]

Rules of justice are a necessary means of the co-ordination of, and co-operation in, activities which are of general benefit. They also specify how individuals and groups may and may not be treated, notably in the sharing out of the products of co-operation. This suggests that principles of international justice are no less crucial than those of justice within the state, and should be thought of as no less binding. Whether a common understanding of such principles exists is a separate question.

The National Interest as a Moral Principle

The denial or demotion of ethical principles in international relations was intended to leave the self-interest of states as the remaining guiding light. The problems of defining what this is are legion. This is a world of pluralist democracies, peasant nationalisms, oligarchies based on agricultural estates or financial empires, kleptocracies in general, and almost every other imaginable political formation. What could constitute a common definition of a national interest in states in which power and influence is so variously distributed as in these?

States' policies which are defended ritually as being unequivocally in the 'national interest' evidently reflect unequally the interests of different classes, political and economic elites, government bureaucracies, and so on. Conversely, the interests of other sections of society are often excluded or damaged by the policies of their governments.[22] An ideal definition of the national interest might have it include 'all the particular interests of those who have a right for governments to represent them'. This is itself problematic. No simple aggregate of particular interests is possible where these interests conflict.

The above definition might also be taken to entail that no interest based upon any activity legitimate within a state should be excluded. But this raises the question of what forms of political expression and articulation of interests are considered legitimate or otherwise in different states. The most powerful voices at home are likely to be the only ones heard abroad.[23]

For Machiavelli, the interest of the state is everything; its salvation and greatness are the sole charge of the statesman. He discards any notion of reciprocal moral obligations between states. Nor does he allow that conventional moral standards are relevant in appraising the conduct of statesmen at home or abroad.[24]

Politics has its own morality, at times irreconcilable with other sorts. Of modern theorists, Hans Morgenthau has provided the most comprehensive defence of the national interest as the basis of statesmen's concerns. He quotes Thucydides approvingly to the effect that the 'identity of interests is the surest of bonds whether between states or individuals'.[25] Moreover, in the sphere of politics, interest is defined purely in terms of power, as distinct from economics, where it is defined in terms of wealth, and so on. Whatever the other objectives of individuals and groups, the realisation of these objectives through the state makes power the primary aim of states.[26]

But Morgenthau is no more of a moral nihilist than is Machiavelli. The defence of the national interest is itself, as for Machiavelli, a moral obligation. It is precisely because international politics is in its practice inhospitable to moral principles that the pursuit of the particular national interest assumes the status of an ultimate moral obligation. Morgenthau cannot accept Machiavelli's cynicism in inverting moral concepts when applied to *raison d'état;* rather, he differentiates between moral and political activity. But he still wishes to defend the goal of the actions of statesmen in moral terms. National interest as a moral rule emerges *faute de mieux.*

Both individual and state must judge political action by universal moral principles, such as that of liberty. Yet while the individual has a moral right to sacrifice himself in defence of such a moral principle,

> the state has no right to let its moral disapprobation of the infringement of liberty get in the way of successful political action, itself inspired by the moral principle of national survival... Ethics in the abstract judges action by its conformity with the moral law; political ethics judges action by its political consequences.[27]

But the statement 'ethics... judges action by its conformity with the moral law' is simply a tautology. 'Political ethics' just *is* a species of ethics. It is difficult to see where 'political consequences' fit in as criteria for judging moral action. If Morgenthau simply believes that ethics and politics have no common form of discourse, he should say so. He cannot, because he wishes to assert the national interest as an unconditional moral principle. But as has been noted, self-interest is just not a kind of morality; not even when it is enlightened. Morals are other-regarding; they involve the possibility that action is required which damages the immediate interests of the agent constrained by them.

Morgenthau recognises the conflict between the pursuit of national interests and national defence as the absolute value of political ethics. He argues that the state, in pursuing its own self-interest, must recognise that of others, and accommodate itself to other national self-interests so far as is possible.[28] Much that is similar to Morgenthau's perspective is also to be found in the writing of Kenneth W. Thompson,[29] who argues for the acceptance of moral pluralism, and for a practical morality based on 'prudence and proportionality'. He too stresses the need to recognise the mutuality and need for accommodation between separate national interests, but unlike Morgenthau denies that the sphere of the political can be separated from the sphere of the ethical, or that 'political ethics' can be understood as an autonomous concept. Nations tend to be 'repositories of their own morality' and tend to debase ethics into the language of material advantage.

Ethical systems distinguish, differently in each culture, between that area of the individual's legitimate self-concerns and the area of his social responsibilities. They also specify where the boundary between the two falls. Morgenthau wants to make the state the exclusive judge of where all its interests lie, and how best to pursue them. To the state is conceded an ethical egoism not allowed to individuals.[30]

2.2   THE STATE AS THE UNIQUE SPHERE OF JUSTICE

For Hobbes, then, justice has no meaning in the absence of an enforcing agency. Justice and property are intimately connected, but property only comes into being where men transfer those natural rights that they have in the 'state of nature' to a sovereign power which, in return, guarantees that security of person and of possession whose absence is the main feature of the state of nature. David Hume, conversely, establishes the need for principles of justice in those circumstances which cause Hobbes to maintain that conditions for justice can never by themselves emerge. These are, essentially, man's limited altruism, and the relative scarcity of resources compared to the voracity of his wants.[31]

Whilst the content of principles of justice is specific to the circumstances of each society, certain constraints always apply. Physical need, and the need for security, are best satisfied by co-operation between individuals in society. When societies form, certain principles are discovered to be most conducive to their peace and security. Hume takes these to be stability of possession, consent when ownership is transferred, and the keeping of promises. These are the principles of justice, but they are recognised and valued because they lead to socially beneficial results.

Justice in itself is an artificial virtue. Man comes first to understand the ideas of property and right, and how they relate to his self-interest. Whatever supports these is called just; whatever subverts them is unjust. But justice is understood always in relation to property, or right, or obligation; these are prior to the concept of justice.

We have seen that Hume's theory of justice is less hostile to international justice in principle than is that of Hobbes. In so far as the context of international relations increasingly comes to resemble that of domestic society, rules of justice can be expected to increase in scope and importance. As for the existence of a state of anarchy in international relations, whilst Hume believes that the state is necessary to give effect to justice in society, the fact of the existence of a society whose individual units manifest a high degree of mutual dependence is sufficient to give meaning to the concept of justice.

Hobbes makes the state the absolute condition of justice. There can be no justice in relations between states since, in the absence of any common higher authority, there exists only the natural right of states. We noted that Hobbes' claim that justice requires the possibility of the enforcement of its precepts is counterintuitive. It would be still more bizarre to say that, because the abstract state itself determines what is just or unjust, the existence of an arbitrary and irrational state prevents us from giving a rational and non-arbitrary account of the nature of justice and rights.

Hobbes is not a precursor of legal positivism. He does not make a strict epistemological distinction between political and legal concepts used descriptively and all normative sorts of argument. Positivism does not deny the normative sphere; it simply refuses to deal with it. But Hobbes is a natural law theorist, albeit of a one-dimensional sort. His account of the relationship between justice and the enforcing power of the state does not depend on any logical separation of moral justice from legal justice. It depends instead on the validity of Hobbes' moral scepticism, on his description of the state of nature among both persons and states, and on the assumption that reciprocal obligation cannot exist where there is no sovereign power.

The Meaning of the 'Interests of States'

If there is no justice in international relations, states retain their full 'natural rights' in Hobbes' sense. These rights are unlimited; they derive from the fundamental right of self-preservation, and those in the state of nature are the only judges of what is required to protect this right. States are seen to have a legitimate self-interest in the same sense that persons have. The nature of that interest is still problematic. Aside from facts such as that public bureaucracies pursue ends of their own different from the public goals they ostensibly serve, the purposes of other 'institutional' interest groups, such as the armed forces or the intelligence community, have a permanence which comes partly, often largely, to define the 'interest of the state'.

Critics of the modern corporatist state identify other groups whose influence has grown to the point where they have become part of the apparatus of the 'para-state'. Critics from the left have stressed, for example, the 'military–industrial complex' whose 'interlocking elites' determine national strategic and economic policy,[32] whilst those on the right have seen industrial organisations – both unions and employer associations – as having similarly hijacked the liberal democratic state.[33]

Even were it granted that national policy can be considered ideally as a complex articulation of broad and representative social interests, rather than simply the interests of dominant elites or classes masquerading as the national interest, the distinction between 'objective' and 'subjective' interests may still be drawn. Here, larger questions of the roles of 'dominant ideologies' and 'agenda-setting' affect the translation of domestic interests into foreign policy. These, along with the problems of cultural relativism and 'ethnocentrism' in the competitive relations of states, are the staples of modern political science and foreign policy analysis, and are beyond the present discussion. They are simply noted to form a contrast with the alternately glib and obscure references to the 'national interest' that appear in much realist literature. It is not denied that in an important sense statesmen feel that what they are about is promoting the interests of their state, in a sense that is qualitatively distinct from the promotion of the particular economic, commercial, cultural or other interests existing within it. How the wider and the narrower purposes of diplomacy are reconciled with each other is a matter for analysis, not uncritical assertion as an absolute moral principle.

It is important to distinguish the state as a concrete political institution from the state as a legal and ethical abstraction. With respect to the latter, it is true that modern realists in general do not go so far as to equate the moral personality of the state with that of the individual, as, for instance, the later natural law theorists did. In this they depart from Hobbes' extreme natural rights analogy of the sovereign as an 'Artificial Man'. Nor do they embrace Hegel's conception of the state as the highest stage of ethical reason, the universal in which the particularity of man's interest and will in civil society is transcended. The ethical complexities of international relations which follow from the natural law tradition are eschewed by most modern realists, as is the ethical absolutism of idealist philosophy. Realists are too sceptical about the nature and significance of moral claims in international relations to endorse such philosophical premises. Realism identifies the state as too often acting only to promote those interests in which the state appears as separate from civil society, as an end in itself, to believe that its 'moral personality' must be wholly derivative of the individual rights and interests it defends.

The fact that realists are sceptical about the absolute philosophical derivation of the state's moral character from the moral characters of the people who compose it does not entail that they are indifferent to the moral significance of the state. Modern writers such as George Kennan see the state as a sphere of relatively secure moral values, the defence of which is threatened by moral entanglements and prescriptions in international relations.[34] For Hans Morgenthau, as was noted, the state's defence constitutes a binding moral principle in world affairs, where otherwise there would be none.

These ethical perspectives still attribute a moral exclusiveness and egoism to the state which we have rejected. But they do represent an advance on scepticism about any sort of principles of justice being binding on the relations of states. For instance, the recognition that the defence of the national interest is a moral value, and that the relations of a state with its society are crucial to the securing of conditions of justice, might be taken to necessitate at minimum some mutual moral recognition between states of their respective duties towards their publics. Even to recognise this much permits an escape from Hobbes' international moral vacuum.

Realists are right to reject the direct moral analogy of states and persons, but they are right for the wrong reasons. To say that states are not like people, that they are not autonomous moral beings, does not mean that the rights and obligations of states are not derivative of the rights and obligations of their citizens. It is precisely because states are not moral beings that they cannot have self-subsistent rights. If states were simply moral analogues of persons, it would follow that the legitimate interests and rights of states could not exceed those of individuals. It is true that, just as individuals' rights are limited in their extent by the rights of other individuals, so too they must be limited by the rights of states, but only where states' rights are themselves an authentic expression of the rights of people within them. States' rights sui generis can never override the rights of individuals.

Since they are not analogues of people, states can only be given unlimited moral licence on the basis of a generalised moral scepticism, or on the assumption of an international state of nature with the moral consequences we have rejected. We have no good reason to think that the rights of states are not limited in their moral scope in the same way as individuals' rights are. This is a consequence of their derivative nature.

Reinhold Niebuhr has described how the moral consciousness and restraint of the individual is lost in the activity of the collective:

> The fact that the hypocrisy of man's group behavior ... expresses itself not only in terms of self-justification but in terms of moral justification of human behavior in general, symbolises one of the tragedies of the human spirit: its inability to conform its collective life to its individual ideals. As individuals, men believe that they ought to love and serve each other and establish justice between each other. As racial, economic and national groups they take for themselves, whatever their power can command...[35] The frustrations of the average man, who can never realise the power and the glory which his imagination sets as the ideal, makes him the more willing tool and victim of the imperial ambitions of his group.[36]

This is more persuasive as a description of the psychology of collective action than as an ethical defence of it. The belief that the limits of the legitimate interests of individuals are transcended when the individual is considered as part of a collectivity is the romanticist heart of totalitarianism. This transcendence is said to be achieved by the subsumption of the individual interest, and the individual will, in the *gloire* of the state, or in the historical destiny of his *Volk*, religious group, or whatever. This transcendence-through-participation serves in totalitarian ideology to liberate the leaders of the state as well as the ordinary citizen from all constraints on the legitimacy of their respective interests. The state's interest is asserted as something higher than the aggregate of particular interests. The abstract state does not come to possess its moral character because it embodies a necessary ethical relationship between itself and individuals in civil society; that is, because of its uniqueness as a constituency of justice. The value of the state is in its reification of an idea, for instance of racial supremacy or religious fundamentalism, which is not itself reducible to the interests of individuals, but whose promotion by individuals frees them of other moral constraints on what they may do.[37]

What is involved here is more than the idea that the interests of the state are in some sense an abstraction of the interests of individuals and groups, and do not correspond with any particular set of interests within society. This, as we noted, is inevitable. What is being asserted is that the state has legitimate interests and rights, which are independent of, as well as greater than, individual interests and rights. The rejection of the view that the moral claims of states depend on the claims of their citizens degenerates finally into this subjectivising romanticism of the state.

The Claims of States and the Defence of Their Peoples' Interests

Hobbes' state brings to an end the condition of anarchy and natural right, and stands between its citizens and the international state of nature, thus doubly protecting their moral interests. But does the state still perform this function, even assuming that this would be a reason for taking the moral significance of states seriously? John Herz has argued that the significance of the era of nuclear weapons has been to break the 'hard shell' of territorial defence. The genesis of the states system lay in the state's unique provision for its people of security against attack. But states no longer have any means of ultimate defence except the psychological calculus of deterrence, and this has in practice meant deterrence between blocs; excluding the superpowers, no state has been able to provide the means of deterring its adversary from within its own resources.[38] Yet this decline in the defensive capability of the state has not led to the questioning of its basic legitimacy, let alone to the obsolescence of the states system.[39]

The defensive role of the state is questionable in other ways. States have historically entered into federations to protect their security, as in the case of the American colonies (and more recently Hawaii) or the Swiss cantons. Such may be the destiny of the European Union. So far from sovereignty being a condition of the external (and internal) security of a territory or a community, the avoidance or the abandonment of a 'lower-order' sovereignty in favour of a 'higher-order' sovereignty may be a requisite of defence. The security function of the state has been questioned on other grounds, too. If states no longer possess the ability to physically defend their territories, then international regime security can no longer be seen as a 'zero-sum game'. Hobbes' version of natural right in the state of nature is without restriction; people (and states) may use any means, at anyone's expense, which they consider necessary for their self-preservation. But if the state's claim to the unconditional right of self-defence, based on its unique capacity to protect its people, is contestable, much more so is the assertion that all claims advanced on behalf of states must be considered legitimate in their own terms so far as they contribute to that end. The history of such claims, usually to the effect that states' security, or economic wellbeing, or prestige, requires the realisation of other, instrumental objectives is not one that inspires confidence. Increased wealth has not brought extra security to states in the modern world. The scramble for colonies in the decades preceding the Great War gravely exacerbated rivalries between the European powers, and made already daunting continental security problems intractable.

The attempts by both superpowers to define interests necessary to their 'defence', not baulking at patronage of systematically unjust and rights-violating regimes, in order to exclude the ideological enemy, have certainly turned out to be costly, in terms of lives, money and reputation. For all the disillusionment these policies have engendered, it is difficult to see that this maximal, global formulation of the extent of 'rights' of national security on the part of the superpowers and their blocs has led to any real increase in the security of anyone. On the contrary, the ever more extensive definition of one's 'vital interests' usually involves a proportionately increasing commitment to defend them. What were supposed to be necessary concomitants of security become the source of permanent vulnerability.

Contractarianism and Social Justice

There are good reasons for scepticism about contractarian justifications of the state. The problem is that the moral autonomy of states is a universal principle supporting the idea of sovereignty. Too many states make the violation of human rights and the denial of social justice almost their first principle. As David Luban has pointed out, the idea that there is usually some 'fit' between community and government is an insidious one.[40] Apart from being a gross mis-description of many states, it conflates the legitimacy of state – the entire government, legislative and judicial apparatus – with that of the government which holds power in the state. One consequence of this is that the possible illegality of the conduct of governments with respect to the constitution and legal order of the state, which could in turn create conditions for just rebellion and (possibly) intervention in support of this, is discounted. One function of the state as a prescriptive legal order is to protect a people against the arbitrary power of its government.

The contractarian idea directly confronts the idea of the universality of principles of justice and rights; it presupposes the priority of the rights of the citizens of a state over those of aliens. For instance, even Locke's proviso for just acquisition of property, that enough and as good be left over for the next man,[41] or Hobbes' stipulation that just title to land does not extend to what is superfluous or unused fails to act as constraints upon the state's absolute assertion of its rights, and of the rights of individuals and groups to which the state gives legal sanction, with respect to other states and aliens. If the claims of the state are taken to be ethically self-subsistent, and if the rights of those outside it do not impinge on its legitimacy, then, in the terms of a strong cosmopolitan critique of the state, the self-assertion of the legitimacy of the state, and its claim to owe a primary duty to its citizens, is on the same level as the Mafia Godfather's argument that the family business comes first. Even if the internal conditions of the state show a high degree of social justice, it does not follow that the state is justified in ignoring the claims of those outside it.

It is too facile to equate 'social justice' with the fairness of the distribution of resources and with the upholding of rights and obligations as seen solely from the standpoint of the individual. The nature of collective rights, and the inter-relationship of individual and collective rights, is obscured by such an approach. There are still domestic principles of distributive justice which must be considered as distinct from, though not independent of, global distributive principles. Also, there are important practical conflicts between a theory which accords the state recognition of the moral legitimacy of its claims contingently and as a matter of degree, and the realities of sovereignty and the equality of states doctrine as recognised in international law.

International law serves in some degree as a vehicle for the advance of international justice. For this reason, the significance of the realities of its understanding of statehood and sovereignty should not be obscured by an ideal moral theory of the state, however important it is to keep such a theory in view.

2.3 CULTURAL RELATIVISM AND THE LIMITS OF MORAL SYMPATHY

We now turn to some other realist arguments against the introduction of justice-claims on behalf of individuals and sub-state groups into the language of international relations. For the realist, some degree of justice in relations between sovereign states, in the sense of reciprocity and respect for one another's interests, is the most that can be expected.

One of these arguments is that there is neither the degree of altruism nor of empathy on the part of either the leaderships or the populations of modern states to support any meaningful project of international justice. Moreover, there is said to be an insurmountable problem of cultural relativism: there is not enough in common among the diverse and antagonistic value-systems of the modern world to support even a minimum idea of international justice, let alone to determine questions of individual and group rights, or the nature of economic justice.

A point to notice here is that, whilst these arguments are related in the realist critique, they do not necessarily imply one another. Problems of cultural relativism are by no means the only source of limited empathy; nor is physical distance between social groups. It would be still less valid to argue that people's identification with their own communities (and states) was only a consequence of lack of empathy and cultural relativism.

Some believe 'Political realism refuses to identify the moral aspirations of a particular nation with the moral laws that govern the universe...'.[42] Following Benedetto Croce, Morgenthau insists on a rigorous separation of the spheres of the moral and the political. With Croce, too, he seems to believe even that ethical principles are contaminated in their sublimity by application to the sordid world of politics.[43]

Here we return to the realist lament about the erosion of aristocratic diplomacy by the open and public 'diplomacy' characteristic of the modern democratic state. Foreign policy is seen to have become just as susceptible to democratic accountability as other areas of policy, not least because the domestic performance of governments, particularly in economic management, has come to depend upon the success of external policy.

The Narrow Scope of International Morality

E.H. Carr tells us why he believes international morality to be more restricted than 'conventional' morality:

> [I]t is... not merely true that the ordinary man does not demand from the group person certain kinds of moral behaviour which are demanded from the individual; he expects from the group person certain kinds of behaviour which he would definitely regard as immoral in the individual. The group is not only exempt from some of the moral obligations of the individual, but is definitely associated with pugnacity and self-assertion... [Whilst] we find the almost universal recognition of an international morality involving a sense of obligation to an international community or to humanity as a whole... on the other hand, we find an almost equally universal reluctance to admit that, in this international community, the good of the part (i.e. our own country) can be less important than the good of the whole.[44]

The eclipse of international morality by 'nationalistic universalism' is exacerbated by the fact that, whilst mass politics has constrained the conduct of foreign policy by the vagaries of public opinion, the state in turn has strengthened its hold over the loyalty of the individual.[45] The era of total war has vastly extended the range of actions which the state can require of the individual, and curtailed his moral freedom to refuse to perform such actions. The steady accretion of power, especially economic and technological power, by the modern state has increased its ability to impose its will upon the individual. In all states to some degree, and in many to a large degree, state power over the public media, and thus over the inculcation of political values that sustain the state, has furthered this process. In totalitarian states, the treatment of political dissent as a threat to state security and the common interest has historically complemented, or supplanted, the more traditional mechanisms of violence and intimidation in states' attempts to guarantee the allegiance of their subjects.

Much of this is hard to deny, but a caveat is in order. Many realist arguments in this vein are plausible at the level of descriptive mass psychology, but provide no good reason for political philosophy to run for shelter under an equivocal empiricism. People do not have to feel obligations towards others for it to be the case that the existence of such obligations can be rationally demonstrated, although a psychological sense of what morality requires is doubtless a condition of the performance of obligations and the respecting of rights.

The Necessary Content of Moral Concepts

Justice as a concept is complex and synthetic; claims for justice are, strictly, arguments. To show that they are rationally valid is to show that we should accept that the principles to which those concepts lead are imperatives. In other words, an argument from justice is an appeal to reason as much as to humanity.[46]

What must be questioned here is the idea that the abstractness of relations between persons or groups is proportionate to the degree to which principles of justice are binding among them. It is precisely when the absence of social immediacy means an absence of responses of altruism, generosity, charity or affection associated with it, that ethical relationships stand most in need of a rational defence.

The value of philosophical argument is not vitiated by the fact that the principles which it establishes are not everywhere adhered to. It would, however, be futile to come up with a set of prescriptions about international justice which are nowhere followed. To do so would suggest that something had been missed out. That something is the fact that the rights, resources, opportunities (social goods) which people value are highly diverse, and cannot always, or even usually, be arranged in a neat order of priority. Certain goods must be recognised as being valued in themselves, and not be seen as derivatively related to other goods. The principle of self-determination, for instance, can be shown to express rights which cannot simply be reduced to the aggregate rights of individuals. Social goods in international relations, as much as in domestic society, are not always linked axiomatically, nor is there one principle from which others derive their value. Such deductive approaches result in conceptions of morality which are too narrow adequately to describe the diversity, and the often conflicting nature, of individual and social values.

The Limits of 'Nationalistic Universalism'

Having criticised the conflation of psychological and philosophical reasons for holding principles of justice to be valid, we may still admit the prevalence of 'nationalistic universalism' in international relations. The significance of Bukharin's and Stalin's 'socialism in one country' was to fuse together the defence of ideological orthodoxy with a much older and deeper Russian patriotism. The use of the Comintern as an undisguised and unequivocal tool of Soviet state interests is testimony of this.[47] The United States' particular conception of freedom is significant in the formulation of national policy at many more levels than that merely of a strategic ploy. The national experience of the US has led to the association of freedom with capitalist enterprise and individualism in the mainstream of political thought. China's international isolation in the Mao era and the ambivalence still shown by its leaders towards the outside world echo a much older mistrust of outsiders, and the persistence of the tradition of the Middle Kingdom, whilst its bitter border disputes with India, the Soviet Union and Vietnam respectively have reflected the strength of Chinese nationalism. China's self-appointed role as guardian of international revolutionary doctrinal purity in the 1960s was a strange backdrop to the aggressive defence of its peculiar national interests, not least against other socialist states.

States do face challenges to the exclusivity of their concerns with the interests of their domestic constituencies, and sometimes these challenges come from within. If we take one example of international justice, the belief that Western advanced states ought at least to fulfil the UN target of the contribution of 1 per cent of GNP in the form of international aid, it is evident that such a demand hardly challenges the practical authority of states. Although politically active people may campaign for greater international distributive justice, the issue in most developed states is for most of the time a peripheral one.

Yet the failure of states to distribute a greater share of their wealth is not merely a consequence of the apathy and selfishness of their publics. Resource transfers have costs; domestic goals have to be sacrificed. Governments must accede to the demands of industry, finance capital or organised labour. However the social and ideological composition of the government affects the nature of patronage towards rival interests, the provision of benefits – industrial grants, regional aid, the maintenance of full employment and a certain level of demand, or the implementation of tax cuts – offers immediate and tangible political advantage to governments. Foreign aid decreases, albeit slightly, the resources governments have for distributing rewards at home, without necessarily providing compensatory benefits in terms of political influence with recipient states, possibilities for economic expansion, and so on.

States have interests which depend upon the fulfilment of sectional interests, and which determine their external priorities. The state represents the interests of groups within it, but in a way which is mediated by the interests of its components, whether these be party governments in fierce competition with rivals within liberal democracies, or bureaucratic and other elite interests in monolithic political systems. The political structures of all states place limits on the level of resources to be transferred abroad. States do not only represent a complex aggregate of particular interests to which relative values are assigned according to the ideological and class make-up of their rulers. By virtue of their authority, and to the extent that the values they represent are widely held in their societies, they are seen to speak for an immutable, homogeneous and necessary interest of 'the nation' in itself – a powerful idea, even if a mainly fictive one.

This does not preclude the justification of valid intra-state distributive principles which must be considered alongside international distributive principles. But it does suggest that any explanation of the limited extent of resource redistribution between states simply in terms of the narrow self-regard of their citizens, and the argument that this offers support to the realist view that the state retains its primacy if not its uniqueness as a constituency for justice, is misleading and even naive as an account of the domestic politics of developed states.

The Primacy of the State as a Focus of Loyalty

What seems best evidence for the view of the state as the appropriate constituency for justice is that it continues to be the focus of people's primary political loyalties, and of their social and economic expectations. In one sense, identification with a state is not to be ranked in the same hierarchy of identifications as region, nation, class or religion, but as something external to, and even deriving from, these preferences. These more immediate, in the sense of more emotively felt, loyalties often issue in the demand for independent statehood.

J.D.B. Miller has argued cogently for the primacy of the state in this respect.[48] The state limits external loyalties. Historically, Pan-Slavic idealism, for example, foundered on the reality of conflicts between states. More concretely, and recently, Pan-Arabism has been frustrated by differences in the attitudes of the Arab states towards Israel, and by inter-Islamic doctrinal differences. Kenneth Waltz has argued that class loyalty as a counterpoint to loyalty towards the state is hardly stronger than racial, ethnic or cultural identity, especially in times of national conflict and war.[49] The support of the socialist parties in Britain, France and Germany for their countries' respective causes in 1914, after repeated condemnations of the imperialist nature of the policies of the Great Powers, provides evidence of this. The ultimate failure of the strategy of the Popular Front governments in 1930s Europe, in the face of strident fascistic nationalism and systematic onslaughts on working class interests and organisations, had still direr consequences. To the sceptic, the ideological disputes of the two major communist states after the schism of 1963, over the confrontation of 'Western imperialism' and the correct attitude to take towards the independence struggles of the Third World, are merely expressions of a much more traditional Great Power struggle for hegemony.

As scarcity produces the need for justice, so it leads to the jealously guarded principle of economic sovereignty. Even the have-not states respect this principle; they challenge the absolute right of states to their resources in the name of distributive justice or the restitution of past wrongs, and of course in the hope of material benefit, but not in such a way as to undermine economic sovereignty generally. The emphasis on restitution rather than on redistribution of resources to satisfy basic rights globally has been favoured by many of the Group of 77 leaders as being more compatible with the principle of sovereignty.

The political and psychological constraints on altruism outside the community of the state do not entail that all or most people are morally wholly indifferent to the external actions of their states, or to the needs and rights of those outside it.[50] Robert W. Tucker attributes what he dismisses as the rhetoric of international justice to the sentimentalism of educated liberal and radical elites in developed states, by his definition disaffected and alienated from the views of the majority of people in these states.[51] But there are reasons not to accept this as a generalisation. The domestic resistance to, for instance, the United States' policy in Vietnam, the deep and bitter domestic divisions caused by French colonial policy in Algeria, or by Britain's policy at the time of the Suez crisis, indicates that the justice as well as the pragmatic wisdom of governments' policies are challenged by others than self-serving, idealistic elites.

Many political systems evidently fail to command the support of most of their populations, and are preserved through the use of force or the threat of it. This is so even where the state is territorially coextensive with a nation towards which individuals have a high degree of identification and loyalty – as was true of Poland before its democratic revolution of 1989 – or where the existence of a political state has, at least to some degree, united disparate peoples in a shared national identity.

Individual Rights, Collective Rights and Cultural Relativism

Realists maintain that even if these barriers to international justice could be broken down, the problem of cultural relativism would remain. One central aspect of this is the relationship between individual action and liberty and the collective good. Western liberalism places the individual at the centre of social thought. From the 'possessive individualism' of the Lockean contract to the radical liberalism of J.S. Mill, the threat of the collective will to the freedom of the individual expresses itself in the rejection of the 'tyranny of public opinion'. Just as Mill rejected Bentham's definition of the utilitarian doctrine as 'the greatest good of the greatest number', and sought to show instead that the safeguarding of the freedom and creativity of the individual was itself an indispensable condition of maximising the welfare of society, so economic liberalism, following Adam Smith, maintained that the pursuit of self-interest by the individual in the market led to the optimal satisfaction of the wants of others, despite the fact that these benefits to others were unintended.

Indeed, libertarian and what are now termed 'neo-liberal' doctrines have been of considerable influence upon the ideology of contemporary Western governments, particularly in Britain and the United States.[52] The collectivist politics of the postwar mixed economy, with its extensive social welfare provision, state education and pervasive state economic intervention, has been seriously challenged by the re-emergence of these doctrines. It is significant that in the impressive resurgence of 'grand' political theory, in the English-speaking world at least, theorists ranging from the New Right libertarian Robert Nozick to interventionist liberals such as John Rawls and Ronald Dworkin have, whilst disagreeing profoundly on the scope of legitimate state intervention in the economy and society, agreed unequivocally that respect for individual rights means that there are certain things which states may not do under any circumstances, irrespective of whether such actions advance the collective 'interest' or 'will' of others.

This unease about the subsumption of individual rights under collective ones, and consequent efforts to make the justification of collective rights depend upon the rights of individuals, has specifically European roots, not least in the Protestant tradition of the direct relationship of the individual and God, without the mediation of church authority. But this primacy of the individual is, some writers contend, largely or wholly absent in other cultures, where the sphere of the individual is conceived very differently. Thus, the traditional Chinese view of the individual places him within bonds of duty to family and state. Obedience and obligation are stressed; these concepts are more compatible with the idea of society as an organic, hierarchical totality than is the idea of a priori right. Islamic doctrine stresses the responsibility of each man to his family, community and, above all, to God, as dictated by the Koran and the shariah. Again, Hindu religion and culture view the individual first and foremost as a member of a caste; *dharma* requires that the individual accept and fulfil his allotted role in society.

Collective rights as well as individual ones are vigorously asserted in modern international politics. The emergence of so many independent African and Asian states in the era of de-colonisation has indeed altered the conception of human rights now enshrined in international treaties and conventions from the individualism of the UN Charter to one that stresses the rights of peoples. Rights to internal and external self-determination are asserted in the International Covenant on Civil and Political Rights, the Banjul Charter of the Organisation of African Unity, and the Algiers Declaration of Human Rights. Rights to national economic development and a just social order have been increasingly asserted on behalf of nations, and not in terms of the economic rights of individuals.

There is another sense in which the traditional rights expressed in international law do not raise problems of cultural relativism associated with rights ascribed to individuals and sub-state groups. Positive international law comprehends the rights of states in the form of treaties and conventions, usually without regard to the cultural specificity of the meaning of such rights. Disagreements have centred on matters of interpretation rather than on the binding nature of international legal provisions.

In Western societies economic individualism and market institutions have been defended on the grounds that inequalities based upon entrepreneurial ability, effort or luck are the means by which the total product is increased. But how to compare these with the organic, hierarchical, and ascetic values practised in, and embraced by, many Asian and African societies? The functional defence of the concentration of great wealth in (relatively) few private hands, and the explicit or tacit acceptance that the poverty and squalor that co-exist with great wealth in capitalist societies are inevitable concomitants of an otherwise optimal system, is entirely at odds with the communitarian, egalitarian traditions of certain underdeveloped and developing states. In this context, the socialist forms of co-operative development in post-Somoza Nicaragua, or in post-independence Tanzania, can be contrasted with the 'development' experiences of vast swathes of the dispossessed populations of Brazil or of the Philippines.

Collective rights as the basis for claims to sovereign statehood and political and territorial integrity are understood quite differently, the sceptic argues. For instance, the European powers finally conceded the principle of self-determination in the sense of the political independence of former colonial territories, only to find that newly independent states were defining self-determination in new and unrelated ways. Highly contestable arguments about rights of self-determination over contiguous territory,[53] associated with contradictory arguments that colonialism itself constituted a permanent form of aggression justifying a forcible response, were used by India in its annexation of Goa and by Indonesia in its invasion and subjugation of East Timor.

Since the nature of the state is understood differently by Marxist-Leninists, liberal democrats and fundamentalist Moslems, it follows that the nature of such principles as non-intervention and self-determination must also be understood differently.

The Ethical Consequences of Cultural Relativism

Whilst many of the facts of cultural relativism are indisputable, the validity of the normative conclusions often assumed to follow from these facts is far less evident.[54] The effect of relativism is that ultimately it will not be the conventions of society, commonly understood and relevant to common needs, which delimit the area of rights, but the fiat of the state. If no ascription of fundamental rights to the individual is allowed, no principle stands to defend him from the state. Of course, it might be objected that no principle can defend the individual from the state in the end, and that only countervailing political action against arbitrary state power can do so. This objection is, however, beside the point. What is under discussion is the nature of principles legitimating such action. Without such principles, there are no grounds on which to criticise states for violating the rights of individuals. This is, indeed, a logical impossibility if states are to be the arbiters of what those rights are.

Many states are essentially in a condition of war with their own citizens, and yet those states are still uneasy about admitting to violations of their citizens' rights. The state's antagonists become enemies of the 'people'. The state never fights them in order to protect itself, but to defend the public. Grossly unequal treatment of groups within the state is attributed to the impersonal workings of some necessary principle (such as the market order) or to bogus 'facts' of racial inferiority, or the incapacity of peoples for self-government. Governments usually attempt to identify some 'rational' and 'relevant' grounds for their treatment of people. To reiterate, hypocrisy is the means by which vice pays tribute to virtue, but it is also the way in which moral understanding shared across the boundaries of cultures and states is made apparent.

Respect for human dignity also requires respect for the social, cultural and religious traditions of a society. The autonomy and unique values of cultures are themselves expressions of the senses of social identity, belonging and security to which individuals have rights. In this sense, respect for cultural diversity is itself a moral principle. However, the sociological understanding of tradition, and of the need of the individual to participate in a common identity, does not preclude an evaluation of the moral and political concepts of that community, and particularly of the rights enjoyed by those within it.

This leads to an important caveat. Respect for cultural diversity and autonomy does not preclude judgement of cultural practices. Such respect is a second-order moral principle. Where cultural practices violate the fundamental rights of individuals, or where they are imposed by dominant elites or by forces alien to a society, they are open to criticism. It is not a case of there being an insoluble conflict between moral respect for individuals and respect for the cultural traditions under which they live. Cultural traditions are valuable because they have positive meaning for individuals. When they come to threaten the fundamental rights of individuals, or even their existence, the defence of the independent value of cultural traditions and practices is no longer possible in these terms.

Collective rights are still more variously understood. The doctrines of both self-determination and non-intervention still have an ambivalent status in international law. But as James Piscatori has pointed out in the case of Islam,[55] the rejection by certain cultures of the philosophical basis of international law, in so far as it predicates the right of nations and states as much as of individuals in a natural law tradition alien to many non-European cultures, has by no means led in practice to the rejection of international law by the majority of non-European states. The leadership of Iran appealed to the United Nations and to the international law of aggression to substantiate its claims that it was doing no more than legitimately defend itself against Iraqi aggression, for one instance.

2.4 REALISM AND THE DOCTRINE OF THE SOVEREIGN EQUALITY OF STATES

Realist theories, broadly, share four assumptions: that power is the ultimate determinant of international relations; that the international system is hierarchical; that the problem of order remains acute (though its solution is to be found in the acceptance and manipulation of this hierarchy); and that these features of the international system are permanent ones, subject only to minor alteration. In order to see how the doctrine of the equality of states causes problems for realists, we should distinguish between what may be termed 'Hobbesian realism' and 'liberal realism'.

Unlike Hobbesians, liberal realists acknowledge that certain principles of justice inform the relations of states. They respect one another's sovereign equality, rights to participate in international organisations, equal obligation to accept the international law principle of *pacta sunt servanda*, and so on. Even the principle of self-determination has gone some way towards becoming a recognised principle of international justice, although the demand for national rights has often threatened the principle of sovereignty – that is, the rights of states – so that international justice strictly understood is not identical with interstate justice. As Hedley Bull notes,

> to the extent that there is a broad consensus that states should be nation-states, and that the official doctrine of most states (even so-called multinational states) is that they are nation-states, there is a measure of harmony between the ideas of interstate and of international justice.[56]

Liberal realists, such as Bull and Martin Wight,[57] accept that international relations are partially characterised by the existence of elements of an international society, which in their view mitigate but cannot displace the central role of power. Both Hobbesian and liberal realists are, however, critical of the doctrine of the equality of states. They see the doctrine as being at odds with the natural and necessary hierarchy of the international system, and therefore as being a threat to international order. It is in their eyes a spurious moral doctrine, giving rise to an absolute proscription of intervention which is both unrealistic and irrelevant in the modern world.

The doctrine of the sovereign equality of states was first formulated in its modern version by Emerich de Vattel, and became the basis of secular, positivist international legal theory:

> Since men are by nature equal, and their individual rights and obligations the same, as coming equally from nature, Nations, which are composed of men and may be regarded as so many free persons, living together in a state of nature, are by nature equal and hold from nature the same obligations and the same rights. Strength or weakness, in this case, counts for nothing. A dwarf is as much a man as a giant is; a small Republic is no less a sovereign State than the most powerful Kingdom ... Since Nations are free, independent, and equal, and since each has the right to decide in its conscience what it must do to fulfil its duties, the effect of this is to produce, before the world at least, a perfect equality of rights among Nations .... [58]

The Different Meanings of the Doctrine of the Equality of States

Julius Stone has identified four 'equivocations' in the doctrine of the equality of states which impinge upon international justice. [59] The first is between equality for states and for other 'group persons'. The effect of claims based on statehood is to exclude non-states and individuals. It is evidence of this equivocation that both the condemnation of anti-colonialism and claims for self-determination hover between claims for justice and the assertion of law. The leaders of newly independent states may support the aspirations of other nations to independent statehood rather than stress the exclusivity of their own rights as states, but the paradox is that as more states gain equality before the law, so the actual material inequalities between states increase.

The second equivocation identified is between the equal legal standing of states, and what Stone terms the 'quantum' of legal rights which proceed from that legal equality. This problem arises especially in international institutions such as the UN General Assembly, where equal voting rights do nothing to conceal the great disparities of military, political or economic power, or the ability to contribute resources to the collective implementation of action decided by the United Nations.

The third equivocation expresses Vattel's central conflict, which Stone terms the 'dialectic of sovereignty', between the equal, sovereign independence of states and their substantive equality. Put simply, this is no more than the question 'does the equal sovereignty of states allow a duty to aid poorer ones?' The fourth equivocation is related to the third; it is between the equality of states or nations as entities, and the equality of all mankind. Is the *jus gentium* binding merely upon the relations between states and nations, or binding in itself upon the whole of humanity? Can we talk about a growing world justice constituency at a time when almost no moral precepts seem to be shared unequivocally?

The Attack on the Doctrine of the Sovereign Equality of States

Some realist writers see more than an 'equivocation' between the state and the nation as the bearer of a right of equality. They deny that there is in the modern world any general coincidence of states and nations, and maintain that the idea of a nation is itself usually a spurious one:

> Nations themselves are mythical concepts that may correspond roughly to realities, or may have virtually no correspondence to them. The corporate personality with which we endow them in our minds is metaphoric and convenient rather than real .... '[60]

For others, the doctrine of the equality of states has led to the anthropomorphism of the state.[61] The doctrine might be based more soundly if all states contained peoples so closely tied together around a common purpose that the voice of the state possessed an exclusivity in articulating the general will of the people. But this is impossibly rare, and even this circumstance would not alter the fact that states are not ends in themselves in the way that human beings are.

The equality of states doctrine is open to attack on two fronts, firstly as a fallacious analogy of sovereign states and persons. For Hobbes and Rousseau, the sovereign power is a moral person. For Hegel, the *Volksgeist* constitutes 'the spiritual principle of the political community'. The insistence on the sovereign equality of states derives from the idea of the inviolable essence of man. But states are not like men; the will of the state is a fictive one. Sovereignty may serve to defend the integrity of individuals, but does not do so without dangers:

> The concept of man possessing an inviolable essence envisages a political society characterised by an equality of concern for all its members. To safeguard the individual's legal and political rights, to create an atmosphere in which man's highest potentialities may flourish, is regarded as a primary objective of political society . . . To further these ends, the myth of state personality may, at certain times and for certain purposes, play an important role . . . [W]hen this happens, the personality of the state may come to have greater value than the personality of the individual.[62]

The consequence of the 'myth of state personality' is seen to be expressed in Article 2 (1) of the UN Charter: 'The organisation is based on the principle of the sovereign equality of all its members.' Standards of justice appropriate solely for individuals are being inappropriately applied to states.

A second criticism is that the doctrine of sovereign equality is at odds with the reality of inequalities of power, and with the workings of the mechanisms of order in world politics. The tradition of great power primacy was reflected in the design of the UN Security Council, and continued until the developing Cold War destroyed the fragile unity of the great powers. But the influx of newly independent states into the UN General Assembly led to the rejection of the idea of the subordination of small powers to the great in the maintenance of world order. Instead, the principle of equal representation, quite detached from the realities of military, economic or political power, but rooted deeply in the idea of states possessing equal corporate personalities, became established. Robert Klein argues that the decline of the 'police function' of the great powers, the idea that responsibility for maintaining international order should be proportionate to a state's power, has led to unprecedented instability in international politics.[63]

Yet the primacy of order as an international value and its conflict with the doctrine of the equality of states continue to be manifested in the realities of intervention in international relations. In the realist view, it is the proposition that states are, or should be, coextensive with nations, which lends itself to the specious exploitation by the great powers of this rivalry of rights between the nation and state as a pretext for exerting power and control. In American policy the doctrine of the sovereign equality of states has not led to the principle of non-intervention being given more weight than fear of communism, or than American commitment to 'common security' in the Western hemisphere. True, interventions in Korea, and later in Vietnam, were justified on the grounds that friendly sovereign governments had appealed for US assistance to repel intervention by revolutionary neighbours, but this hardly seems a plausible explanation or defence of US intervention in the Dominican Republic, Grenada or Panama, let alone of the covert but highly effective intervention in Chile in 1973. The doctrine of the equality of states serves to obscure the reality of power politics by making bogus excuses for it.

Nuclear Proliferation and the Equality of States

From this highly critical perspective, it would seem that the belief that formal legal equality carries with it certain substantive rights has led small powers to view the Non-Proliferation Treaty of 1968 as an institutionalised form of discrimination against them. At the same time, the acquisition of nuclear weapons by an increasing number of states threatens to make the management of international order more precarious if not impossible. It is thus the most pernicious consequence of the belief in the equality of states, representing the ultimate disjunction between the 'natural' hierarchy of states and the imperatives of maintaining international order. At the same time, proliferation offers, for the prophet of 'world order' solutions, the best evidence of the obsolescence of the existing, hierarchical international system. These two sets of critics differ in their prescriptions, but there is little doubt that proliferation presents an equally grave problem for both.

The proliferation of nuclear weapons threatens to undermine an international order based on the natural inequalities of states. Size of population, natural resources, stage of economic development, conventional military power or strategic position provide no certainty of a state's ability to coerce a weaker enemy when the latter possesses nuclear weapons.

States want to acquire nuclear weapons for many reasons.[64] Security concerns may be focused on actually or potentially hostile neighbours who are suspected of developing nuclear weapons themselves; or on powers (including the superpowers) outside a region whose intervention is seen as likely to threaten the security or even the existence of the proliferating state; or the state may, by virtue of its pariah status, value nuclear forces as the only means of confronting a number of permanently hostile powers, as in the case of Israel or apartheid South Africa. Whatever the motives, if the disjunction between traditional sources of national power and military capability undermines the maintenance of order in the international system, the principle of sovereignty which was the cornerstone of that system has by no means diminished in importance. In fact, by the act of proliferation the state affirms its unlimited political sovereignty, and its lack of obligation to the citizens of other states and to humanity generally in so far as it intends to use such weapons. The dismantling of hierarchical international relations has led not to the mutual respect for and accommodation of sovereignty suggested by the philosophical justification of the doctrine of the sovereign equality of states, but to an aggressive and unqualified assertion of sovereignty.

For the realist critic of the equality of states doctrine, the confusion of the formal and substantive equality of states has led the governments of the major powers to acquiesce in the idea that the right to possess nuclear weapons is somehow inherent in the nature of sovereignty. The cosmopolitan critic of the international system can draw little more comfort from the facts of proliferation. They seem to point further away than ever from solutions based on the transfer of political authority to global institutions. The reality of global proliferation shows both the persistence and the dangers of the assertion of national sovereignty.

Vattel's concept of *droit nécessaire* is not the same as Hobbes' natural right: it does not preclude justice in relations between states, but merely asserts that none but the state may act as judge of its own actions. The questions raised by the first two 'equivocations' which we examined, concerning the equivalence and respective rights of nations and states, the viability of new states and their ability to participate in the international system, and the substantive content of their rights considered as something distinct from their legal, formal equality, are the central issues of the right of self-determination. The 'dialectic of sovereignty' and the duty of aid are the essential problems of international distributive justice. The question of the nature and extent of the *jus gentium* determines the answers to the questions 'who are the subjects of international law and international society?' and 'how far does international law operate as a vehicle of international justice?'

The National Interest and the Interest of States

The realist tradition in general can be seen to contain a serious conflict between its defence of the primacy of the national interest, and its evaluative criteria of the moral significance and comparison of rival interests. This conflict seems from the Hobbesian standpoint to be irresolvable. Since the Hobbesian tradition treats states as persons, and attributes natural right equally to them, it has no grounds on which to weigh their claims differently. Natural right involves, as Hobbes says, that

> every one is governed by his own Reason; and there is nothing he can make use of, that may not be a help unto him, in preserving his life against his enemyes; It followeth, that in such a condition, every man has a Right to everything....[65]

Yet there is clearly a sense in which it is preposterous to say that, for instance, Cape Verde or Honduras must be understood as possessing the same quantum of rights as France or Russia. But if the 'quantities' of states' rights are to be considered unequal, this must follow from the argument that those rights are derivative of the rights of the people – that section of humanity – who compose them. Liberal realism defends the state as having a positive value as the expression of a constituency of justice, and not just as providing the necessary degree of force which gives justice its only meaning, as the Hobbesians contend. The moral character of the state and the extent of its legitimate claims are related, albeit obscurely and indirectly, to the rights and needs of the community within it.

It might, therefore, seem a relatively easy step for liberal realists to reject any implication that the formal, legal equality of states gives any support to claims for equal substantive rights. What is, however, disturbing about the idea that the rights of states are directly proportionate in content to, say, the size of their populations, is that the 'moral authority' of large and powerful states may come to be carried over, spuriously, to the rectitude of their actions. Moreover, if some threshold of minimum rights attaching to a state is not permitted, then the rejection of the equality of states doctrine in favour of some 'proportionate' account of state (and national) rights undermines many safeguards for the protection of the rights of communities and individuals. Rejection of the equality of states doctrine on the grounds we have reviewed might become a justification of imperialism or worse.

Liberal realists do not regard states' rights as being entirely derivative of the rights of persons in the sense that the natural law theorists did. Rather, states are assigned a special moral autonomy in so far as they do protect and enshrine principles of justice for their citizens. The reason is that an acceptance of the wholly derivative nature of the state's personality would mean that states cease to be moral entities in their own standing. If this concession is made, then there is no longer a good reason to rule out claims of individual and cosmopolitan justice, as liberal realists do.

This dismissal by realists of individual and global justice is defended by reference to the supposed incompatibility of those claims with international order, and on this point Hobbesian and liberal realists are united.

2.5 JUSTICE VERSUS ORDER IN INTERNATIONAL RELATIONS

The conflict between order and justice in international relations is described with great acuity by Rousseau:

> The first thing I notice, in considering the condition of the human species, is an open contradiction in its constitution which causes it to vacillate incessantly. As individual men we live in a civil state subject to laws; as peoples we each enjoy a natural liberty; this makes our position fundamentally worse than if these distinctions were unknown. For living simultaneously in the social order and in the state of nature we are subjected to the inconveniences of both, without finding security in either. The perfection of the social order consists, it is true, in the conjunction of force and law. But this demands that law guides the use of force; whereas according to the ideas of absolute independence held by Princes, force alone, speaking to the citizens under the name of law and to foreigners under the name of *raison d'état*, removes from the latter the power, and from the former the will to resist, in such a way that everywhere the empty name of justice serves only as a safeguard for violence.[66]

Hobbesian realism may be distinguished from liberal realism in that it views the conflict between order and justice as especially acute and unequivocal. It cannot accept that there are circumstances in which order should be sacrificed in the interests of greater justice. Hierarchy and the use or threat of force preserves order in international relations, and preserves the sovereign state which is the condition of justice.

Scepticism About the 'New International Economic Order' Debate

Robert W. Tucker has argued that demands for a 'New International Economic Order' based on global economic redistribution, and the 'new political sensibility' of liberal elites in the (predominantly Western) developed states, are at odds with the requirements of world order.[67] They ignore the fact that inequality and hierarchy, deriving from unequally distributed natural resources, are endemic to the international system.

Demands for greater international economic justice made by least-developed countries (LDCs) are, in Tucker's view, paradoxical. Sovereignty over resources, which is insisted upon as a principle as much by LDCs as by developed states, is incompatible with the insistence that wealthy states have a moral duty to share their resources. Most LDCs are very far from wanting to undermine the system of independent, sovereign states of which self-help is the mainstay. In Africa and Asia, the preoccupation of recently independent states with border disputes and contested claims to control of resources and the simultaneous commitment to the principle of non-intervention of the OAU or ASEAN testify to the continuity of the 'old' international order in the Third World. The LDCs seek only to enhance their standing within the international system, not to transform that system itself.

There is, on this account, nothing novel about the claims of the LDCs. Optimists of a cosmopolitan persuasion hope that international economic organisations can promote the conception of international welfare, and that the growth of complex interdependencies between states will make the use of force counterproductive. It is argued against such a view that the opposite of ameliorative reform of the contemporary states system is occurring. Interdependence increases the scope for international conflict – witness the hostility of the American and European responses to OPEC oil increases, and the resentment among radical LDCs that Arab petrodollars were used to maintain liquidity in the Western banking system rather than to assist fellow, and poorer, developing states. The process of development has, if anything, increased the power of the state throughout most of the Third World, particularly as individual states have come to serve the interests of powerful domestic elites. Rivalry between LDCs themselves has grown. The unity of the Non-Aligned Movement, or of the fledgling 'Group of 77', has been eroded by the success of new 'tiger economies', which no longer express solidarity with the most backward. Not a new type of international order, but a new hierarchy within an international system showing most of the features of the old order has emerged. Old inequalities based on religion or metropolitan/colonial relationships have been replaced by the inequality of national resources, and by social and cultural constraints upon development in certain states. Inequality remains systemic.[68]

On this view, the sources of order within this 'new' international system have been diminished by the accession of the major powers to the demands for justice of developing states. A disjunction between power and order has emerged. Order in the international system was previously maintained by the exercise of power on the part of dominant states.

At present, the danger is that those states that seek to benefit most from a shift towards greater economic and political equality will simply be unable to maintain order within that system, whilst the great powers have needlessly limited their ability to use their power at a time of growing disorder. This has been manifested, *inter alia*, in the reluctance of elites within the dominant states to intervene, or to intervene decisively, to protect their vital interests, as a result of a naive and excessive respect for the rights of weaker states. The separation of power and influence within the United Nations is another example of this disjunction between power and responsibility, most graphically illustrated at the time of the Uniting for Peace Resolution of November 1950, by means of which responsibility for international security was transferred to the UN General Assembly in recognition of the impotence of the Security Council in organising collective action.

In Tucker's view, states such as the US have overestimated the cohesiveness of the LDCs, and the extent of Western vulnerability to their pressures. Those states that are of economic or strategic significance must be distinguished from those that are not. The former tend to be those states at the upper end of the scale of developing states – Taiwan, South Korea, Singapore, Brazil – that have a less vociferous and urgent interest in aid or trade concessions, or any of the other paraphernalia of 'greater international economic justice'.

Conservative critics of demands for a 'New International Economic Order' have offered other reasons for scepticism about international resource transfers.[69] Domestic demands within donor states pose countervailing pressures: national publics are manifestly unwilling to

bear the costs of resource transfer when they stand to suffer notice-
ably from them. Moreover, the domestic distribution of funds received through aid is always uncertain: national prestige projects,
investment in production for the demand of privileged Third World
elites, or simple corruption may prevent such funds having any real
effect on the welfare of the people they were intended to help. Most
importantly, the emphasis of proponents of the 'new political sensibility' upon the welfare of individuals, and the consequent down-
grading of the role of the state that this emphasis is said to have
produced, are seen to fly in the face of facts about the nature of the
international system. The paradox is that the state remains the only
mechanism of redistribution and justice, whilst the states system is the
major obstacle to that process on a global level. Demands for greater
international justice are only marginal with regard to the nature of the
international system itself, whilst the need for order remains para-
mount.

International order can be understood in two senses: as a synonym
for the arrangement of the elements of the international system as it
actually is, with no statement of value implied in the description; and
as a condition of that minimum of security, stability and settled
expectation which is the condition of other desirable goals, including
justice. It is the second sense that is important here. It is also necessary
to distinguish between a particular order that exists at any time, and
order as a general condition. International order for the Hobbesian
preserves the state as the vehicle of justice; to talk of a trade-off
between order and justice at the international level is therefore mis-
guided.

The Liberal Realist Response to the Conflict Between Order and Justice

Liberal realists, such as Hedley Bull, argue that a degree of justice
between states as well as within the state is compatible with the
preservation of order, but also concede that there are circumstances
in which justice may be the higher value when it conflicts with a
particular order in which justice is denied. This is to make a compromise in a particular instance; it is not to subvert order as a condition to
the demands of justice in an absolute sense. Justice continues to
require order.[70] The cosmopolitan theorist, conversely, assumes that
it is the very condition of order which exists among states and the
mechanisms used to defend it which preclude the realisation of global
justice.

Hobbesian realists and cosmopolitan theorists, then, share a belief that sets them apart from liberal realists, although they share it for opposing reasons. They believe that there is a radical antithesis between the conditions of justice within the state, and the conditions of international or global justice.

Against this, Bull rejects the 'all or nothing' approach to order and justice, and accepts that a just international order is likely to be more durable than an unjust one.[71] The tension between justice and order takes place along a continuum. At one end, the subordination of order to justice may be relatively short-lived, and may issue in a new, tolerably stable order which incorporates values considered to be more just. In such a situation, a large degree of consensus on the need to secure such values may precede the transition, though this consensus need not be shared by the parties to the conflict. Such a case is the period of decolonisation after the Second World War. Relatively orderly progress to independence was aided by the illegitimacy of colonialism in the eyes of new members of the international system, particularly after India's independence, and by the pressure brought to bear by the United States upon its European allies. The degree of violent disorder was also limited by the economic and political weakness of the former imperial powers. Although this was not without exception; the savagery of French policy in Algeria harkened back to a much older and darker era than did the relatively restrained British response to the Mau Mau in Kenya. With the departure from the international stage of the pariah roles of Salazar's Portugal and Smith's UDI Rhodesia, South Africa remained the alienated legatee of the colonial era; and Pretoria long insisted that South Africa's role had been one of maintaining regional (and ultimately global) order in the face of a pervasive communist threat.

Certain justice-claims lead ineluctably to a starker choice between justice and order, in circumstances where no international consensus exists. Many Third World states in the United Nations have taken the position that apartheid was itself a form of international aggression, whilst Krishna Menon argued that the centuries-old Portuguese occupation of Goa constituted permanent aggression. Such purported principles of justice as these have been seen by liberal realists to gravely threaten international order. The declaration of certain types of domestic political regime as being de facto illegitimate, and the positing of an unrestricted post-colonial right to the annexation of territory on the basis of contiguity found little general acceptance, even amongst those states that occasionally find such devices useful to employ.

The Conflict of Order and Justice and Their Mutual Necessity

A minimum degree of order is required to defend just social arrangements once achieved, and the ultimate value of order lies in the fact that the security and dignity of the person depend upon it, as they also depend upon the securing of justice. In this sense, order and justice are always mutually dependent conditions.

Demands for cosmopolitan justice are seen by realists generally as especially inimical to world order. Proposals for justice conceived globally require, at best, co-ordination on policies of resource transfer, immigration, ecological protection and the safeguarding of religious, social and cultural practices about which there exists no international consensus. Indeed, the consensus which obtains is that such matters are within the exclusive competence of states, except where, as in the case of regional arrangements such as the EU or the former COMECON, or generalised ones such as GATT, states voluntarily limit their sovereignty for specific purposes. The legitimacy of demands that make reference to the needs of a 'community of mankind' may be questioned, on the grounds that no representative political process of the sort that exists in (some) domestic political systems exists at the international level to authenticate such demands. They should be seen rather as ideological in nature than as articulations of real interests of real groups or persons.

Demands for individual justice, which normally come under the rubric of human rights, are seen by realists as inherently conflicting with international order. As already noted, the realities of international power politics intrude in such matters, as states themselves specify the criteria for human rights. Whilst international resource transfers may be justified on grounds of individual welfare, governments and not persons are the immediate beneficiaries. The United States' government classification of non-democratic governments as either 'totalitarian' or 'authoritarian' is supposed to determine whether the denial of human rights is endemic to the political system, or is a lamentable by-product susceptible of reform. Unsurprisingly, most of America's hemispheric allies turn out to be merely authoritarian in their political make-up.

Where individuals are made the subjects of international justice in the sense of personal criminal liability for political acts, as in the cases of the Nuremberg and Japanese War Crimes Tribunals after the Second World War, such treatment is equally selective. Such attempts to introduce human justice into the international arena do not reflect any consensus about the rights and duties of individuals; rather, the fact that only victorious states are able to impose such responsibilities upon the subjects of their defeated adversaries precisely demonstrates the lack of such a consensus. But what is most subversive of international order about human or individual justice from the realist perspective is that it posits individual responsibility towards individuals who are not subjects of the same state, and towards alien states and governments. The corollary is that individuals have not only the right but the duty to disobey their own governments in certain circumstances.

In the realist view, international law itself essentially expresses the status quo; the facts of conquest and annexation must ultimately come to be recognised. International law can never achieve primacy over international politics, since it derives from the acts of will of sovereign agencies, and depends upon these for its execution. Since international law is subject to *raison d'état*, abstract principles of international justice are likely to be of yet more peripheral relevance to states' actions.

The Exaggerated Antithesis of Order and Justice in International Relations

The liberal realist emphasis on mutual tolerance as a source of order is oddly out of place in a world where profound conflicts over values ultimately precipitate violence. It was, as noted, only the peculiar circumstances of the post-World War II world, especially the weakness of the imperial powers, which enabled the national liberation of the former colonies to take place with only moderate violence.

For the realist, some claims of international justice are more threatening to order than others. Claims of justice addressed to a prospective world community (cosmopolitan justice) threaten to eclipse states' rights entirely by positing the 'global interest' as the only grounding for principles of justice. International resource distribution would replace economic sovereignty, and, ultimately, the idea that states stand in any unique relation of legitimacy and obligation to their publics. But the cosmopolitan view of justice is not all of a piece; it too exists along a sort of continuum. Most of those theorists who conceive of justice in global terms, and who allow no particular moral weight to the state, are reconciled to its remaining the basic unit of pluralistic global political organisation. The degree to which states have been willing to concede sovereignty in the interests of co-operation in the common interest has been limited. The institutions of the European Union, for example, have become the means of the management of conflicting national economic interests among European states rather than an arena to reconcile them in some supranational conception of the general welfare. Similarly, COMECON existed to serve the economic interests of its member states, predominantly of course of the former Soviet Union, rather than to realise a common welfare amongst socialist states; thus the rejection of Mozambique's application to join, and the general detachment of COMECON from the development needs of the Third World, certain favoured but marginal states such as Mongolia, Vietnam and Cuba excepted.

Kant argued for the necessity of nation-states as an expression of natural cultural pluralism, and accepted the idea of the national interest as a legitimate one.[72] The most problematic feature of the cosmopolitan argument is not the unequivocal political opposition it expresses to the states system, but the philosophical conflict between its values and the persistence of the state as the actual constituency of justice and welfare for most of the world's population.

Again, it is alleged that the safeguarding of diverse cultural practices is incompatible with cosmopolitan principles of justice. Doubts about the significance of cultural relativism for a theory of justice have been expressed, but it was argued that respect for pluralism in cultural, national and religious practices and values was intimately related to respect for the autonomy of individuals. In this regard, the difficulties of designing cosmopolitan principles of justice do at first sight appear intractable. For one thing, the acceptance of the value of cultural diversity implies the principle of tolerance. This runs counter to the fact that many sorts of belief, from Stalin's variant of Marxism-Leninism, via the exclusivist and hostile 'super-patriotism' of the McCarthy era in the United States, to the radical resurgence of fundamentalist Islam, have as their defining condition that no rival values are to be tolerated.

Justice for individuals is said to be too selective to operate as an international principle. There is always the danger that states will seek to justify the use of arbitrary force on the grounds that it is being used to protect the rights of those outside its borders, and to use such force against individuals said to have been in dereliction of their duties. The problem of this selectivity in the international enforcement of rights and obligations is graphically illustrated by Noam Chomsky's comparison of the war guilt of the Nazi and Japanese wartime leaders and the 'pacification' policies pursued by the US military leadership during the Vietnam war.[73] When individual responsibility is attributed to those individuals and groups that have been directly responsible for state policy, or even when individuals come to be held collectively responsible for the actions of their states, the line between individual and state, between private and public action might seem to become so confused as to be meaningless.

These criticisms are important, but to reject the punishment of individuals or of groups, or even as in the case of reparations after the Great War of entire nations, on the grounds that it is merely victors' justice, is to miss an important point. Hans Kelsen has argued that what is essential to the idea of a law is that there be a sanction applied in the event of a transgression of that law (a 'delict' as he describes it), and that this is as true of international law as it is of domestic law.[74] In the international sphere, this sanction need not be enforced against a recalcitrant state by the entire community of nations. One nation, or a group of nations acting in consort, may impose the sanction.

The idea that the execution of a sanction does not need unanimous assent provided that the law itself specifies the sanction, as the Hague Conventions and the Kellogg–Briand pact provided the basis for the trial of Nazi war criminals, is an important one. We may not agree that the fact that an action is capable of being punished is a necessary condition for holding it to be just or unjust.[75]

Dependence, Interdependence and the Value of Sovereignty

As more and more of the international economic product comes from an increasingly international division of labour, and as the value consumed within the borders of states shows an ever greater discrepancy with the value produced there, principles of international resource distribution grow in importance. But the facts of interdependence relate not only to that increment of the global economic product that derives from transnational productive activity: they describe the problems of access to resources, the constant threat of producer cartelisation, the vulnerability of the international banking system to debtor defaults, and the growing intractability of international exchange control. Interdependence increases the area of possible conflict in international relations, and exacerbates the problem of international order.

The approach taken to the New International Economic Order (NIEO) debate by the Trilateral Commission (Falk, Brandt, Brszinski *et al.*) and their associates highlighted the threat of this growing interdependence. But realist and conservative critics remain sceptical about how far even likely beneficiaries of resource redistribution are committed to fundamental reform of the international system. They point to continuing disputes between developing states as evidence that the principle of national sovereignty is alive and well.

More disputes between these states have arisen as a result of the colonial borders that they inherited upon independence than from conflict over economic resources. Thus in Africa, disputes arising from the demands of groups for self-determination or secession within colonially established states and rivalry between groups over the inheritance of political power after decolonisation have been the chief sources of conflict and civil war. This was the case in the Congo in 1960–1, in the Nigerian civil war of 1967–70 (although in this instance, the presence of large reserves of oil did introduce an element of conflict over resources), in Angola after Portuguese withdrawal in 1974, and in Ethiopia after the overthrow of Haile Selassie in 1974 (where both secession and succession contributed to the continuing civil war). None of these conflicts was confined to the disputants; in each case, intervention by either the former metropolitan powers or by the superpowers ensued.

In addition, the extent of possible economic co-operation in the common good between Third World states has often been limited by their dependence upon external powers. Thus, in West Africa, critics of the CFA franc zone have complained that development in the region is being hampered by dependence upon French 'imperialism'.

When realists accuse Third World states of double standards about international economic and political reform, they ignore the crucial value of the principle of sovereignty to developing states, particularly in respect of economic control. That principle – itself an import from the European states system so far as almost all of Africa and large parts of Latin America and Asia are concerned – has been closely associated with the ability of developing states to exercise any influence over the welfare of their populations. For example, the power of the multinational corporation is confronted in the poorer of the underdeveloped and developing states solely by the power of the state itself, and this power is largely a negative one. Where primary exports are the principal sources of the income of a country, as is usually the case, the ability at least to impose conditions over the rate and extent of the exploitation of mineral and agricultural resources, and to provide some minimal benefits for those outside the small minority of the population that constitutes the management and technical elites, the comprador classes who benefit from the trade provided by multinational operations, and the small skilled proletariat that staffs those operations, by means of taxation and other measures, lies only in the hands of the state.

National sovereignty and the diversity and conflict of the interests it gives rise to have led to the erosion of the initial solidarity shown by the Group of 77 states at the time of UNCTAD 1 (1972) and the policy of 'bloc confrontation' of the North. Rivalry has increased between the 'less developed countries' and the 'newly industrialising countries' (NICs). Growth rates and increases in export revenues in the latter have been much higher than in the underdeveloped world. As Joan Spero notes,

> Such disparities in growth may undermine the Southern perception of a common interest in joint action and may encourage states to concentrate on national or regional policies to the detriment of Southern unity. Moreover, the success of the NICs raises the question of whether they will be co-opted into the North. The advanced developing countries may find a growing interest in keeping the international economic structure intact, and may begin to share Northern apprehensions about radical reform.[76]

The success of OPEC in dramatically raising oil prices also had a divisive effect. If the poorer developing states thought that OPEC members would cast their bread upon the waters, they were disappointed. Instead, growth prospects in developing states were worsened by the sudden increase in the cost of oil imports. This rivalry within the developing world threatens future joint action for resource transfers, and suggests too that any account of international distributive justice would have to include the transfer of resources from NICs as well as the developed powers to the poorest states.

Conservative critics of NIEO proposals challenge the idea that there is a genuine interdependence in relations between developed and developing states. Northern states are said to have no dependence on Southern ones that corresponds to the latter's dependence on trade with the North. There is some economic evidence to support this: the proportions of trade, investment and income generally between developed and developing states as a proportion of their respective global totals have remained low. The classic Lenin–Hobson explanation of imperialism as a means of exporting economic surplus has lost much of its validity as developed states have largely managed, through policies of demand management and redistributive taxation and domestic transfer payments, to absorb much of their economic surpluses internally. However, other forms of dependence, actual or potential, remain. They include the constant possibility of cartelisation and denial of vital resources by Southern states, the debt crisis, and the continuing problem of maintaining economic growth in the developing states, which still makes the search for new markets imperative. Resource dependence can only worsen as irreplaceable natural resources are used up, though this may improve the bargaining position of the developing states in the short run. It is complacent, to say the least, to maintain that global interdependence poses no significant threat to the existing international order. On the contrary, the need for international economic co-operation is acute. Principles of international justice exist to define the terms of such co-operation.

The argument that the effective use of national power is more likely to preserve international order than the pursuit of any concept of justice dismisses the case that the stability and durability of the international order are themselves related to the degree of justice within it. In so doing, this argument overlooks the fact that regional conflict brought about by perceived injustices increases the risk of intervention and military involvement, carrying with it the ever-present risk of escalation. In the contemporary world, the danger of using force to achieve objectives is that any proportion between the degree of force that may need to be used, the costs of using such force, and the value of the objective to be achieved, can quickly be lost sight of. The United States' experience in Indochina, and the Soviet Union's in Afghanistan and Chechenia, have already demonstrated this; the disutility of force must become ever greater in a world of many nuclear powers. Realist arguments often reveal a nostalgia for the paternalist use of force, ignoring how far such paternalism historically created the problems of injustice that remain today.[77]

An Alternative to Realism

We have criticised the moral scepticism of the realist theory of international relations, both in its tendency to assert the uniqueness of the state as a constituency of justice, and as a description of the international state of affairs. Most importantly, the tortuous and unsuccessful attempts of realist theorists to devise a dualist morality with effectively independent domestic and international spheres, or to assert the national interest as an ethical principle *faute de mieux*, are avoided by the clear and separate identification of the two realms of law that is central to the natural law tradition. We have earlier described elements of natural law tradition which give some idea of its candidacy as an alternative to the realist conception of the state and international justice. What is postulated is a body of international ethical first principles by means of which both domestic and international positive law is ultimately to be judged, but which continues to recognise the practical integrity and efficacy of these spheres in a diverse and imperfect world.

The realist defence of the primacy of the state in terms of justice, and of the independent moral value of *raison d'état*, either proceeds from, or collapses into, an organicist conception of the state as being greater than the (ethical) sum of its parts, with or without the associated view that the state is progenitor of the justice-claims of its subjects. The natural law tradition, however, never allows the practical recognition of the critical role of the state in upholding values to degenerate into a critical acceptance of the state as a self-subsistent ethical order. The state is never allowed as an end in itself; its claims are always to be seen as derivative of those of the people who compose it.

Any 'complex instrumentalist' theory of the state must draw heavily on the insights of the classical natural law tradition. In so doing, it seeks to avoid the ambivalence of the realist tradition towards the sovereign equality of states, an ambivalence that derives from the contradiction of *raison d'état* as a moral absolute and the unacceptability of the analogy of states and persons. There is nothing in the form or nature of justice-claims asserted by the leaders of states that is qualitatively different from those of individuals or groups. Neither is there any unique or novel moral character lent to the state by its mediation of these claims. The contradiction is between the moral personification of the state and the desire to avoid ethical statements in the realist description of international relations.

Nevertheless, we must separate the descriptive and normative levels of realist theory. We may concede that parts at least of the former are valid without allowing that the latter follows in any obvious and direct way from it. The state does represent for the vast majority of the world's population the best, even the only, chance of securing justice and rights. Its contingent nature as a constituency and vehicle of justice must be offset against the dangers and impracticalities of alternative global political institutions of the sort examined in the next chapter. Neither of these aspects of the state is morally insignificant. The instrumentalist theory of the state never loses sight of the tension between the ideal and the real in international political theory.

The clear distinction between natural law and the 'Law of Nations' characteristic of natural law theory in the sixteenth and seventeenth centuries continues to provide a richer source of understanding of international ethical conflicts than the sterile opposition between justice and order found in realist writings. The recognition of the contingent but highly significant role of the state in securing justice, and the practical recognition of the independent rights of states, avoids the moral perfectionism, and certainly the reckless pursuit of utopian moral principles, which realism justifiably abhors. Yet the ethical content of the natural law tradition provides standards of reference for the adjudication of matters of dispute, whilst recognising that positive international law must provide for the degree of tolerance of political and cultural pluralism that international security requires.

3 The Cosmopolitan Theory of International Justice

The cosmopolitan theorists see the state, so far from being the condition of human justice, as an obstacle to its truly global implementation. In addition, whilst the arguments to be considered here neither assert, with the realists, the primacy of the value of international order, nor, with advocates of revolutionary change, subordinate order to the realisation of justice, these arguments do stress the intimate relationship between justice and order; the one is highly precarious without the other. The states system as presently constituted is seen to be as much a threat to international order as to justice.

3.1 KANT: THE STATE AND UNIVERSAL RIGHT

Immanuel Kant is, strictly speaking, a republican political theorist but, following Martin Wight's interpretations, it seems to me to be quite reasonable to regard him as a major progenitor of modern cosmopolitan theories.[1]

In Kant's political philosophy, the concern is with 'Universal Right' as an ideal, rather than justice in any of the more confined senses in which we have so far used the term. Man's rational nature means that he must respect others as equally rational agents, and thus as ends in themselves, and that he be himself bound by the universal laws which his rational nature decrees. In Kant's famous definition, 'the Categorical Imperative can ... be expressed thus: Act on maxims which can at the same time have for their object themselves as universal laws of nature.'[2]

Kant asserts the primacy of the moral over the political. His ethics are deontological; man discovers the principle of right as the basis for all law, and is obliged to obey not only the precepts of that law, but to extend its scope as far as possible; and this is true of the law of international relations as well as of the law of domestic society. Kant means by 'peace' not simply the absence of conflict or violence, but a state of affairs which is at once the condition and the goal of the common acceptance of universal, binding laws embodying Universal Right. Peace is not an impossible ideal: it is wholly compatible with the rational element of human nature. Right reason can discover the conditions of perpetual peace which nature in any case ordains: 'Nature inexorably wills that the right should finally triumph. What we neglect to do comes about for itself, though with great inconveniences to us.'[3] Just as reason leads to the establishment of universal laws in the state necessary for the preservation of all, so nations unite under international law as a result of self-interest (particularly as revealed through the necessity to regulate trade). These arguments form the central themes of Kant's great work on international relations, *Perpetual Peace*.

Kant's belief in the providential plan of nature,[4] and in the moral improvability of man,[5] leads him to envisage an institution of Universal Right to overcome international insecurity, and to avoid the domination of states over one another which the anarchy and hierarchy of international relations produce. Although Kant has no faith in the conventional mechanisms of global order, such as the balance of power, to preserve either order or right, he does not argue for a universal institution in the sense of a global state, but rather for a federation of states.

Perpetual Peace

The first article of *Perpetual Peace* provides that 'The Civil Constitution of Every State Should be Republican'[6] and founded upon principles of political equality, expressed through representative government. The relationship of democracy and the peaceful conduct of states' policy is for Kant a most important one. If the consent of the citizens is required for war to be embarked upon, then states will be less likely to embark upon it. In undemocratic states, the ruling individual or oligarchy does not have to bear the costs of war, but 'if the consent of the citizens is required in order to decide that war should be declared (and in this [democratic] constitution it cannot but be the case), nothing is more natural than that they would be very cautious in commencing such a poor game, decreeing for themselves all the calamities of war.'[7] Athens in the late fifth century BC and the modern 'totalitarian democracies' come to mind as counter-examples to this hypothesis, and as evidence of a close link between certain types of democracy and militarism. Still, Kant's belief in the power of democracy to prevent wars is unwavering.

The second article decrees that 'The Law of Nations Shall be Founded on a Federation of Free States.'[8] The republican league would be a league of nations, not a world state, as the latter implies the idea of subjection, which cannot exist among states. Kant's idealism is found in his insistence that, whilst the natural condition of international relations is one of war, war may decide issues, but cannot decide questions of right. As for international law, Kant denies that this can specify occasions for just war. War is the unilateral use of force to settle issues; it is the denial of law, which is the only means of the enforcement of right.

Kant goes on to develop his argument that his republican league of states does not require the subjection of its sovereign components to a supranational authority. Kant makes use of an argument analogous to that of Hobbes which we encountered earlier:

the obligation which men in a lawless condition have under the natural law, and which requires them to abandon the state of nature, does not quite apply to states under the law of nations, for as states they already have an internal juridical constitution and have thus outgrown compulsion from others to submit to a more extended lawful constitution according to their ideas of right. This is true in spite of the fact that reason, from its throne of supreme moral legislating authority, absolutely condemns war as a legal recourse and makes a state of peace a direct duty, even though peace cannot be established or secured except by a compact among nations. For these reasons there must be a league of a particular kind, which can be called a league of peace, and which would be distinguished from a treaty of peace by the fact that the latter terminates only one war, while the former seeks to make an end of all wars forever. This league does not tend to any dominion over the power of the state but only the maintenance and security of the freedom of the state itself and of other states in league with it, without there being any need for them to submit to civil laws and their compulsion, as men in a state of nature must submit.[9]

The third article states that 'The Law of World Citizenship Shall Be Limited to Conditions of Universal Hospitality.'[10] Here Kant makes use of some of the principal ideas of the natural law tradition, such as the idea of an initial common ownership of the earth's resources, the inevitable physical proximity of persons and the consequent need for tolerance, natural co-operation to facilitate mutually beneficial trade, communications, and so on.[11]

Whilst Kant considers states as moral persons, their authority is far from absolute. They depend for their legitimacy upon the relationship between ruler and ruled. For instance, as he argues in the essay 'Metaphysical Elements of Justice', the right of a state to send its citizens to war depends upon whether the state treats its citizens as autonomous moral 'ends' in Kant's sense.[12] This requires, at least, that war should be declared only with the consent of the mass of the people, and that war be prosecuted honestly and openly by the state in such a way as to make plain that it is the general interest which is being served, and not hidden private interests opposed to the general good. The idea of just war comes to depend on the idea of contract.

Kant argues for the necessity of independent states, although this has constituted a state of war. For all states to pass under one power would lead to a 'soulless despotism'. Language and religion are nature's means of separating and preserving the identity of peoples. The separation of nations contradicts the ultimate hegemonic will of states, which is the union of all nations under one state.

Yet Kant shows an equivocal attitude towards this possibility, for, whilst maintaining that world government is not possible, he still argues that the evolution towards a 'state of many nations' is desirable. The problem is to combine this inevitable separation of humanity with the preservation of peace embodying Universal Right:

> For states in their relation to each other, there cannot be any reasonable way out of the lawless condition which entails only war except that they... adjust themselves to the constraints of public law and thus establish a continuously growing state consisting of various nations (*civitas gentium*), which will ultimately include all the nations of the world. But under the idea of the law of nations they do not wish this, and reject in practice what is correct in theory.[13]

Instead, 'there can be... in place of the positive idea of a world republic, only the negative surrogate of an alliance which averts war'[14] – the necessary but inadequate alternative in an imperfect world.

Kant clearly intends his idealised state composed of all the nations to possess a logic opposed to that of the hegemonic logic of the particular state, and yet acknowledges that in practice it would not be viable – in part because the re-emergence of mutually antagonistic 'corporations' would lead back to the state of war. Nonetheless, only such a state could ultimately achieve perpetual peace, which therefore itself remains an ideal, incapable of final achievement, but towards which nations, and the Law of Nations, must aspire. The rule of law is a metaphysical idea, one to be achieved gradually, and not through revolution involving the annihilation of the 'juridical state of affairs'.

Kant's grounding of moral laws in man's rational nature has two positive consequences. Firstly, the voluntaristic account of morality offered by realist scepticism is rejected. Kant's theory offers criteria of universalisability and impartiality in moral action: as a rational agent, any behaviour or interest of my own which I may legitimately defend must be such as I would be prepared to acknowledge on the part of another. Morality is not merely a species of enlightened self-interest; on the contrary, any special pleas of privilege destroy the universal essence of moral precepts. If a man stakes a claim on behalf of himself, or of his state, which he would not be prepared to acknowledge as a just claim on the part of others in a similar position, he cannot justify his demand on moral grounds. The misleading notion of 'political ethics' as a halfway house between politics and morals is rejected.

The second consequence is that arguments of cultural and moral relativism, or of limited human empathy and the significance of personal and social proximity, as devices to limit the scope of our (or our states') obligations to others are dismissed. For Kant, the question of states having simply empathetic *feelings* as motives for action is quite irrelevant. Actions are only truly moral if the agent could wish the precepts of his actions to be universal ones.

The Criticism of International Practice

Kant's theory does not provide any complete system of substantive moral principles, but it does provide a basis for moral criticism, and a means of distinguishing between statements about justice, rights and duties in a moral sense from legal, sociological or anthropological statements. It establishes a position to defend against the moral and cultural relativism of the realists. The central difficulty in the relativist approach is that when, for example, rights are taken as meaningful only within a particular legal, political or cultural context, and when particular persons or groups are identified as the holders of these rights, the concept of rights becomes qualified in so many mutually exclusive ways that any significant, common meaning to the concept of rights used in these contexts seems to recede altogether. The effect of evaluating rights, and moral precepts generally, according to a test of rational consistency is to produce constraints on the moral consequences of cultural relativism.

A difficulty arises, however, when such a formal, anti-consequenti-alist moral theory as Kant's is required to yield practical results. We are said to have duties towards other people we don't know which we feel no inclination to perform, but if the material interests and welfare of others are not in themselves criteria of the rightness of an action, how could we know what the content of our obligations was? This problem is resolvable, it appears, only by going beyond what Kant himself intended in his theory. Benn and Peters have expressed the point well:

> the rightness of the intention depends upon the general principle of which it is an application. And when we ask 'How could it be if everybody acted on this principle?' how can we exclude from con-sideration the interests of the persons affected? People have interests or needs which they put forward as claims. The criteria of impartia-lity and respect for persons are satisfied when these claims are assessed on relevant grounds, and privilege excluded as the basis for allowing a claim. In so far as we consider people's claims we consider their interests, and therefore we are making decisions which affect their welfare...[15]

We no longer have a purely formal and rational basis for ethical imperatives. The consequences of Kant's theory thus interpreted pro-vide a necessary moral basis for the satisfaction of individual and collective rights, and for principles of distributive justice. The attempt to apply a theory constructed in this way to the practical world may lead to a violation of its strictly metaphysical status, but its rational force is not thereby impaired. The moral equality of persons on which the theory insists points beyond abstract impartiality to a substantive equality of treatment.

International Law, the State and War

The Categorical Imperative expresses itself in the incorporation of Universal Right into international law. Immediately it confronts the problem that, as Kant asserts, subjection is alien to the nature of the state. Nor does Kant seem to believe that 'subjection' in the sense of a state being bound by unconditional and universal moral precepts is less alien than is political subjection. This seems clear when Kant refers to the 'self-interest' of nations leading them to unite under international law; prudence discovers what reason itself reveals. The Categorical Imperative is, as noted, a deontological principle:

'self-interest' is no part of its criterion for moral rules. Kant's use of the notion of self-interest implies an area of discretion.[16]

This view of the relative moral autonomy of the state sits uneasily with Kant's conception of international law. No law can give rise to a just war, since the settlement of disputes by violence violates Universal Right. Only law can decide matters of right; war is a violation of reason, which sanctions peace absolutely. It might be argued that Kant's concept of Universal Right is an idealistic one, a means by which international behaviour may be judged, whilst it is accepted that it can never conform to such a rigorous moral standard. Yet Kant is unequivocal about the nature of law, even though he recognises a political paradox in the simultaneous defence of a 'league to end all wars' and of the sovereignty of states.

Kant does acknowledge war to be a continual possibility even under his proposed global federation. The problem with Kant's strict adherence to the view that law can have nothing to say about the justice of wars is that international law, especially in this century, has attempted, albeit with limited effectiveness, to restrict the scope both of *jus ad bellum* and of *jus in bello*. In the former category are the Kellogg–Briand Pact of 1928, and Chapters Six and Seven of the UN Charter concerning the pacific settlement of disputes and collective intervention against international aggressors, whilst the latter category includes the Hague Conventions of 1899 and 1907, the Geneva Convention of 1925 and, more recently, the 1972 Biological Weapons Convention. It may be argued, as Osgood and Tucker have at least come close to doing, that the legalist paradigms of the just war tradition have proved irrelevant in the age of nuclear weapons,[17] but this does not show that law has no business in principle to address itself to problems of justice in warfare when warfare persists as an endemic feature of the international system.

Kant's denial that war can ever settle questions of right is an epistemologically necessary truth; right is a matter of universal reason manifesting itself in the Categorical Imperative, and not the arbitrary and ephemeral outcome of a conflict of forces. But Kant appears to go further, and deny that force may be legitimately used to enforce a just law. The question is, how is right to be upheld if states turn away from the path of moral reason? If states with a just cause renounce the use of force against an evil-doer, the latter's willingness to use force is the cause of its success. This inversion of the moral order is the central paradox of pacifism; but Kant is not a pacifist. Kant's position is that actions are only good in so far as they conform with the objective moral principles whose criterion is the Categorical Imperative. Now, if states intervene, whether individually or collectively, to enforce the provisions of a just law on a malefactor, just as much as if states prosecute a just cause in a purely moral sense without international legal authority, they will be motivated by self-interest, and by no means only by rational adherence to Universal Right. So far as this is the motivation for states' actions, these actions can be neither praised nor blamed from a moral point of view whatever their consequences.

Again we encounter the problem of interpreting Kant's moral criteria without reference to the interests and needs at stake in political action. The Kantian level of abstraction offers only a procedural means of testing moral judgements. Political actors are confronted with the problem of how it would be to act in a certain way in the concrete circumstances of the present, rather than in a morally more perfect order of the past or the future.

In his conviction that democracy avoids war, Kant anticipated neither the power of elites within the modern democratic state to manipulate public opinion, nor the degree to which the private person comes to identify himself with the purposes of the state in times of war. Moreover, inasmuch as the individual's prosaic and closely bounded sphere of private activity is transcended by his participation in the aggressive assertion of the collective personality, governments often find it difficult to resist domestic clamouring for hostile action. The age of mass politics has become the age of total war for more than technological reasons. It is not necessary to share Morgenthau's desire to return to an era of diplomacy conducted by an 'aristocratic international' to accept that the rational calculus of costs and benefits in the choice of foreign policies, so far from being assured in democracies, is subject to pressures which autocratic and oligarchical governments do not experience.[18]

Universal Right and Contractarianism: the Ambiguity of the Universal State

The liberal state is one in which government authority is limited by the recognition of a sphere of rights possessed by individuals. Government authority is defined and circumscribed by law, is exercised in such a way as to treat all individuals within the state as ends in themselves and to exclude no-one's interests from consideration, and is itself from time to time accountable to the population.

Kant's proposal for a world federation depends upon a contractarian form of authority. His ideal state is itself a juridical order predicated upon Universal Right. His fundamental premise is that the problem of justice has found its solution within the contractarian state, in which law comes from the rational agency of autonomous individuals. All that remains is to transfer this solution from the level of the state to that of the global federation. Yet the appeal of social contract imagery cannot hide the fact that it is difficult enough to point to examples of contractarian or consensual power within states, let alone to find evidence for its viability as a universal political principle. Moreover, if the participation of free, rational individuals, necessary for the achievement of a just order in Kant's uncompromising sense, is the rare exception rather than the rule within the state, the law and the authority of the proposed global federation would still be at one remove further from the agency of individuals.

Kant insists that the universal state would be qualitatively different from states as we know them in that it would not aspire to global hegemony, and thereby destroy national and cultural diversity. But there are no good grounds for believing that some 'superstate' of the future would be less hegemonic than have been states in our historical experience. Such a state, no matter how unjust, no matter how systematically it violated human rights, might eliminate all the rivals to which its citizens could flee. In recognition of this possibility, Martin Wight has argued that the possibility of political asylum that it provides is an important justification of the system of sovereign states.[19] Better the international state of nature, with its partial and separate political and juridical orders, than a monolithic world-order, which might lead to annihilation of all possibility of justice.

What Kant has in mind, however, is not a universal state as the political agency which ushers Universal Right into being, but a state which is itself the embodiment of this; it is the expression of pure reason, and this is always higher than any contingency of historical experience. No such state could exist, but only such a state can ultimately preserve peace and justice.

3.2 FUNCTIONALISM OR REGIONAL SOLIDARITY: DISSOLVING THE POLITICS OF INTERNATIONAL HIERARCHY

Functionalist theories make human needs the grounds for the international distribution of resources. The state, the 'sphere of the political', is seen as an obstacle and a threat to the global satisfaction of needs. Functionalists have stressed the technical and supposedly non-controversial aspects of governmental conduct, and of weaving an ever-spreading web of international institutional relationships on the basis of meeting such needs. They would concentrate on commonly experienced needs initially, expecting the circle of the non-controversial to expand at the expense of the political, as practical co-operation became coterminous with the totality of interstate relations. At that point a true world community would have arisen.

Conflict and disharmony arise in society in so far as authority is exercised by politicians and not by technicians. In the state, power, rather than the common good, is allowed to determine policy. For Ernst Haas, the displacement of 'politics' by technical management is both inevitable and desirable.[20] Only in this way can the technological and industrial forces for progress lead to an improvement in the general welfare. The true nature of this will only become apparent when people's loyalties cease to be 'penned up within the territorial confine of the exclusivist nation-state'. The 'unnatural state' obliterates the 'true common good' of 'humanity at large' and has a distorting effect with respect to 'the possibilities of human fulfilment'. The modern state has come to 'displace' society, understood in terms of genuine participation and identification amongst individuals.

Security, rather than the common solution of problems, has become the principal goal of the state, and thereby of society. But the condition of the alleviation of economic problems is also the condition of ending the causes of wars; it is the overcoming of the particularity of the state, the ending of the circumscription of co-operative social activity by its borders, and the restoration of a sense of global human unity.

In functionalism, the state strives to make itself superfluous. The loyalty of the individual passes to the various international functional agencies upon which his welfare comes increasingly to depend, and, indirectly, to the international community which they serve. International agencies serve as a source of an eventual 'world community of sentiment' which is the essential precursor of world government; the individual comes to see how intimately and effectively his welfare is linked with the securing of the common good. The possibility of building an international consensus in which 'national modes of thought' are effectively undermined is asserted.

David Mitrany sees the growth of institutions and arrangements for international co-operation – UN specialised agencies, the World

Bank, and so on – in a similarly positive light. Taken together, they represent the remarkable first signs of a

> sense of world community, of international responsibility for local conditions everywhere. The idea of the welfare state, new as it is even in our own countries, is already broadening out into a sentiment for a welfare world.[21]

Mitrany does not view the 'new nationalism' of the international system, engendered by the number of new states which have recently become members of it, as necessarily inimical to functionalist progress. On the contrary, he claims, the new nationalism concerns itself with social rights, and is indeed to be understood in terms of these rights, in contrast to the cultural basis of the nationalism of the nineteenth century.

The argument of Mitrany's *Working Peace System* is that the organic complexity of economic and social life provides a common interest in global co-operation which is contradicted by the reality of the division of humanity into formally independent units. Whilst historically the growth of nation-states protected individual and collective rights, the rights of nations to states of their own no longer guarantee, or are even relevant to, the former rights.[22] Increased international division of labour, need for raw materials, and other features of modern interdependence produce common interests which are seen as the objective basis for the transfer of loyalty to international welfare agencies, which can provide what states in isolation are no longer capable of providing.

A New Understanding of the Equality of States

The process by which sovereignty is to be transferred from the state to functional agencies is expected to be a gradual but cumulative one. Sovereignty is to become 'pooled' rather than simply alienated. But what about the conflict between the doctrine of formal state equality and the reality of the grossly disparate power of states? Will small states be happy with the preponderance of the great powers in such organisations? This is not expected to be a major problem, because

> Smaller states have accepted and even invoked the leadership of the great in times of international crisis, and there is no reason why this should not continue to be the case with respect to functional tasks

also. Instead of the legal fiction of equality there would thus be an evident and factual inequality in certain spheres...[23]

This is the important feature of the functionalist theory with respect to international justice, which is understood in an egalitarian sense, and is to be promoted by functional institutions. In return for the acceptance of inequalities of function in certain areas that undermine the principle of the formal equality of states, greater actual material equality would be obtained. Mitrany assumes that questions of international distributive justice such as those that relate to international investment, basic resources, migration, transfer of skills and technology, would be effectively addressed by functional arrangements. The resultant increase in economic equality would pave the way for closer political association. State sovereignty, and especially economic sovereignty, is to a large degree avoided as an obstacle to greater international economic justice.

The Limitations of Functional Agencies

The functionalist disparagement of the sphere of the political ignores the uncomfortable fact that the operations of agencies largely depend on political will, especially on the part of the major powers which provide the resources for such agencies and control the political, diplomatic and military context in which they operate. The International Labour Organisation, the quintessential functional agency to which Haas devoted his book *Beyond the Nation-State*, suffered from US withdrawal in 1967, a few years after Haas' work was published. More recently, UNESCO has been severely affected by the withdrawal of first American and then British financial support. It was the ultimate placing of security forces under the control of a supranational agency which was to be the harbinger of the truly functionalist era, yet the almost complete absence of concerted, collective intervention under the auspices of the UN Security Council to promote international security since the time of the Congo crisis (1960–63) and the limited and abortive role of UNIFIL in the Lebanon during the early 1980s augur badly for this prospect.

Ultimately, functional agencies exercise only delegated authority. Not only may this be withdrawn, but states clearly make a distinction between recognition of particular agencies for particular purposes and a general sacrifice of sovereignty in return for some 'non-political' advantage. The autonomy of any international agency is always only relative. The delegation of authority by a number of states to a range of functional agencies need not imply agreement about the ultimate goals of those agencies, or about which of the functions they perform is of greatest importance.

It might also be added that economic problems, far from constituting an autonomous sphere, are in the modern world the principal political problems.

Global Issues of Justice

There exist issues in respect of which global conceptions of justice do arise. The most prominent of these is the persistence of mass poverty and starvation. The justice-claims to which this gives rise are more than the simple aggregate of individual justice-claims, since these problems overwhelmingly affect particular races and regions, and are often evidently beyond the capabilities of governments to solve. It is only in terms of a conception of a 'world interest' that global poverty can be comprehended and tackled. Problems of global distributive justice certainly challenge the economic sovereignty of the state, but this is not to say that the state as a constituency of distributive justice becomes irrelevant.

Another problem that gives rise to a conception of justice formulated in terms of a 'world interest' is that of environmental pollution. Whilst the benefits of, say, electricity production are confined to the particular state, the costs are distributed amongst its neighbours, and often globally. The process of controlling pollution by international agreement is slow and often unsuccessful, but it is unclear that any global authority would necessarily be more successful in solving the problem than are contemporary states.

There will in any case be other powerful vested interests with which to contend. And in the absence of the state as an authoritative mechanism of allocation the conciliation of conflicting interests might be more problematic still. The outcome would be sure to depend as much upon the degree of influence exerted by the representatives of those interests over the conciliating authority as does present international agreement upon the influence which dominant interests currently bring to bear on their governments.

Whilst it may be pointed out that problems of global justice have ethical solutions that are independent in their validity of the political feasibility of implementing them, any additional costs that cosmopolitan solutions to global justice problems would be likely to bring must be weighed against the limitations of the present self-help principle of sovereignty. States can at least exert pressure on one another to modify their behaviour. World governments, or even interlocked functional agencies, have no sovereign rivals.[24]

The Nature of Needs

The functionalist view of human needs as essentially non-controversial and thus 'above politics' is by no means an obvious one. The nature of needs has been the source of ceaseless dispute.

In Marx's utopian communism, 'from each according to his ability, to each according to his needs' was to be the canon of distribution. But Marx distinguished between the satisfaction of material via man's struggle against nature, which is said to be the driving force of all history, and the growth of increasingly artificial desires and whims masquerading as needs. This latter development he famously derided as 'commodity fetishism'.

More recently, the themes of the alienation of man both as producer and as consumer of commodities in modern bureaucratic–capitalist societies have been developed by such writers as Herbert Marcuse,[25] whilst the process of the creation of spurious 'wants' and 'needs' by the manipulative power of manufacturing and retailing corporations has been explored with great insight by J.K. Galbraith.[26] On the right, economic theorists such as F.A. Hayek and Robert Nozick have disputed the contention that basic needs, even if these can be coherently identified, give rise to any legitimate rights-claims.[27] Social justice is seen as chimerical. We need not enter into these controversies here. The point is that if such a debate about the nature of needs persists at the level of the state, which at least provides an authoritative mechanism for the resolution of these disputes, the functionalist contention that needs considered at the global level present no special problems seems at best optimistic.

The Transcendence of the Political

The contention that the spheres of the technical and the political are empirically (or even logically) separable is a challengeable one. Those writers who, following Weber, have most carefully described the emergence and growth of bureaucratic and technical power in modern industrial society – the 'managerial revolution' in James Burnham's terms,[28] or the 'technostructure' in Galbraith's – have certainly not argued that this process has amounted to a 'depoliticisation' of modern social relations. Weber saw bureaucracy as constantly threatening to usurp its instrumental function, and to enter the realm of the truly political.[29] For Weber, the belief that bureaucracies pursued interests entirely separate from those of the social class from which they were drawn, as in the case of Plato's Guardians or Hegel's Universal Class, was no more than naive.

Functionalism is essentially a liberal doctrine, but it is in important respects in conflict with the liberal tradition. Both the liberal-pluralist conception of politics and the cosmopolitan rejection of political activity make the common good their object, but here is the crucial difference between them: the cosmopolitan tradition imagines the common good to be the expression of a spontaneous, universal moral order once the parochial and insidious institution of the state is abolished. Conversely, the political view expects there to be individuals and groups who will, if unrestrained, pursue their own interests beyond the point at which they can be reconciled with the common interest, as well as those who disagree irreconcilably about what the common interest is, and who will resort to violence to impose their will on others. We may notice too that the functionalist conviction that economic conflict is the principal cause of war begs many questions about the systemic, psychological and other sources of international conflict.

Functional Agencies as Rival Objects of Loyalty

A legal order protecting individual rights, machinery for the political representation and conciliation of conflicting interests, and a central agency for the implementation of public policy have as yet no analogues at the global level. Nevertheless, functionalists maintain that the nation-state itself is bound to decline as a source of people's identification and loyalty. Whether this prediction turns out to be true or false, there is little evidence that people's loyalty has been or is likely to be transferred to functional agencies.

It might be more accurate to say that loyalty, which in functionalist usage expresses a subjective pattern of identification, a sense of a patron–client relationship, rather than the mere existence of 'objectively' interdependent relationships which give rise to no such identification, is more often demonstrated towards the idea of trans- and supranational authority than to the actual institutions which embody such authority.[30] This might be argued in the case of the commitment of European political parties, especially social-democratic ones, to the European Union as an ideal which exceeds the present institutional reality.

If the concept of loyalty is restricted to meaning mere acceptance of authority, and recognition of the usefulness of having certain commonly binding decision-making procedures, then such institutions as the European Court do provide examples of functionalist success in creating a sense of 'loyalty'. This is, however, a more restricted and less positive form of identification with authority beyond the state than functionalist writers have in mind. The coming into being of functionalist organisations with a principally legal capacity was seen by these writers as a stage beyond the development of administrative agencies. It seems instead to represent the limit of functionalist progress thus far.

Those features of the state that attract loyalty are absent in other institutions. Whilst it is certainly possible to find examples of states that are fundamentally unviable because they enclose irreconcilable communities, the state retains the potential to secure loyalty as a political expression of a common experience. The state also secures the transcendence by the individual of the sphere of his particular interests through his identification with the purpose of the state, as we have noted. The dark side of the identification of the individual with the state is revealed in time of war. But at the same time, in such extremes, the state receives its practical confirmation as the expression of a communal identity.[31]

Why could not functional agencies come to attract such loyalties? One reason may be that the identity of the group requires that the extent of the group be determinate, and based on some shared characteristic that others outside the group lack. For a group to constitute a community, there must be patterns of identification between the individual and the collective on a multiplicity of levels. If not all groups are communities however, all communities are groups in the sense that to know who is in the community, one must know who isn't. This does not require that others be regarded as enemies, though this follows with depressing frequency, but only that they be excluded. The problem is that there is neither exclusivity in relations between individuals and functional agencies, nor many-layered patterns of identification. Instead, these agencies have client groups according to the service they provide.

Whilst this is also true of the relations between individuals and functional agencies within the state, this is not (necessarily) a problem

in that there are other aspects of communal 'belonging' that complement the economic and social aspects of those relations. Thus, whilst
the collective provision of education and health care is considered by
interventionist liberals and socialists both to express and to increase
the sentiment of community, such economic and social provision is
not strictly necessary to this.[32] In the global sphere, however, the
other aspects of community outside and beyond the state are not
sufficiently developed for functional provision alone to lead to a sense
of international community. Even those racial and religious sentiments that do transcend the boundaries of states – Nkrumah's Pan-
Africanism or Arab solidarity – are limited by the facts of state
sovereignty. The functionalist might say that this proves the point
about the essential artificiality of the state, given other forms of
existent identification. It is an indication of the power of the state as
a source of political identification that it is able to resist such emotive
objects of rival loyalty.

Welfare, Nationalism and Collective Rights

The idea of global welfare is seen to proceed from the gradual extension of the welfare state in developed countries. Even if economic and
social rights as a major element of fundamental human rights define
the limits of cultural and ethical relativism about the treatment of
human beings, there remain serious cross-cultural disagreements
about the scope of welfare provision and people's entitlement to it.
Such a maximalist conception of global welfare as the functionalist
one would certainly encounter such problems, especially as the experience of collective provision of even minimal economic and social
welfare is almost entirely limited to developed states. It is, moreover,
in these states that the challenge to collective welfare has come most
strongly under attack. In addition to the philosophical arguments
already mentioned, the welfare state has been charged with ineffi-
ciency, maldistribution, undermining self-reliance and initiative and
creating attitudes of dependence, and with inhibiting economic
growth by stifling enterprise and imposing punitive tax burdens on
the productive side of the economy. The desirability of extended social
welfare is less widely accepted than it was when Mitrany made his
optimistic forecasts of future global welfare.[33]

This was itself to be the condition of fulfilling the rights asserted by
the 'new nationalism', which could not be satisfied by states acting
alone. This nationalism was not seen as a threat to functionalist

progress; rather, the demands it gave rise to were viewed as reducible to purely social and economic components. This analysis may be challenged in several ways. The contention that the division of humanity into states is made anachronistic by increasing interdependence and international division of labour assumes a mercantilist view of the nation-state as the primary unit of production and trade. Yet as John Herz finally acknowledged,[34] the 'failure' of the state on the levels of economic autarky and military defence has not led to its being challenged as the primary unit of political organisation.

There is a deeper problem in cosmopolitan approaches to international justice. The emphasis on questions of welfare and social justice generally assumes that to talk of collective rights is no more than a shorthand way of referring to the aggregate of individual rights, so that asserted rights of national autonomy, immunity from external intervention and so on are only comprehensible, and only legitimate, when they further the rights of individuals. There are no collective rights *sui generis*. Yet the values of the individual are bound up with those of the collectivity. The value of the principle of self-determination is that the national community is the mediate entity through which the individual participates in the 'community of mankind'. Membership of a subordinate group diminishes the individual, often in his own eyes as well as in the eyes of others. There is a necessary relationship between individual rights to autonomy and self-respect and collective rights to these values. Certain rights must be enjoyed collectively for it to make any sense to say that individuals enjoy them at all.[35] This is how such rights differ from those that functionalists count together under the rubric of social justice, principally concerning matters of economic and social resources and that range of positive and negative rights which, crucial though they are, are only ascribed to and enjoyed by individuals considered in themselves.

The problem with the functionalists' preference for global agencies rather than federations, on the grounds that states would not be prepared to cede power to a possible rival institution, is that any agency or group of agencies with significant influence over the internal affairs of states becomes a rival, in so far as it may challenge the legal as well as the political aspects of state sovereignty. But there is room for practical doubt about the ability of functional agencies to address themselves to international distributive questions. Conflicts between international agencies and contributor states, currently acute at a time when contributions made by major states to international organisations are relatively insignificant as a proportion of their national budgets, would very likely become unmanageable if the budgets of functional agencies grew to rival those of major states. Conflicts between agencies themselves must also be considered.

It must be stressed, however, that this is a criticism of the optimism of functionalist theory, not a defence of the irrefragability of the moral authority of the state, nor a denial that human rights, the most important limit of any conception of 'common interest' are to be conceived in universal terms. Yet the practical problems which beset cosmopolitan conceptions of international justice must be confronted. If a perfect conception of justice is destined to remain only a utopian possibility, it is necessary to strive for justice in the world of the possible. In such a world, the value of the sovereignty to governments, especially those of developing states, in allowing them even minimal control over the welfare of their societies is considerable – though a state's authority may, of course, become itself the major threat to its people's welfare.

A Regionalist Approach to Greater International Equality

The 'regionalist' model of international organisation presented by Rajni Kothari[36] as a response to the injustice which he sees as endemic in the social and economic global order shares some of the assumptions of the functionalists, but attaches greater significance to national and regional identities, and to the role of the state.

This model is not strictly a cosmopolitan one in the sense in which we have so far used the term. But state sovereignty is only accepted subject to severe restrictions at the regional and global levels, and these restrictions are justified and necessitated by a conception of justice in the development process, and in the distribution of resources in all societies, which is wholly cosmopolitan in its nature. Its moral assumptions are held to be valid for all societies, though this does not of course mean that Kothari's ideal of social justice is meant to transcend political and ideological differences. Far from it: capitalism, at least in its free market variant, seems definitely to be rejected as a social system.

Greater solidarity among developing states is to be encouraged through closer co-ordination and co-operation in international agencies, building upon the modest successes of the Group of 77 states, but most importantly at the regional level. This co-operation is to involve states 'pooling their economic, political and military resources'.[37] The strength which weaker states could gain thereby would act as a counterweight to the dominance of the powerful, particularly the 'superpowers'. Since it is these latter states which have themselves made greatest progress towards 'solidarity' in organisations such as the former COMECON, the EU, or NATO, the need for integration among the weaker states is thereby made still greater.

Kothari argues for the inevitability and value of cultural and historical distinctiveness, and rejects the idea of a centralised world government. Rather, regional federations are to be seen as steps towards ultimate world federal institutions. What he envisages at both levels are essentially functional agencies. At the global level, ECOSOC would become the principal executive agency of the United Nations, with contributions from members according to their GNPs. It would also have powers to undertake large development projects in the underdeveloped world.

Economic and administrative co-operation at the regional level is intended to promote general welfare, too. Along with the achievement of greater self-sufficiency by developing states, co-operation would lead to greater equality in relations among states making up regional federations. Here are stressed the strong historical links between states in regions such as Southeast Asia, Latin America, the Middle East and West Africa, including historical trading and commercial links, which have been disrupted by 'artificial' relations between such states and the colonial powers.

Associated with this regionalist perspective is a conviction shared by many writers on Third World development that growth is not enough to ensure greater justice, although it may be a necessary condition of it. Most of all, if development is to improve the general welfare, the acquisitive ethos of the rich countries must be avoided. There should be economic maxima as well as minima. It is not only that there is an interconnection of wealth and poverty; excessive and ostentatious consumption is rejected in itself. This egalitarianism rejects the conception of distributive justice as depending upon the results of growth. Here, again, we find some assumptions held in common with functionalist writers.

The Limits of Transnational Solidarity

Another problem limiting the significance of transnational sentiments in terms of practical politics is the fear of groups within states that their identities and interests are being subordinated to those of elites within a dominant state with which some transnational bond is shared. The reasons for the collapse of the United Arab Republic of Egypt and Sudan indicate the sorts of conflict which might arise elsewhere.[38]

And the debacle of the United Arab Republic illustrates the divisions of class, status, culture and faction that prevent the integration of sovereign states, even where they are geographically proximate and their societies share common ethnic and religious traditions. Each state plays a unique role in preserving social rank, economic position and the particular forms of a common culture. When a change in the nature of sovereignty seems to threaten the social order, especially when one of the states about to merge is perceived by its people as the weaker partner, the threatened political submergence of that state is experienced as a threat against the security of society as a whole. The state as a result attracts the loyalty and support of its people.

This might seem, and to some degree is, a more apposite criticism of functionalist proposals for world order reform. But the jealousy with which sovereignty and national independence are guarded at the regional level is likely to constitute a problem for Kothari's proposed regional federations. Though neither the merging nor the loss of sovereignty is proposed, fears that one or more states will come to dominate federations, and to impose their wills on weaker partners are likely to be real, and probably justified. This should serve as a cautionary note for proponents of cosmopolitan solutions of world order and justice who believe that such 'restrictive' principles as cultural autonomy and political self-determination must decline in importance with institutional progress towards the supersession of the state.

The regional model is intended to promote greater global equality, through co-operation within regional federations as well as through resource transfers facilitated by world agencies. Significant resource transfers between units in each federation would, however, be required in the interests of distributive justice. For example, relatively wealthy Taiwan or Singapore might be obliged to aid, respectively, Macao and Tibet, or Burma, amongst the poorest countries in their regions. Conversely, India, with its own problems of deprivation and even starvation, might be obliged to transfer resources to still-poorer Bangladesh. This situation could be ameliorated by major international resource transfers, including transfers to states that are themselves aid-donors in their regional context. However, the attitude of the major economies, capitalist and socialist alike, to matters of global deprivation and injustice might be that these had now become essentially regional problems, and that aid from outside would only serve to deter regional co-operation, self-reliance and initiative as means of escaping from poverty. Regionalism is unlikely to solve problems of international justice when their solutions lie with states beyond the region.

Inequality and Economic Growth

That a strict egalitarian model of development best promotes the collective good is open to question. Such egalitarianism is more easily defended as an 'end state' conception of justice than as a feature of developing societies where the total domestic resources available are insufficient to provide a social and economic minimum for all the population. Thus, whilst growth is certainly not a sufficient condition for greater social justice in poor societies, it is almost certainly a necessary one. It seems at least plausible to argue, following John Rawls,[39] that greater differences in wealth and income than would be justified in a society in which a social minimum for all is possible may be justified if such differences are necessary incentives to the economic growth required to make the provision of universal welfare possible. In other words, a higher degree of social inequality, over a time, than could otherwise be considered just may be an inevitable concomitant of securing the conditions of social justice.

Nor is this the case only where there is capitalist enterprise. The experience of forced economic accumulation in post-revolutionary socialist states has been hardly less harsh or unjust. The most striking condition of state-socialist growth has been physical expropriation and gross political repression, but the forced collectivisation of the Stalin era was certainly akin to the structural exploitation of workers which Marxism identifies as the condition of capitalism. It seems that the requirements of initial economic growth and of justice may pull in different directions. If the paradoxical consequences of this at the level of theory are to be avoided, the inequalities that are concomitants of necessary growth are better described as justified rather than as just. The conflation of the two expressions bedevils much of the liberal theory of justice.[40]

3.3   THE 'PREFERRED VALUES' OF THE WORLD ORDER MODELS PROJECT

Against the optimism of the functionalists, 'World Order Models Project' (WOMP) writers, maintain that, if the growth of functional agencies is to remain compatible with state sovereignty, the consequence must be that when an agency attains 'any tradition or capacity for independent action' it must inevitably run foul of national governments. Indeed, 'the very achievements of these institutions may in part be a consequence of their irrelevance to the high matters of state that cause wars'.[41] The WOMP approach emphasises the growth of cultural, economic, scientific and political activities across the borders of states in creating 'transnational reference groups' which increasingly attract the loyalty of participants. Such activities promote international understanding and common values.[42] The assumption is that it is ignorance of one another's cultures which underpins much of international conflict: 'It is not diversity of language, culture, ideology or race, but a structure of stratification based on these diversities that produces misery and assures the persistence of the war system'.[43]

Richard Falk accepts the argument that regional organisations of states may bolster the bargaining position of weaker states in their relations with the strong; but they may also embody relations of ideological affinity as opposed to a genuine sense of the need for transnational co-operation to tackle problems, or embody forms of coercion and dominance. The dominant actor may use regional organisations to justify and disguise the exercise of force, as in the Warsaw Pact's 'support' for the invasions of Hungary, Czechoslovakia and Afghanistan, or the joint US/OAS action against the Dominican Republic in 1965. Again, the purpose of regional organisations may be to enable members to compete more effectively against outsiders, rather than to make any progress towards the transcendence of the nation-state.

Current developments in the EU show how far benefits secured within a framework of co-operation tend to impose costs on outsiders. The Social Chapter of the Maastricht Treaty and the Single European Market of 1992 will, their architects hope, lead to greater social justice within the Union, as well as greater economic efficiency. It is hoped to promote the standardisation of welfare rights, employment policies and regional assistance. But all this may worsen the lot of other groups, notably migrant workers. Open borders mean greater freedom of movement within the EU, and consequently much tougher restrictions on entry from outside. More developed social policies within the Community can only add to the perceived need to exclude non-EU nationals. Already we see Italy taking a much harder line on residence permits. It is not hard to think of other examples where greater social justice within a community has led to greater exclusivity and the denial of benefits to outsiders.

The WOMP project is concerned to 'demythologise the state'.[44] Without the state there would be

> no world structure that is able to exalt or protect its adherents, ... no enemy against whom to organise, and ... no widespread sense of bondage to men who belong to a different tribe or speak a different language or worship different gods or believe in a different kind of a political system.[45]

It is the state itself, with its concomitant parochialism of political identification, which is the cause of world conflict, and of our inability to address tasks that exceed the competence of individual states, or ad hoc groups of states.

The Transformation of the State

Paradoxically, the state is both too large and too small to sustain world order. Falk and his colleagues maintain that states ought as far as possible to correspond to national boundaries.[46] Secession and self-determination would be allowed to produce smaller and more homogeneous states, with less need for repression against disaffected minorities at home, and less opportunity for external intervention on their behalf. Such a transformation would engender a more moderate and co-operative form of international relations. However,

> the interrelatedness of modern life requires larger, not smaller, units of policy-planning and execution; larger function units would, of course, be consistent with smaller political units.[47]

The system of sovereign states is seen as unable to respond to the main global threats of the twentieth century: resource depletion, over-population, pollution, the threat of nuclear war. The logic of the 'national interest' precludes co-operation between states to achieve common tasks. In the act of unifying disparate elements within itself, the modern nation-state depends upon 'the potency of symbols of nationhood and sovereignty', as Alfred Cobban remarked.

The WOMP critique of justice in the contemporary states system is an uncompromising one. The self-help principle among states perpetuates injustice. Some writers, such as Robert Johansen, explicitly reject the nation-state as the principal constituency for justice, and deny the exclusiveness of any of its claims:

the value framework proposed here rests upon the assumption that the human race is the important constituency to consider in policy-making.... The traditional approach gives priority to the people of one nation. It also provides more benefits for the governmental elite and its supporters within the nation than for the national population in general.[48]

In Johansen's conception, the 'human community is expanded horizontally to include all nations, and vertically to encompass all classes'.[49]

The current international system is beset by the 'paradox of aggregation', which may be understood in the form of the fable of the 'tragedy of the commons'. Each farmer in a village grazes two cows on the common pasture. If each were to graze three, all would gain extra yield in the short term, but ultimately the land would be ruined and all left destitute. From the point of view of any one farmer, the extra income he would get from a third cow greatly outweighs the marginal loss of yield per cow which would result from one more animal, provided that the others do not follow suit. If a particular farmer were, however, to consider the long term interest of the community and keep only two cows, whilst his less public-spirited neighbours opt for three, he will miss out on the extra yield which they will receive before catastrophe befalls them all. WOMP writers argue that this situation is inherent in international relations. In the absence of a common superior authority, or of a heightened sense of the common good among mankind, it will be in the interest of no state to do what is ultimately in the interest of all states.

WOMP writers describe 'preferred values' as the basis for a new world order.[50] They include non-militaristic forms of security, production for need rather than for market profit, the recognition and implementation of universal human rights, including economic ones, and a universal commitment to forms of economic development that preserve the 'ecological balance'.

Ambivalence about the State

For Falk and Johansen, the idea of a 'world government' possessing the centralised, hierarchical and authoritarian features of current state governments is rejected. Many older versions of world government theories are criticised as being too statist; they seek to install on a universal scale that very institution which global reformers should recognise as the fundamental source of inequality and injustice. They both share the conviction that the task should be 'building downward from the state with respect to economic and political concentrations of functions, and building outwards from the state to encompass the functional dimensions of interdependence'.[51]

They assume that states will be prepared to accept simultaneously a disintegrative principle of self-determination (or at least effective devolution of authority), and the emergence of ever-growing and powerful functional agencies to rival and ultimately displace their power and influence. The internal and external aspects of sovereignty are dissociated to the point where the potency of the former as the force of unity and cohesion in civil society is transformed into a relatively weak and anodyne force in the latter.

The critical tension is between the need to co-ordinate global efforts to achieve justice and avert impending threats, which suggests structures of authority of a degree of centralisation and interventionary capability hitherto unprecedented, and the desire for the decentralisation of economic and political power to undermine the domination and exploitation of man by man.

Another tension exists between these writers' deprecation of the sense of hostility towards the outsider, which they view as the inevitable concomitant of the sense of solidarity within communities isolated from one another by the boundary of the state, and their adherence to a strong version of the principle of self-determination which recognises this solidarity as the essential basis of political organisation. An uncoerced sense of belonging to a community and the right to self-government by all peoples are the necessary conditions for avoiding internal repression and external interference; but the very parochialism of political identification within the state which stands condemned by the WOMP creed is here asserted as unavoidable. In other words, the condition of security and justice within the state is identical with the condition of war and the denial of justice between states.

Diversity, Dominance and Conflict

Ambivalence proceeds from the belief that it is only when the state interposes itself in the otherwise healthy and creative relations of diverse cultures and beliefs that this diversity becomes conflictual. It is the state itself which is ultimately pathological, even if it is pragmatically necessary to accept it. What is not entertained is the idea that human diversity itself may be a source of conflict. The implication must be that if individuals, groups and entire societies are able to communicate with one another without the corrupting intermediacy of their governments, a more truly global society could come into existence. But as a prominent sceptic about world order reform proposals has noted,

> All governments have opportunities to control and distort mutual awareness and contact, and even when the conditions for awareness of other societies are most favourable, what one society knows about another is always selective and partial. Moreover, awareness of other societies, even where it is 'perfect', does not merely help to remove imagined conflicts of interest or ideology that do not exist; it also reveals conflicts of interest or ideology that do exist.[52]

In addition, transnational contacts are as likely to lead to the regional or global dominance of one culture over another as to a global environment of mutual tolerance and respect. This cultural dominance may find its political expression not in the transcendence of the state, but in the subjugation of one state's sovereignty by another. The relations of the United States with some of its hemispheric neighbours are illustrative of this effect.

Social Justice and Cultural Criticism

It seems reasonable to suggest that certain general categories of just and unjust behaviour, on the part of authority as much as on the part of individuals, find recognition across cultural boundaries as a result of 'the basic fact that human beings with certain innate propensities have to live together somehow'.[53] This is the social premise of natural law theory, argued by Grotius and Pufendorf to be as valid in international relations as in domestic society. More recently, the general categories of justice have been described by Barrington Moore Jr as

> failures of authority ... to control the instruments of power, failures to keep the peace, demands and exactions that run counter to or exceed the prevailing definition of collective purposes, and punishments that violate a sense of what human beings are or what they ought to be. In the division of labour we have found indications that there is a considerable area of agreement across time and place about what constitutes desirable and undesirable forms of work.... Finally, at the point where the division of labor connects

with the distribution of the social product there are indications of a widespread feeling that people, even the most humble members of society, ought to have enough resources or facilities to do their job in the social order, and that there is something morally wrong or even outrageous when these resources are unavailable...[54]

The wideness of these categories should not obscure the fact that the importation of a particular and alien criterion of the distribution of resources, rights or obligations from one culture to another may have highly costly and disruptive consequences. It is true that when we criticise others' cultural practices from an ethical point of view, there is an implied universal content to such criticisms.

Yet the condemnation, or enforced prohibition, of cultural practices by outsiders may lead to a loss of sense of autonomy, and with it of self-respect, both by society as whole and by individuals as members of society. Moral and cultural censure tends to engender complacent superiority on the part of those who pass it, and an erosion of self-belief and self-esteem on the part of those who are its constant recipients. The latter have historically responded with resentment and moral anger. The obdurate response of the American South to Northern criticisms of slave-owning is evidence of this process, as is the shattering of the self-confidence of Africans by the political violence and moral and racial disparagement practised by colonialism against their indigenous culture, and movingly described by Frantz Fanon.[55] Still more recently, the anger generated amongst African women in the World Health Organisation by Western feminist criticism of the practice of female circumcision has provided a graphic example of the perils of criticising cultural practices.

None of this means that the costs of the criticism or prohibition should never be borne. Gross and systematic ill-treatment of racial, cultural or religious groups, 'untouchable castes', or women, the persecution, political disfranchisement, or deprivation of livelihood of minorities (or majorities), arbitrary arrest, torture, child labour, and so on, are not practices that should be allowed to shelter behind blanket prohibitions against 'paternalism' or 'cultural imperialism' let alone 'interference in another country's affairs'. This appears only as a form of moral dereliction. For one thing, since the victims of oppression within cultures can hardly be said to consent to their ill-treatment, their oppressors are at least as vulnerable to the charge of cultural despotism as are those outside the society who condemn oppressive practices. However quietistically and resignedly the victims of Hitler or Stalin, or the lowest castes of Hindu untouchables, have contemplated their fates, we do not require evidence of virulent psychological or physical opposition in order to be able to say that their rights were being violated.

The ascription of moral rights is categorical, and therefore universal. Only such a concept permits any criticism of actual, substantive rights to economic provision, personal liberty, and so on.[56] It is certainly true that the leadership of many societies seek to suppress any such criticism violently; but to suggest that the failure of a person to recognise, or even to dream, that he possesses rights as a moral agent is tantamount to his ceasing to have any is not only to write a dictator's charter, but to debase the concept of rights as the primary and essential moral concept in favour of a purely voluntarist, and in effect trivial, understanding of rights.

But WOMP values encompass more than the basic content of human rights. They are, essentially, the values of the white, Northern hemispheric, liberal tradition, with large elements of socialism and utopia included. This fact has inevitably produced hostile reactions, from critics 'averse to the hollow sounds of comfortable, angry men... hopping from one continent to another in a bid to transform the whole world – the latest edition of the white man's burden'.[57]

There is more shared international understanding on moral questions, and better prospects for international society and international law as vehicles of justice, than the realists can ever allow. But the facts of cultural diversity must be recognised. The imposition, should it ever become a real possibility, of the cosmopolitan values of WOMP, the functionalists, or even the grand Kantian moral schema upon societies with traditions markedly different from those that gave rise to these intellectual theories seems more likely to produce conflict and resentment than to eliminate them. Most especially, the WOMP values, though they incorporate, as we noted, a quasi-religious conception of *humanitas*, are at bottom secular and rational values. The myth, ritual and eschatology which sustain the ethical and cultural codes of most societies do not lend themselves well to such impositions.

These reflections are more apposite than the usual criticism of WOMP and other cosmopolitan schemes, which is that the values they espouse are not authenticated by having emerged from a representative political system. Such systems are still comparatively rare exceptions in the world, and in no political system do values or policies emerge untainted by the covert or overt influence of the dominant interests of social groups. Given the source of so much political belief in the control and manipulation of information which the modern mass media and official and semi-official agencies of government and state have at their disposal, it seems arbitrary that philosophers and others should be excluded from devising 'preferred values', even if they show a certain naivety about the consequences of implementing them.

Intervention and Social Inequality

Internal and external facts of sovereign power are acknowledged by Falk and Johansen in their rejection of any 'statist' model of world government.[58] Their desire to build both 'downwards' (the decentral- isation of power within the state and the regaining of autonomy by civil society) and 'outwards' (the slow displacement of the exclusivity of state power by functional agencies) is itself a desire to harness and control the power of the state.

At this stage, the irresolvable problem which underlies the WOMP approach as much as that of Mitrany and Haas becomes apparent. It is the tension between the need to co-ordinate global activities so as to solve problems which are beyond the scope of independent sovereign units, a process itself requiring constant intervention in and direction of social and even individual affairs, and the wish to break down structures of coercion and exploitation, and to return that degree of autonomy and self-motivation to people's lives which the modern industrial state is thought to have destroyed. To achieve those neces- sary global objectives that imply the transcendence of the state, and to support agencies that are certain to challenge and conflict with the state's sovereignty, would require a political apparatus that threatens to replicate all the worst features of the state from the cosmopolitan point of view.

A constant theme in WOMP literature is that the existence of sovereign states obstructs social justice by preventing the free move- ment of economic resources, not least human talent and skill, to produce the optimum satisfaction of human need: by arbitrarily favouring one limited section of humanity to the exclusion of others; by denying many nations the basic economic and social minimum provision which give the right of self-determination and other collective rights meaning; and by preventing a just distribution of resources within society, by means of restrictive and self-interested conditions attached by donor states to their foreign aid as much as by leaderships of recipient states, who favour already privileged elites and tolerate or encourage corruption.

Much of Johansen's critique of the relationship of the state to social justice is in keeping with the central themes of this study. We have already rejected the scepticism of the realists about moral obligations between states and communities, and the idea of the state as a self-enclosed and unique constituency of justice. We have suggested that the legitimacy of the state and of its external claims must depend upon its safeguarding of collective rights as well as its maintaining conditions of social justice. It is when the state *per se* is rejected as an insurmountable obstacle to justice, and above all when it is implied that its abolition is in itself a guarantee of greater social justice, that serious problems with the cosmopolitan conception of justice become evident.

There is a greater sense of interdependence, and perhaps of solidarity, between elites in metropolitan and former colonial countries than there is between the subordinate classes of those countries. As already noted, centre–periphery elite linkages operate across a broad spectrum of cultural, ideological, financial, military and strategic areas of dependence and interdependence. Conversely, the mass populations of developed and developing states often stand in a conflictual relationship, so far as they come into contact at all, as jobs and living standards in developed countries are threatened by cheap imports and undercutting of labour costs in economic competition which, especially in times of recession, is of an acute and zero-sum nature. This asymmetry in relations of elites and masses is undoubtedly an expression of profound economic and social division within states and across state borders; but there is little reason to believe that the demise of the state would see the end of dominant elites and social classes, indeed of the whole structure of social inequality.

In many developing and underdeveloped states, political elites are straightforwardly identifiable by their direct control of the apparatus of government and by the social institutions from which they originate, whether it be the landowning class, comprador bourgeoisie, a dominant tribe, or the military operating on its own behalf or on behalf of any of the former. In advanced societies, however, social and economic power rests with elites in the economic technostructure, in the welfare bureaucracies characteristic of modern states, in mass media, marketing, and political lobbying at least as much as with the formal political elites. Possession of scarce knowledge and organisational skill is increasingly the basis of social and political power, especially when this possession goes along with the ability to control the dissemination of knowledge to outsiders. It is not too cynical to suggest that there is much in the World Order Models Project approach that would be congenial to such elites.

3.4 WORLD STATE, IDEAL STATE OR NO STATE?

The nature and explanation of elite power lies in the total economic and social system. In the present world it is as anachronistic to consider economy and culture to be bounded by state frontiers as it is to consider political power and economic exploitation as occurring only within the state. But Johansen and other WOMP writers at times come close to suggesting that the state alone guarantees the continuing existence of dominant classes.

World Government and International Class

However dominant classes use the machinery of the state to further class interest, these classes are not coextensive with states, nor are state mechanisms the only ones which they could imaginably use to further their interests. If the global system of production itself issues in unequal class relationships, and patterns of elite dominance, then utopian political proposals for the limitation or abolition of states fail to confront economic reality.

Proposals for world government have come largely from the developed world, a fact to be contrasted with the stress placed by developing and underdeveloped states on sovereignty. The abolition of the states system would not remove the threat of elite and class domination and exploitation within a new system of global authority as long as the underlying economic and social system remained in being. The weaker societies of the world would face not only 'private' coercion from multinational (now global) corporations, banks or other institutions. Just as in the contemporary states system, international organisations such as the World Bank, IBRD or IMF have been used by governments to further the interests of economically, and therefore politically, powerful groups within their societies, so the less powerful and less prosperous justifiably fear that class interest and corporate power would co-opt transnational or global institutions and direct their policies in favour of privileged interests.

The United Nations has inevitably formed the focus of schemes for creating institutions of 'global solidarity', yet from the standpoint of the Group of 77 states, it hardly offers much prospect of global egalitarianism. Great powers dominate the machinery of the United Nations still more than they did the League of Nations.[59] Should the United Nations ever show signs of evolving into anything approaching a world government, the interests currently canvassed by the major countries might be thought to have a head start in influencing institutional design and policy formation. What the WOMP approach and to some degree all the cosmopolitan approaches underestimate is the value of the state as a counterweight to preponderant economic and social power, and the injustice which proceeds from such power.

Economic Power and Political Authority

The assumption, then, that cosmopolitan theorists make about global institutions is that they would not be co-opted by powerful economic, national, ideological or other interests. This is odd, because it is a major contention of most of the theories examined here that the contemporary state does come to serve the interests of dominant social elites and economic classes. Why should not these groups, given the transnational linkages and common interests between them, come similarly to exercise dominance over world authorities?

Cosmopolitan writers believe that powerful interests are disproportionately represented because states are limited in size. It might be argued, and more plausibly as a historical thesis, that states have been limited in size because of the nature of the interests they have primarily served. But this alternative understanding offers even less comfort for cosmopolitan theorists. In an era of global economic interdependence, dominant interests are no longer limited in geographical extent to the confines of the state. The need to establish influence, if not control, over world authorities would become vital for transnational economic interests.

The relationship between the sovereign state and the multinational corporation, for example, is an ambivalent one. The centrality of such corporations in global production affects the calculations of all governments' economic policies, particularly in the case of primary exporters. Multinationals play one government off against another by differential investment policies, transfer pricing, and by means of the flexibility they enjoy in moving operations from country to country. Despite this capacity, multinational corporations still confront the governments of host countries as sovereign entities, providing the legal context for operations, and retaining the ultimate powers of expropriation and nationalisation. Therefore, multinational corporations must compromise with individual governments, and this limits the degree of rationalisation and efficiency of their global operations. To offset this need to compromise, or because compromise is difficult or impossible given the political composition of the government, multinationals seek influence over ruling elites. Where this is not possible, as in Chile during the Allende government, connivance with military forces to overthrow governments is an alternative.

It is possible to imagine a world government of some kind existing in the context of a world economy in which the multinational corporation retained its economic primacy. Such corporations would find it essential to control the world government. The benefits of global operation without the need to placate hostile governments, or to be tied to fixed commodity prices, limits on transfer pricing, rates of profitability, and so on, would be very great. Reinforcing the requirement for control of global policies would be the fear that if political factions hostile to multinationals gained control of world authorities, no selective compromise or exploitation of conflicting interests between different states would any longer be possible. The very basis of multinational operations would be threatened.

The 'global reach' of multinational corporations and the vast problems of regulation which this creates might be considered an argument for some type of world authority. The economic independence and political power of states are certainly diminished by the current nature of global production; but the political authority of the state remains intact. This authority may be a shadowy and paltry thing in the particular instance, but in general the diffuse nature of political authority in the system of sovereign states serves at least to prevent the effective hijacking of governmental power that might occur under some future world authority.

The WOMP approach also tends to underestimate the role of the state in promoting social justice. If we consider the modern developed state, representative democracy and the political success of radical and reformist parties have made at least some inroads on structural inequalities. Redistributive taxation, the welfare state, provision of public education, (relatively more) open entry to public office: all have increased personal and social opportunities. Competing

ideologies and evolving conceptions of social justice have been necessary but not sufficient conditions of this success, at least in Western
societies. More important has been the requirement of political parties
aspiring for government to build broad coalitions of support in a
competitive political environment. Social reform may be limited in
its possibilities in liberal-democratic states; but detailed specifications
of how representative and competitive political processes might be
sustained are almost entirely absent in global institutional designs. So
too are convincing reasons to believe that monolithic bureaucracies
are susceptible to control of their ultimate purposes without the
application of constant, countervailing political power.

If problems of economic conflict are not merely artificial constructs
of the state, then the questions of the 'paradox of aggregation', and of
military force and economic wastage, take on new dimensions. Only
in a world of pure altruism, or of the thoroughgoing regulation of all
forms of private and corporate economic activity, or both, could the
paradox of aggregation be entirely resolved. This is not to deny its
seriousness; but it is not clear that its regional or global agencies
would find it any easier to overcome vested economic interests to
prevent the over-exploitation of scarce resources than would the continuation of more piecemeal efforts by governments to control their
domestic industrial operations, and to seek co-operation with other
governments to control environmental damage and wastage of resources.

In the case of armaments, it is impossible to deny the gross wastage
of global resources they represent, and the heavy price world hunger
pays for them. But one may still doubt that a world divided by
ideology, religious doctrine, racial hatred, and above all economic
scarcity could ever be one in which division did not express itself in
armed conflict, however 'irrational' in cost–benefit terms. It is not
only that violence remains a latent possibility where the facts of
human aggression and vulnerability persist. Force, including
revolutionary force, may be necessary to achieve justice.

False Analogies of the State and Global Authority

The cosmopolitan approach to international justice rejects the state,
for two conflated but ultimately contradictory reasons. One is that the
state is said not to be able to deliver what it is supposed to deliver in
terms of social justice, rights, environmental protection, and so on.
This is because it cannot exert control over the external factors upon

which its success in providing for its citizens depends, or alternatively because its actions are directed primarily towards the interests of dominant classes and elites. The second argument is that problems of global justice and order require the sort of institution(s) globally that are analogous in many respects to the state. In fact, the ambiguity of cosmopolitan accounts as to whether what replaces the states system would itself have the characteristics of a state derives from a misplaced contractarian analogy of the problem of justice within the state, and the problem of global justice.[60]

The legitimacy of global political institutions is to be understood exclusively in terms of their relationship to individuals and groups in the provision of welfare and the securing of conditions of justice. Whatever the resemblance of the form of such institutions to the form of the state, there can be no direct analogy of content, because global institutions are meant to protect justice and rights to a degree transcending the capabilities of the state.

The cosmopolitan critique of the existing international order posits what is in effect an ideal state. It overestimates what the state or any other central authority can achieve in terms of justice.[61] The state, projected globally, is supposed to achieve at the global level what in contractarian terms it is unable to do for domestic society. At the global level it is less likely that questions of justice could be determined consensually and through an accountable, representative machinery, rather than be determined by the use of force by the dominant group. What is more, states are often unable to ensure domestic order. The defence by a state of its own internal authority may be incompatible with its own survival as an entire unit, as in the case of Indian partition, or the Lebanon of the 1970s. If, however, global institutions, or a global government, were to collapse, it is unclear how transition to another political order would come about.

Conversely, what is essential about the state in securing justice is also ignored.[62] We have noted the lack in cosmopolitan theories of an account of the individual's rights and needs when he is considered in relation to his national, ethnic, religious or cultural group, and the narrowly utilitarian account of individual and group values, especially as this serves as a basis for their expectations of the state. Justice and rights are universal concepts, but this does not mean that all and every minute detail of the application, conflict, or cultural interpretation of questions of rights and justice may be illuminated by reference to a small number of clear and absolute principles.

Justice and Order Again

It is the case that some general categories of justice are common among societies and cultures, and that the justice-claims within these categories have of their nature a universally attributable content. At the level of practice, however, debates about justice in domestic society are often irreconcilable in terms of a general consensus. An agency of adjudication and enforcement is needed. Either the authority of the state alone or that authority operating above a representative political system, in which economic and social consideration is given to those excluded from the effective political majority and in which there is a possibility of constitutional change of governmental authority, serves to preserve the political – if not the social – unity of the state.

The diversity and antagonism of political philosophies and economic, military and strategic interests are, it is almost truistic to say, vastly greater at the global level than within any state. Amongst other obstacles to global pluralism is the opposition of the principle of tolerance to the facts of the intrinsic intolerance of many cultural practices.

The ability of the state to 'settle' questions of justice in an often rough and ready way is itself a form of sacrificing justice to order. There are times when societies will sacrifice order, at least temporarily, in order to overcome injustice. But the general disorder which results from the absence of any effective authority over a society of fundamentally conflicting interests and beliefs may prevent either the achievement or the stable enjoyment of conditions of justice. A trade-off between justice and order is the inevitable result, though the terms of this trade-off are themselves, of course, amongst the most highly contested questions of justice.

The central difficulty of the cosmopolitan theory of international justice is that, whilst the state is able to address the problems of domestic justice in ways which it is far from clear any global authority could do, its own primary principle is the preservation of order. Because of this, it is an imperfect vehicle of justice. The same trade-offs between justice and order which arise in domestic society must occur under any global authority. Since the models we have discussed do not include any convincing mechanisms for the maintenance of global order, the result of violent disagreements about global justice in the absence of an effective authority above the disputants could be imagined as preventing either order or justice. The trade-off becomes larger on both sides, perhaps uncontrollably so.

When the global authority is conceived as some constellation of global and regional functional agencies, it confronts the fact that it possesses none of the mechanisms by means of which the state reconciles the imperatives of justice and order, a reconciliation which is itself a prerequisite of justice. When the image is of a world state, it confronts the limitations of the effectiveness, and even the durability, of the state in the face of the problems of justice and injustice.

World Authority as a Threat to World Justice

None of the cosmopolitan approaches to justice seems likely to meet with practical success, at least barring some unforeseen global catastrophe. But at the level of hypothesis, it is difficult to see how separate functional agencies, confronted by the problems of co-ordination of their own activities, and ultimately of eliminating the challenge of the sovereign state, could avoid becoming a world government.

The most intolerable part of the Hobbesian theory appeared to be that questions of justice could only be decided by countervailing force; justice becomes a matter of government fiat. We rejected this conception of justice; yet we have also argued that, in the absence of states, the problems of world justice would become more, and not less, intractable. The real difficulty is that there would be nothing to stop a world state from implementing its version of just economic, social, cultural and political arrangements, whatever the real merits of the issues. For want of rival agencies of representation, authority, arbitration or enforcement, justice by pure fiat would be all that remained.

A form of global authoritarianism seems more than possible. A unitary state would be the purest form of arbitrary power if effective, since no rival to it would exist. Nor would individual rights be enhanced by the ferocity of the likely competition among groups to control the apparatus of such a state. Since this would constitute the sole global authority, the stakes for control over it must be dramatically increased over those in most domestic societies. In addition, states are obliged to tolerate rivals by the facts of the distribution of global resources, population, and so on. A world state might be more jealous of its power, because the tolerance of political and ideological pluralism enforced on states by the facts of countervailing power is no longer a necessity. Indeed, the fear that secessionist rivals could come to challenge the authority of the world state, either by asserting their independent sovereignty, or by seeking to usurp the position of sole global authority, could be imagined to result in the violent suppression of pluralism in order to preserve the monolith.

So the idea of a full-blown global state exposes the limits of contractarian justice as a practical analogy for world justice, if not as a philosophical model, and reveals the degree of injustice and violence the anti-contractarian monolith could employ in the absence of external constraints. The weaknesses of lesser alternatives are clear: those mechanisms of the state that can create social justice are absent, and the risk of global anarchy is present.[63]

An Alternative to Cosmopolitan Theory

We noted whilst discussing Kant that the universality of moral principles by no means leads directly to the specification of their content. How can we go from a Kantian account of obligation to the description of the particular obligations existing between states? This is especially problematic if those obligations are thought to concern transfers of wealth and resources. International welfare cannot be the object of a universal, categorical moral law because its content is highly particular in its social, cultural and historical dimensions.

The specification of the positive content of international obligations requires a defence of a theory of substantive rights. If the state provides only a limited and contingent context for the securing of these claims, its disadvantages from an idealistic point of view must be heavily discounted against the practicality and immediacy of the state as an existent institution, and against the greater dangers to the rights secured – however imperfectly – by the state that is posed by the very global, or at least superstate, institutions proposed by cosmopolitan theorists.

The existence of a plurality of independent states provides for the individual who is oppressed by his own state, in principle at least, the possibility of asylum elsewhere. It also permits the exertion of moral, political and diplomatic pressure upon recalcitrant states to improve domestic conditions of justice and rights.

In this context, it should be noted that the natural law tradition has always maintained that, whilst the ethical principles binding upon states are not qualitatively different from those binding on individuals, the need for co-operation between states is of a lesser degree of urgency than that of co-operation between individuals, because of the greater autarky of states as compared to individuals, and because the existence of the state itself provides for the basic security of those living within it, both from the exigencies of the state of nature and from the depredations of other states.

Cosmopolitan theory provides the clearest examples of the conflict between the principle of state sovereignty and the claims of justice and rights, at both the empirical and the normative level. A complex instrumentalist theory offers no easy way out of this opposition. It does not prescribe the abolition of the state, though it accepts as an unavoidable fact that the full range of human rights and legitimate claims for justice cannot find their complete satisfaction within the state. But the coupling of natural law assumptions about the general existence of mutual obligations among states with a definite account of human rights based on the idea of agency goes a long way towards the resolution of this dilemma. It will be shown to provide us with an account of international justice that offers more than the sterile rehearsal of arguments for the opposition of state sovereignty and the logic of justice and rights which are so central to both the realist and the cosmopolitan viewpoints.

If rights and other justice-claims relate to provision of physical, social and economic resources as well as to the protection of security and property and the traditional range of civil and political rights, then global inequalities will require rectification according to principles of international distributive justice. The defence of the state as a vehicle of international justice requires such principles, if one considers that without them the misfortune of having been born in one state rather than another may literally render life impossible.

Even so, such severe stipulations for the future viability of the states system cannot blind us to the immediacy and practicality of the state in the securing of justice and rights, nor to the often ill-understood theoretical contradictions and practical dangers of alternatives to the state. The natural law defence of the state remains possible without any corollary of the ethical absoluteness of the state, or claims that its existence alone gives meaning to the ideas of justice and rights, and without ceasing to recognise that actual human beings are the constituents of international society, and the ultimate subjects of justice.

4 Justice in a Society of States

Cosmopolitan theorists cannot live with the contradiction between the logics of sovereignty, and of justice and rights, which is perhaps another way of saying that they have no real sense of political tragedy.

The main aim of this chapter is to defend the continued relevance of the natural law or 'society of states' tradition of international relations thought, of which the conception of the state and international justice offered here is a development, and to show that its basic normative conception of international relations is sufficiently defensible in philosophical and practical terms for it to serve as a substantive theory of the state and international justice.

We need to show that sufficient international ethical understanding exists, and is reflected in practice; to substantiate the idea of international society as a viable context for principles of international justice; to identify the members of that society; to distinguish the legitimate from the illegitimate uses of natural law theory; and to show that the role of international law in the settlement and management of issues of international justice is sufficiently effective for it to be reasonable to characterise the former as a vehicle of the latter. We shall see also in what senses it is meaningful to speak of moral principles of adjudication and evaluation other than, and in some senses above, that of positive international law.

Natural Law and International Relations

In the wake of the Reformation and the break-up of the unity of Christendom, natural law theorists sought to ground the relations of the new sovereign states in principles of natural law, derived from the old Roman concept of the *jus gentium*, which right reason as well as divine revelation showed to be binding upon all human beings, as well as upon the relations between their states.[1] Elements of co-operation and common interest between states to be regulated by such principles were stressed. Trade and commerce, rather than war or utopian moral obligation, became the paradigm relations between states. At the same time, the realities which the other two traditions described were not overlooked. The latency of war in human affairs was acknowledged.

Grotius' greatest book is *The Law of Peace and War*.[2] In contrast to the Hobbesian rejection of moral standards in states' relations, Grotius is concerned to define the just occasions for war, just practices in time of war, and the circumstances in which the aggrieved state itself or the entire community of states may intervene to punish an aggressor. Human beings are the ultimate subjects of natural law, and the ultimate bearers of rights and duties. States are only the mediate, though practically the dominant, subjects of natural law. The law which pertains to them is the Law of Nations, which is subordinate to natural law.

The natural law tradition provides us with an integrated and powerful body of international moral theory, in contrast to the scepticism and pessimism of the realists. It shares with cosmopolitan theory the view that states' moral claims are essentially derivative, and that the state can never come to constitute a moral end in itself. But it rejects as impractical the cosmopolitan urge to transcend or eliminate the state. The state is instead viewed as a necessary, but by no means sufficient, condition of human justice.

The application of the society of states perspective, and of the philosophy of natural law generally, to the modern international system immediately raises an important problem. Domestic society clearly involves more than the idea of proximity or common sentiment. It involves the regulation of social institutions and practices, and the prescription of rights and obligations, by a popularly understood and recognised system of law. If international society is worth the name, a system of international law which bears resemblance at least in some important respects to domestic or municipal law, and which serves as at least a rudimentary vehicle for international justice, must be shown to exist.

4.1   THE IDEA OF AN INTERNATIONAL SOCIETY

We should expect a society to possess at least the following characteristics.

Firstly, there should exist significant interdependencies among groups and individuals in the creation and development of the material and cultural conditions of their existence. In 'primitive' societies the ends of individuals are subjugated to the common social purpose, so that the degree of interdependence is very high. In developed, 'pluralist' societies, which comprise many and more variegated ends, interdependence does not confront each individual as an immediate and primary social fact, though it may remain objectively significant. In other words, the objective facts of social interdependence do not always issue in a subjective, social sense of mutual interests and reciprocity.

Secondly, there exists some body of moral values revealed by recurring social judgements of right and wrong and which moves the concepts of justice, rights and duties beyond the realm of metaphysics and into that of practical morality.

Thirdly, whilst profound divergences of belief and practice exist in most societies, the idea of a society requires that there be no division or coincidence of divisions of so unchanging and impermeable a nature that no common moral understanding across them is possible.

Fourthly, the concept of society implies common institutions, practices and principles of co-operative behaviour, however rudimentary, which regularly inform the behaviour of the members of that society, and may be said to be part of the 'socialisation' process, as opposed to the mere codification of rules of self-interested prudence compatible with a Hobbesian view of man.

Fifthly, some or all of these practices should be regulated by a formal structure of law, which itself comes to embody, more or less, the values of society.

The view that no common culture, and therefore no common ethical ground, exists at the global level has become current in much recent writing about international relations. Adda Bozeman maintains that the plurality of world cultures often reflects profound and unbridgeable cultural divides which preclude the growth of any unitary world culture or common moral understanding.[3] These divisions include that between the rationalism of the West and the mysticism and reverence for tradition of Oriental cultures; the Western stress on the individual human being as the source of thought and the bearer of rights, as opposed to the collectivism of Confucian or Hindu cultural and religious teaching, which stresses that all things, including human life, are expressions of a cosmic unity, and makes the rights of the individual wholly subordinate to the interests and security of the organic, hierarchical society.

In contrast to those who propound a culture of modernity, either as a result of the assimilation of Western ideas or as the inevitable consequence of industrialisation in developing states, critics of the idea of an international society often argue that the penetration of European traditions is, in the long run, limited. Westernised elites stand astride two cultures, becoming remote in culture and sympathy from the mass of the population over which they rule, whilst often themselves retaining a residual antagonism towards Western culture, perhaps as a result of the recognition that its permeation of their own education and lifestyle has cut them off from their fellow country-men.[4]

Cultural Atavism and Ideological Divisions

The persistence or reappearance of indigenous religious and cultural rites in post-colonial societies, such as the burning of widows on their husbands' funeral pyres in India, may be seen as a deep-seated form of protest against Western values, and as a restatement of customary values. The revolt by indigenous cultures against Western influence has certainly reappeared with a new ferocity in the last twenty years, ranging from the Khmer revolution of 1975 in Cambodia to the fundamentalist Islamic revival signalled by the Iranian revolution of 1979.

The anti-Westernism of Mao Tse-Tung or Kwame Nkrumah seem in retrospect to have had much in common with older, more traditional and less ideologically frenetic nationalist sentiments. Despite their respective espousal of international anti-imperialist solidarity and Pan-Africanism, both were confronted with the persistent reality of the nation-state, and had to accommodate their vision to that reality. Unlike these examples, other, more recent forms of revolt against Westernised elites – the Khmer Rouge, the Shining Path movement in Peru, or even the bizarre military successes of the tribal witch Alice in Uganda – have deep and obscure, even occult, origins in disturbed societies and make the conventional language of ideological and nationalist revolt inadequate. At the very least, international cultural homogeneity is weakened by persistent strains of anti-Westernism in developing states, at both mass and elite levels; important elements of non-Western cultures have not been eclipsed. Nor is it only Western influence which is resented, as the continuing troubles in the former Soviet Union's southern republics testify.

Other global divisions have been attributed to the pernicious effect of Marxism upon both Western and Westernised elites, leading to a loss of confidence on the part of the former in their own institutions and values, and the employment by the latter of exploitative imagery as a means of disguising their own responsibility for the conditions of their societies. In conservative eyes, the concept of the state is itself seen as being under attack; the use of private violence, terrorism (including state-sponsored terrorism) and the prevalence of arguments, used both by non-aligned and communist bloc states, that colonialism constitutes a permanent form of international aggression and that self-determination is an unconditional right, have led to the undermining of international consensus on what constitutes war or peace.

Martin Wight has been typically forthright in rejecting the belief that a growing international society is taking shape around a new moral consensus, or that the fledgling institutions of such a society have done much to improve the moral climate:

> the United Nations has enhanced the power struggle between the have-nots and the status quo powers. The existence of the United Nations has exaggerated the international importance of the have-not powers, enabling them to organise themselves into a pressure group with much greater diplomatic and propaganda weight than they would otherwise have had. The paradoxical consequence has been that powers which, taken collectively, exhibit a low level of political freedom, governmental efficiency, public probity, civil liberties and human rights, have had the opportunity to set themselves up in judgement over powers which, taken collectively, for all their sins, have a high level in these respects.[5]

These illustrations of cultural and political diversity are significant, but we shall see that they do not demonstrate the absence of common moral understanding as one foundation of international society. National societies of extraordinary cultural diversity have historically organised their common social life around moral and political principles which have come to serve as inspiration and ideals uniting disparate elements. The United States' Constitution is a major historical example of this.

Shared Ideas of Justice and Constraints on States' Behaviour

Individual or collective conviction about the morality of practices is no argument against rational analysis and discussion of moral concepts. To say this, however, is to invite another attack on the idea of moral consensus as an element in international society. This is that moral consensus as an integrating force requires beliefs to be deeply experienced and internalised, and not just to provide philosophical grounds for possible agreement. On this view, common beliefs about international justice are too few and too feeble to explain or judge comparatively the justice of different social practices or government policies.

Two replies to this objection are possible. One is that governments do recognise common normative principles even, or especially, when they are violating them. Thus military intervention becomes disguised as a response to the request of a legitimate government for aid against an external aggressor (the Soviet Union in Afghanistan), or as a countermeasure against a government denounced as illegitimate because supposedly supported by an external aggressor (the United States in Nicaragua), or as a response to real or imaginary rights-violations (humanitarian intervention). Conventions for the limitation of warfare have widely been accepted; when, for example, Iraq resorted to chemical weapons in its war with Iran, it was at pains to deny it, or to claim that Iran had used them first.

Israel's leaders, and its foreign supporters, have denied that either the pre-1967 Israeli state or the occupation of the West Bank and Gaza constituted a violation of the right of self-determination for Palestinians. This is not because a nation is said not to have such a right, but because it is denied that the Palestinians constitute a nation.

The climate of moral expectation of states' behaviour can act as a significant constraint on what states feel free to do, and is not necessarily seen as instances of intervention threatening to the principle of sovereignty.

The second objection to the argument from moral relativism is still more important. When grossly rights-violating regimes reject all and any outside criticism, the usual consequence of this denial is not to defend the cultural and moral autonomy of individuals or societies, but to bolster governments whose policies are themselves the gravest threat to that autonomy. In any case, the moral relativist is left with precious little to say.

Westernisation and International Society

The westernisation of elites inevitably poses problems of cultural conflict in developing societies. We should distinguish between the effects that elite linkages between centre and periphery states have had on economic development and inequality in the latter (together with the alienating and disruptive effects that Western culture in its most commercial and insidious forms has had upon developing societies), and those effects that the political culture of the West has had upon different social structures. The latter effects seem more beneficial. Indeed, the claims that representative democracy and constitutional legality represent alien forms imposed upon tribal societies not yet 'ready' for them, or that they are in some way alien to traditional patterns of government and authority in those societies, seem to indicate both a lack of respect for and confidence in those societies rather than any real commitment to diversity of political forms.

Conflict, Consensus and International Understanding

The next criterion of an international society was that divisions within it should not be irreconcilable or permanent.

Among the more obvious divisions in world politics are those arising from nationalism, ideology and the familiar proposition of the zero-sum nature of international security. Elie Kedourie has attacked the modern doctrine of self-determination as a principle of international disorder in a world in which states and nations patently do not coincide.[6] At the same time, it has been argued that the grounds for self-determination have changed from the demand for the political autonomy of a territory (statehood), whether or not the territory was coextensive with a nation, to a demand for national and ethnic autonomy, compounded with other, and often contradictory, principles, such as that of territorial integrity which India used as grounds for occupying the Portuguese colony of Goa.[7] This might, indeed, be seen as a limited reversion to the irredentism of the nineteenth century as a precondition of constructing nation-states. The first demand was directed against colonialism: it did not threaten the end of the sovereign states system, only its expansion in numbers. The new variant of self-determination poses a much greater threat to international order.

The influence of ideological divisions, according to the sceptics, has been to compound the subversive aspect of self-determination and to reduce all international politics to conflict and domination. Third World Marxism-Leninism is held mostly to blame; its proponents argue both for national sovereignty and for class warfare. Another major problem of self-determination is the proliferation of small and often politically unstable states, 'imitation' states as they have disparagingly been termed, which lack the means effectively to participate in international society, and which are seen by realist and conservative critics as a challenge to the precarious principles of legitimacy and responsibility which exist.

In response to these arguments it may be noted that the spectre of self-determination as a radical and permissive principle, challenging the integrity of sovereign states in a revolutionary way, has not materialised. The Soviet Union could once claim, as in the early days of its support for Castro, that the rights of a people to political and economic liberation were aspects of its right to self-determination, and justified a request to a fraternal power in order to achieve that right. But claims that later actions were merely counter-interventions in response to interference and subversion by 'imperialism', as in Afghanistan, did much to damage the image of the former Soviet Union in the eyes of the Third World. One must think more recently of Chechenia.

As to the view that the purported right of self-determination engenders constant interventions and disruption of international order, the historical experience in much of the world is that when the principles of self-determination and non-intervention have come into conflict, the latter has usually won. Thus, neither the Indian intervention in Bangladesh, during a struggle for self-determination, nor the Vietnamese intervention in Kampuchea, during a struggle which had the aspect of self-determination for a large part of the population, was justified by the protagonists on the grounds of legitimate support for self-determination, but instead as a justified act of self-defence against aggression.

The post-independence history of Africa, where artificial colonial boundaries raised especially acute problems of self-determination, also provides examples of the importance attached to the non-intervention principle. Indeed, on those (relatively few) occasions where the OAU has been divided or equivocal about intervention in conflicts, as in the cases of Katangan secession in the Congo or Biafran secession in Nigeria, or about which of the contending forces to support as in the Angolan civil war, the opportunity to intervene has been seized not by African powers hoping to change the political or territorial status quo in their favour, but by external powers (including, in this context, South Africa).

The viability of independent states as a determinant of their international legitimacy raises problems for a liberal realist like Morgenthau, who defends mutual respect for the defence by states of their interests, and of the duty of statesmen to their publics in so doing, as principles of 'political ethics'.[8] The size of a state does not obviously affect its claims to be the best, or only, judge of the national interest. The viability doctrine runs still more counter to the Vattelian idea of the immediate analogy of states and persons. Personality is not a question of size.[9]

The critique of viability presents fewer problems for the two extremes of the traditions we have examined so far. Hobbesian realists, or political neo-Darwinians such as E.H. Carr and especially Herbert Spencer, certainly do not believe that respect for states' rights or integrity is a moral absolute. Nor do cosmopolitan theorists, whose wholly derivative view of the state's authority and legitimacy appears to necessitate the conclusion that a state with a large population has prima facie greater entitlements (to resources, for example); and therefore they must challenge the legitimacy of a state which by virtue of small size or impoverishment is unable to provide for the fundamental rights and needs of its people.

The relationship between cultural understanding and conflict in international relations is far from obvious. The systemic conception of conflict,[10] or the view that problems exist as autonomous entities independent of the perceptions of those who must grapple with them, may be questioned without our being committed to the view that greater mutual knowledge leads ineluctably to an accommodation of perspectives. It is the essence of the determined ideologue that the acquisition of knowledge is a highly selective process, serving the primary purpose of buttressing prior convictions.[11] But the simultaneous ignorance and hysteria encouraged in the participation of mass publics on both sides of the cold war lend some persuasiveness to Morgenthau's desire for a return to a calmer if more paternalist era of diplomacy.[12] If it is rash to suggest that knowledge always breeds tolerance, it is rasher still to deny that ignorance has the converse effect.

Common Institutions and Coexistence

The third criterion of international society was the existence of common institutions, another target of sceptics. Again, the question of the viability of states is at the core of the problem. It is argued by sceptics about the idea of international society that decolonisation has taken place, often through unilateral decisions by the metropolitan powers, without thought as to the ability of the states to accept international responsibilities, or to the costs for the former colonial populations, or to the inappropriateness of Western forms of government. 'Tribalism' is seen to be necessarily at odds with European structures.

Nor, on such a view, has the expansion of the international system and of international diplomacy seen a parallel extension of the most basic international rule of co-existence. Instead, as we noted, anti-colonialism and self-determination have been extended to 'internal' or 'settler' colonialism, giving rise to forcible intervention to bring self-determination about, even where the majority do not wish to be 'free' from the colonial power. Relations between Third World states threaten disorder which might escalate to a global level, as in the case of India and Pakistan. The threat to the principle of the immunity of envoys, graphically witnessed in Iran, the sponsorship by governments of national liberation movements committed to using terror beyond the borders of the state in which the struggle occurs, the problems of adequate compensation for nationalisation of foreign assets: all these have been seen as sources of new international divisions.

Others have attacked the idea that the United Nations serves as a vehicle for international solidarity, and have seen too many discrepancies of power and responsibility. They point to the absence of shared values in the 'hypocrisy' of UN Resolutions.[13] A case in point was the 1967 referendum on self-determination for Gibraltar organised by the United Kingdom in accordance with the UN Charter's commitment to the equal rights of peoples. When union with Spain was hugely rejected, the General Assembly responded by passing Resolution 2429 XXIII condemning the 'colonial situation' in Gibraltar. Again, the failure of the General Assembly to condemn human rights abuses in Uganda represented to conservative critics a wholly spurious and morally corrupt form of racial solidarity, in marked contrast to the General Assembly's usual enthusiasm in condemning other human rights abuses at that time. Small states are seen to cling tenaciously to the meaningless (on this view) 'equality' bestowed upon them by their votes at the UN General Assembly, but lack the material and the moral resources to sustain any valuable international role.

One problem of accusations of tribalism, aside from the fact of the responsibility of the colonial powers for artificial political boundaries which often ignore ethnic identity and solidarity, is that the term is pejorative. It suggests the presence of something less than a nation, without the rights to which the dignity of nationhood gives rise, but without defining either term in order to show the moral superiority of the claims of one over the other. The practical consequence of this is that the horrendous costs in social and economic disruption and in loss of life involved in those national and religious conflicts that began in the late Middle Ages and culminated in the modern European nation-states system are ignored. The struggle of European nations for statehood is, it is implied, historically sui generis, a positive and necessary development in the history of civilisation, whilst African or Asian nationalist struggles are merely disruptive tribalism – even forms of barbarism.

This stands up to analysis no better than does the contention that conflicts between the new states threaten in themselves to disrupt international order. The role of great powers and superpowers in the genesis and the continuation of these conflicts is overlooked. If these conflicts threaten global order, they do not do so as independent variables, but because they are, or were, the only spheres in which East/West rivalry could partly struggle free of its nuclear straitjacket and express itself by proxy. The conflicts which threaten the very idea of an international society are not, for the most part, occasioned simply by the admission of new members to that society. They are rather manifestations of much older divisions in that society's history.

The claim that doctrines of 'internal' or 'settler' colonialism have been used to justify intervention to enforce self-determination, whether wanted by the majority or not, encounters the problem that there are not many examples of this happening. India's annexation of Goa perhaps qualifies. So too might Indonesia's invasion of East Timor, were it not for the fact that the Portuguese colonists had already gone. The Argentine invasion of the Falklands was the result of a dispute about historical possession. But the refusal of the UN General Assembly to accept Britain's claim of both legal sovereignty and of the moral and political rights of self-determination of the islanders, and the UN's equivocal attitude towards the status of Gibraltar, are examples of the assumption that 'settler colonialism' may justify the denial of rights of self-determination even to large majorities in such circumstances.

As for the more general criticisms of the new states in the UN, they manifest a tendency to associate material resources with moral capacity in an almost Calvinistic way which fails to recognise that it is not the mere fact of hypocrisy or moral inconsistency which is alarming, but the consequences of the policies which follow from that fact. That condemnation of injustices in developing states has been avoided out of sophistry or bogus solidarity has, on occasion, been the case. It would be harder to argue that American interventions originating from the policies of 'containment' or Soviet interventions to combat imperialism or even in the case of hapless Hungary recrudescent 'fascism' have caused less moral and material damage than the petty obscurantism of some Third World governments.[14]

The Expansion of International Society

The extension of the states system has generally witnessed the 'export' of state theory and reciprocal behaviour.[15] A degree of shared aspirations and even common acceptance of rules to limit armed conflict have emerged, although an undermining of the moral legitimacy of force may lead simply to more subterfuge about its use. Still, international society is hard to opt out of, as witnessed by the attempts of the Afrikaners to isolate themselves from global scrutiny and criticism.[16]

The existence and significance of an international society has been well summarised by Bull and Watson:

> It might be thought evidence of the underlying strength and adaptability of the international society created by the Europeans that it has been able to absorb such a vast accretion of new members, interests, values, and preoccupations, without giving rise to any clear sign that its rules and institutions are collapsing under the strain, or that the new states have repudiated them. Indeed, the most striking feature of the international society of today is the extent to which the states of Asia and Africa have embraced such basic elements of European international society as the sovereign state, the rules of international law, the procedures and conventions of diplomacy and international organisation. In all these areas they have sought to reshape existing rules and institutions, to eliminate discrimination against themselves and to assert their own interests forcefully, but all of this has been against the background of the strong interests they have perceived in accepting the rules and institutions, not only because of their need to make use of them in their relations with the erstwhile dominant powers, but also because they cannot do without them in their relations with one another.[17]

There is in the long term little hope of promoting common interests and shared moral perspectives where these are viewed as fraudulent and skewed on the side of the dominant powers and the class interests their policies represent. It is certain that such a view will be taken in the absence of greater economic or distributive justice. The institutions and practices of international society are limited by the fact that so much of the world's population is marginalised in its ability to participate even in its own society by deprivation or ignorance. The benefits of international co-operation are of little value if the minimum social and economic provision which makes such participation possible is absent in domestic societies.

The adaptation of international institutions in the interests of greater economic justice, which *inter alia* will require the relinquishing of the absolute political veto provided by the voting system of such institutions as the IMF, the World Bank, and the IBRD, and the granting of political autonomy to key economic agencies, requires the mutual accommodation of political sovereignty, including its partial relinquishment on both sides, and neither the transcendence nor the absolute assertion of sovereignty.

4.2   THE MEMBERS OF INTERNATIONAL SOCIETY

We said that natural law may be defined as those rules discoverable through reason and experience that are necessary to preserve social co-operation and primary conditions of security.[18] Hugo Grotius identified the positive law, or the Law of Nations (*jus gentium*), as essential to coexistence between sovereign states,[19] though this law was less perfect than natural law, but argued that the precepts of the Law of Nations must come more closely to resemble the natural law, decreed by God but knowable in addition by right reason.[20] He argued for a necessary interdependence between the two forms of law; the Law of Nations, though reflecting the exigencies of international relations and the imperfection of human nature, was not the limit of moral and rational constraints upon states. The two forms of law are not wholly separate, in the sense that the obligations of natural law are both a part of the Law of Nations, and of a higher order in comparison to it.

Natural law exists in Grotius' theory alongside a contractarian prescription of state authority, reflecting a belief in the innate rationality, sociability and moral autonomy of man. What is true of man in the pre-social condition is, for Grotius, true of states, as James Brown Scott has noted:

> States as such are, according to ... natural law, free and equal, as having no superior. But, no more than individuals can they live in isolation; they are not sufficient unto themselves; for their preservation they are bound to associate. They are like individuals in the state of nature, and the natural law applies to them as well as to individuals. But this primitive law may be perfected. How? By

contract between the states. The natural law which imposes itself
and the law between the states which is created by custom, consent,
or contract. The promise of states, like that of an individual, gives
rise to an obligation and contractual law, just as natural law,
executes itself. Thus we have the law of nations.[21]

Here is a sharp contrast with the cosmopolitan tradition. The
contractarian conception of the state is not used to justify some
analogous, higher authority which aims to replace the sovereign state.
On the contrary, the latter is preserved, and is in conformity with
natural law, whilst the contractarian analogy gives rise to a society of
states. But the idea of contract between states does not entail that
international law is solely the product of the wills of sovereign states.
The *jus gentium*, the part of international law based on consent, is
considered by Grotius to be only one part of international law. States
are bound by the precepts of natural law with the same force as are
individuals, since states and individuals are recognised as being essentially identical from a moral point of view.

Most importantly, Grotius stresses that individuals are ultimately
the subjects of natural law, and of international society conceived in
the light of this law, although states are the subjects of the law of
nations, the voluntary law which proceeds only from the will of
nations. Thus,

> the members of international society are ultimately not states but
> individuals. The conception of a society formed by states and
> sovereigns is present in [Grotius'] thought; but its position is second-
> ary to that of the universal community of mankind, and its legiti-
> macy derivative from it.[22]

Grotius is insistent that states are bound by principles of justice just
as men are, even if they do not derive such immediately obvious
advantage from living under a system of law:

> But, not to repeat what I have said, that law is not founded on
> expediency alone, there is no state so powerful that it may not some
> time need the help of others outside itself, either for purposes of
> trade, or even to ward off the forces of many foreign nations united
> against it.[23]

In international relations there is no common superior, so law is not
self-executing. Each state has the right to pursue justice against others
injuring it. War is just on three grounds; 'defence, recovery of what

belongs to us, and punishment'. The enforcement of sanctions against transgressors of the Law of Nations is also the right of the community of nations as a whole, although Grotius is aware that the exigencies of the law may lead to constant upheaval, and so does not make of this right a duty. Such wars should themselves be prosecuted with restraint, in accordance with natural law. He maintained, unlike Vattel and the positivist international lawyers who came after him, and who insisted that international law must remain neutral as to the justice of a war, that there was right and wrong to be determined in conflicts, in accordance with natural law principles. *Raison d'état* is no better an excuse for lawless action than selfish advantage on the part of an individual:

> For just as the national, who violates the law of his country in order to obtain an immediate advantage, breaks down that by which the advantages of himself and his posterity are for all future time assured, so the state which transgresses the laws of nature and of nations cuts away also the bulwarks which safeguard its own future peace.[24]

Whilst the necessity of effective enforcement of law over recalcitrant individuals makes the state legitimate, neither its authority nor its policies are absolute or beyond moral challenge. Natural law may be regarded systematically as the minimum necessary content of a common, binding international morality.

The Growing Distinction between Natural Law and the Law of Nations

With Christian Wolff, the distinction between natural law and the voluntary law of nations becomes much sharper.[25] The latter is seen to consist entirely of extant international law made between states. In this way, Wolff's voluntary law becomes more limited than Grotius' Law of Nations. The distinction is made by reference to a *civitas maxima*, a purported world society. Nations are to be considered as analogous to persons living together in the state of nature. Both nations and persons have rights and obligations deriving from natural law. But just as men entering into civil society acquire actual rights and obligations which differ from their natural rights and obligations, and which may exceed the latter in some regards whilst being less exhaustive in others, the same is true with respect to the law created by nations among themselves as they come together in the *civitas maxima*. Since individuals were assumed by Wolff, following Grotius, to be bound by the laws without which their society could not subsist, so nations were bound to preserve the great community of nations to which they belonged. The fiction of the *civitas maxima* posited an international society whose positive laws were not different *in esse* from those of domestic society.

The duty of each nation is to 'perfect' itself. This is, for Wolff, the 'purpose of its state', that is, the promotion of the civil, intellectual, moral and spiritual potential of its people. This is the justification not only of the state to which each nation has entitlement, but of nations' duties to one another:

> Every nation owes to every other nation that which it owes to itself, in so far as the other does not have that in its own power, whilst the first nation without neglect of duty towards itself can perform this for the other.[26]

Here we begin to see a much more explicit concession to the self-interest of states than we find in Grotius. The 'natural liberty' of nations and their right to self-preservation make nations their own legitimate judges of when aid to other nations is possible without damage to their own vital interests:

> every nation must be allowed to stand by its judgement, as to whether it can do anything for another without neglect of its duty towards itself; consequently, if that which is sought is refused, it must be endured, and the right of nations to those things which other nations owe them by nature, is an imperfect right.[27]

National interest justifies the subordination of natural law precepts to the positive law of nations.

Wolff was not ready to ascribe an independent moral personality to the state, as would be Emerich de Vattel a few decades later.[28] Vattel rejected Wolff's image of a *civitas maxima*, maintaining instead that as nations were less dependent and vulnerable than individuals, they were therefore not naturally obliged to unite in civil society. The *civitas maxima* is, for Vattel, a pointless fiction in the absence of a common sovereign above states. He distinguished between the 'necessary' law of nations, which was broadly equivalent to what his predecessors had meant by natural law, and the 'voluntary' and 'customary' law of nations, arising from, respectively, explicit and tacit recognition by nations. The state's highest duty was to promote the welfare and security of its members. But the state now comes to possess a self-subsistent moral personality, having its own affairs and interests: it deliberates and takes resolutions in common, and it thus becomes a moral person having an understanding and a will peculiar to itself, and susceptible at once of obligations and rights.[29]

Whilst nations were bound by natural law to contribute to the welfare of others, and to promote the natural society of nations, for Vattel as for Wolff every nation was to be judge of when assistance to other nations became incompatible with its duty towards itself. But for Vattel, for one nation to make demands of another beyond this point was to violate the rights of a free person. The necessary law gave rise to 'perfect' rights; that is, rights against nations that could always (in theory) be enforced. Voluntary law produced 'imperfect' rights, rights that were contingent upon the nation fulfilling them, not sacrificing its own interest. These rights were termed respectively *droits nécessaires* and *droits volontaires*.[30]

Vattel did not adopt the unequivocal position of the later positivist lawyers that international law must be silent on the question of the justice of a war, but argued that states must tolerate even that conduct of other states that violates the laws of conscience in order to protect the liberty of states. Whilst there is a sense in which individual human beings are the ultimate subjects of the reduced version of the natural law to which Vattel still adheres, the state is the necessary condition of their wellbeing, and thereby acquires an inviolable status. Intervention is the denial of that status. Intervention by a state, or by the community of states, in interstate conflict according to the criteria of *jus ad bellum* proposed by Grotius amounts to a claim asserted generally on the part of states to be competent to judge one another's affairs, a competence which Vattel's equality of states doctrine explicitly denies.

The 'Essential Identity' of States and Persons

As Sir Hersch Lauterpacht shows in his commentary on Grotius,[31] the moral unity of mankind is stressed at the expense of the Machiavellian doctrine of ratio status. Military security and economic interdependence necessitate rules of just conduct. The analogy of individuals and states is also used by Grotius, but quite differently from Wolff or Vattel:

The analogy is much more simple, more direct, and more convincing. The analogy – nay, the essential identity – of rules governing the conduct of states and of individuals is not asserted for the reason that states are like individuals; it is due to the fact that states are composed of individual human beings; it results from the fact that behind the mystical, impersonal, and therefore necessarily irresponsible personality of the metaphysical state there are actual subjects of rights and duties, namely, individual human beings. This is the true meaning of the Grotian analogy of states and individuals. The individual is the ultimate unit of all law, international and municipal, in the double sense that the obligations of international law are ultimately addressed to him and that the development, the well-being, and the dignity of the individual human being are a matter of direct concern to international law.[32]

In fact, Vattel pays mere lip service to the idea of natural law in promoting an analogy of states and persons which leads to the complete moral independence of states. Three consequences follow from Vattel's doctrine. *Raison d'état* becomes the supreme moral principle of states' conduct, and the just war theory of Grotius disappears; states' actions cannot be practically challenged, however unjust they may be by the precepts of natural law, without destroying states' moral autonomy; and mutual aid is limited. Indeed demands for assistance among states run so directly counter to the doctrine of absolute sovereignty over resources found in Vattel, that such assistance is effectively limited to the restitution of past wrongs.[33]

It is clear that Vattel's highly constricted idea of international justice is not constructed from the same sources as is that of Hobbes. Vattel does not claim that justice is meaningless in the absence of a sovereign authority; natural law still operates, although there is no international community analogous to civil society. Nor are international relations characterised as a state of nature; they are more akin to the pre-social situation described by Locke. But in holding that the justice of the action of the state is beyond practical challenge, because the state is the condition of the welfare of its citizens, Vattel's doctrine is subject to the same sorts of criticisms made of the Hobbesian conception of international relations in Chapter 2. If the state has a right, indeed a duty, to look after its own, the assertion of this as a supreme moral principle in a world of finite resources is contradictory. The function of the state with respect to its citizens, its duty to 'perfect itself' as Wolff puts it,[34] cannot become a universal maxim when its realisation by one state prevents its realisation by another. Co-operation is essential if the moral precept of the state in the abstract is to be attainable by actual states. That is to say that the limitation of that precept, and with it the limitation of sovereignty, is essential if the precept is to become concrete.

This presents no problems for the Hobbesian theory, since the assertion of the absolute natural right of self-preservation in a state of nature rules out any further conception of natural law based on the existence of society or respect for mutual obligation. But in asserting sovereignty against the duty of assistance to other states, and in prohibiting intervention even against unjust actions, Vattel throws away what is essential to the natural law tradition, a tradition which by this point has become little more than an encumbrance to him.

Difficulties with the Analogy of States and Persons

Another problem with the Vattelian analogy comes to mind. To intervene against a state, argues Vattel, is to violate its moral 'autonomy'. But it seems odd to argue that to prohibit, with sanctions, certain actions, or to restrain a person about to commit them, or to punish him for having done so, is to violate his moral autonomy. On the contrary, it is to remind him of his obligations to others, and of the limits of his rights where others' are endangered. It is to treat him as a moral agent, who is capable of recognising these rights. Even the use of violence need not alter this recognition, provided it goes no further than is necessary to prevent or punish a criminal act. This is the essence of Hegel's aphorism that 'punishment is the right of the criminal'. Why should the case be different for states if they are analogues of persons? Why should they be immune from the law?[35]

There are other reasons to believe that Vattel's doctrine collapses in practice into something similar to Hobbesian moral scepticism. If the state is to be uniquely competent to determine the extent of its obligations towards itself, and of its external obligations, then it acquires what is essentially the unconstrained 'natural right' which Hobbes ascribes to states as analogues of persons in the state of nature – something we have already rejected. The earlier natural law tradition of human beings as the ultimate members of international society is wholly abandoned where the personified state alone specifies its obligations to those excluded from it. Since we are offered no convincing criteria for distinguishing *droits nécessaires* from *droits volontaires*, this determination by the state can be nothing more than arbitrary fiat.

The natural law tradition preserved in Vattel's doctrine becomes a hollow shell. The failure of the Vattelian analogy undermines the idea that states have a moral character different from that of the people who make them up. The international society to which natural law has given moral content has human beings as its members precisely because there are no other candidates. There are no 'analogues' of persons.

The Origin of States' Rights

None of this tells us, of course, exactly what rights states may claim. And it must be repeated that any criticism of the cosmopolitan tradition must make the state a vital element in human justice. But it does tell us that those claims, whatever their legitimate content, are never *sui generis*. They derive from the legitimate claims of individuals. As Lassa Oppenheim notes,

> While it is of importance to bear in mind that primarily States are subjects of International Law, it is essential to recognise the limitations of that principle. Its correct meaning is that States only create International Law; that International Law is primarily concerned with the rights and duties of States and not with those of persons; ... when we say that International Law regulates the conduct of States, we must not forget that the conduct actually regulated is the conduct of human beings acting as the organ of the State. As Westlake said, 'The duties and rights of States are only the duties and rights of the men who compose them.' If that view is accepted, then it is scientifically wrong and practically undesirable to divorce International Law from the general principles of law and morality which underlie the main systems of municipal jurisprudence regulating the conduct of human beings.[36]

Hegel's Moral Theory of the State

We have viewed individuals as ethically prior to the state. For Hegel and his followers the state is, at least in a sense, ethically prior to the individual. The state is the unique basis for the ethical community. The purely private interests found in civil society are both preserved and transcended in the state. The state is freedom, not in the sense of guaranteeing arbitrary choice of action by individuals, but by revealing to the individual his own essential nature, as an agent whose freedom, and whose interests, are inseparably bound up with others, and thereby with those of the state, which upholds private interest.

This is 'rational freedom'. The state 'embodies man's highest relationship to other human beings':[37] it reveals to him his existence as part of an ethical whole. The state embodies reason in that it unifies the particular will of the individual with the universal will. The individual experiences the laws of the state not as an external imposition but as an extension of his self-consciousness as a social and ethical being:

> The nation state is mind in its substantive rationality and immediate actuality and is therefore the absolute power on earth. It follows that every state is sovereign and autonomous against its neighbours. It is entitled in the first place and without qualification to be sovereign from their point of view, i.e., to be recognised by them as sovereign. At the same time, however, this title is purely formal, and the demand for this recognition of the state, merely on the ground that it is a state, is abstract. Whether a state is in fact something absolute depends on its content, i.e., on its constitution and general situation; and recognition, implying as it does an identity of both form and content, is conditional on the neighbouring state's judgement and will.[38]

It must be borne in mind that Hegel is describing an ideal or abstract state, not any particular state actual or possible. Nor is he describing any necessary form of political system. The idea of representation is an ethical one, and not in itself a democratic concept, or even a political one in the true sense. Actual states may fall far short of Hegel's ideal type. Thus, recognition of sovereignty is a right of a state which fulfils its 'idea' in Hegel's terms; it is not an entitlement of any particular state claiming it. When Hegel speaks of the state as an 'ethical substance', he is not asserting the absolute moral autonomy of the state, as his many detractors have suggested, nor is he making a case for totalitarianism. Rather, he is saying that the ethical being of a particular state depends upon its substance. What this means is that the moral personality of the state depends upon its relationship with its people; the sort of claims it may make and the sort of rights it may assert against other states depend upon the nature of this relationship.

Hegel does not mean that the rights and obligations of states are aspects of the essential identity of states and persons in matters of moral accountability. He understands something unique when speaking of the state as an ethical substance. Yet, although the theory of Grotius still appears to me the best way to understand the ethical nature of the state, Hegel's account is more satisfactory than Vattel's in that the use of a misleading analogy of states and persons is avoided, and the moral character of the concrete state comes to rest upon more than an arbitrary dictum.

We need to explain why Hegel defines the state as the limit of ethics and as the highest embodiment of reason. He regards international law as purely volitional, the expression of sovereign wills which cannot, of their nature, be unconditionally bound. The answer lies both in the ideality of Hegel's theory of the state, and in the more prosaic fact that international law in his day was largely the law of treaties, supplemented by customary practices in the matter of diplomacy, treatment of prisoners, and so on. It was the international law of war, which was for Hegel the cardinal feature of international relations.

Modern international society did not exist, nor did the range of international political and economic institutions, nor the mass of modern international law. There was no idea of international welfare provision through supranational agencies, nor global management of macrocosmic problems through international co-operation.

We must conclude that Hegel's concern with the ethical uniqueness of the state arose from the fact that in his day the state was effectively the only sphere in which the interests of the individual had any influence, and in which his rights could be secured. International law was fragile and embryonic; it had neither the interlocking complexity nor the significance for the regulation of social life that it has today. Nor did it have anything to say about the rights of individuals.

That the extent of international society as an element in international relations exceeds what Hegel observed has, it is hoped, been demonstrated. To show that international law is more than purely volitional, the occasional unimportant expression of sovereign wills, is our next task.

4.3 INTERNATIONAL SOCIETY AND INTERNATIONAL LAW

It was noted earlier that the very idea of society is bound up with the existence of a body of rules. At the level of the state, these rules have the status of laws. A major objection to the claim that international society in any way resembles domestic society is that international law is quite unlike domestic law. A range of writers from Hegel to Austin[39] have denied that international law really counts as law at all.

Differences Between Domestic and International Law

Domestic law has three principal features – a comprehensive system of the administration and execution of justice (criminal and civil courts), mandatory penalties in the event of infractions of the law, and the most fundamental premise that obedience is non-optional – which seem to have no equivalents in international law. Let us look at these supposed differences in slightly more detail.

Firstly, no mandatory mechanisms of arbitration or of deciding matters of jurisdiction or legal competence may be said to exist. States must agree to subject themselves to such processes, and any such self-binding may be tolerated only for limited areas of judicial competence and for limited periods, and is in any case revocable. Nor – it follows – does any machinery for the review and improvement of existing international law exist. Only multilateral revision of treaties, usually involving substantial renegotiation, is possible.

Secondly, no system of sanctions for those states that violate international law exists (at least not of the organised and predictable nature of sanctions in domestic society).

Finally and most importantly, international law is said to be voluntaristic in its nature. It consists chiefly of treaties entered into by sovereign states, supplemented by customary international law based upon observed regular practice, by the 'soft' law of United Nations Resolutions and Declarations, and by expert legal opinion as an occasional and informal means of legal review. States are self-subsistent legal orders. That is another way of saying they are sovereign. No external body stands in the relation to the state that the state does to its people, so sovereigns cannot be bound to obedience in the way that subjects of domestic law may be. International law, being of an essentially voluntary nature, is therefore seen by many writers as being marginal to any notion of international society.

H.L.A. Hart's Theory of International Law

In examining these apparent differences between domestic and international law, it will be informative to contrast the positions of two prominent modern legal theorists, H.L.A. Hart and Hans Kelsen.

Addressing the first difference, that of the roles of jurisdiction and arbitration, Hart distinguishes in a domestic legal system between 'primary' rules of obligation and 'secondary' rules specifying procedures for adjudication, legal review, etc. The latter rules are lacking in international law, as are 'centrally organised sanctions', the subject of the second difference. This makes international law analogous to the law of 'primitive' societies. Further,

> It is indeed arguable...that international law not only lacks the secondary rules of change and adjudication which provide for legislature and courts, but also a unifying rule of recognition specifying 'sources' of law and providing general criteria for the identification of its rules.[40]

In the absence of rules of recognition, international law constitutes only a 'set' of rules, and not a 'system'. There is no ultimate provision from which the validity of international laws derives; nor is there any a priori validation of general classes of laws. Formal rules of recognition could arise (for example the binding of non-signatory third parties to treaties), but it is not clear that any such rules, which would make the process of creation of international law a 'legislative act', have yet emerged. In the meantime, 'In the simpler form of society we must wait and see whether a rule gets accepted as a rule or not.'[41]

That it lacks secondary rules does not prevent Hart from counting international law as law. He remarks that

> Bentham, the inventor of the expression 'international law', defended it simply by saying that it was 'sufficiently analogous' to municipal law. To this, two comments are perhaps worth adding. First that the analogy is one of content not of form: secondly that, in this analogy of content, no other social rules are so close to municipal law as those of international law.[42]

Hart does not believe that international law is vitiated by the absence of sanctions. Because of the vulnerability and relative equality of persons in domestic society, law requires effective sanctions as deterrents and restraints. It is usually the case that the majority will support effective action against malefactors; therefore, there is little danger that the use of sanctions will lead to generalised conflict and disorder. But in international relations, the 'public use of violence' remains both dangerous and unpredictable. Effective sanctions imply the threat or use of force, up to the level of warfare. International peace is itself often more durable than peace in domestic society, because the dangers of war are enough to deter on most occasions the use of violence. It is enough that international law should serve to safeguard order by encouraging predictability and therefore stability in the conduct of states. Its rules are 'thought and spoken of' as binding, and are generally observed and regarded as valuable, even in the absence of centrally organised sanctions.[43]

It is not in their having precisely equivalent mechanisms that international law and domestic law resemble one another; it is in their respective roles in social regulation that the similarity lies. The purely normative component of obligation exists as much in domestic law as in international law. It is not a matter of indifference to society that someone should break a law provided that a sanction is enforced upon him in consequence. The idea of 'ought' is inextricably connected with the idea of law as a form of social regulation; sanction is not enough to convey the entire meaning of law as a system of social rules. The preservation of reputation, and conformity with the 'climate of moral opinion', however nebulous that at times may be, is of importance to states.

There are weaknesses in the analogy of domestic and international law which beset Hart's attempts to assimilate the two. States are able to opt out of the provisions of international law with relative impunity, as shown by the refusal of the United States to accept judgement by the International Court of Justice on its mining of Nicaraguan harbours. The ability of states to refuse to be bound by such legal rulings or to otherwise exempt themselves from international law is not politically neutral. The recourse to international courts was the most effective, indeed the only effective, pressure a state such as Nicaragua under the government of President Ortega could bring to bear on the United States. From the latter's standpoint, international law is virtually an irrelevance in the panoply of military and economic pressures that can be brought to bear on tiresome and recalcitrant states. The volitional element in international law inevitably makes it at least partly a servant of the status quo.

Whilst we must recognise the normative element of law, it is hard to deny that this very fact seems to require the existence of the sanctions which Hart denies to be necessary. It is the usual attitude of society not only that its members ought to obey the law, but that if they do not, they ought to be punished. Conversely, what retribution there has always existed in international relations has seldom had the sanctification of law.

Hans Kelsen's Theory of International Law

In complete contrast to Hart's theory, Hans Kelsen makes the concept of sanction the essence of his legal theory.[44] A legal order is a normative hierarchy, in which each norm is created by a higher norm, in a regressive series. This 'pure' theory of law seeks to avoid the pitfalls of the Austinian or 'command' theory.

The circularity problem in the latter is that if, following Austin,[45] the command of the sovereign is taken to be the unique origin of law, then the problem arises, by what means other than legal recognition is the nature or exclusiveness of the sovereign power itself determined? The basic norm is the rule whereby the other norms of the legal order are validated. Its validity is the condition of the validity of the entire legal order. The basic norm, a 'legal postulate', specifies the basis of legal authority (in Britain, for example, Parliament).

More generally, it is of the form that the constitution ought to be obeyed. That this basic norm should be independent of any other is the condition of a sovereign; that is to say, a self-sufficient, legal order. These norms are not merely hypothetical; they must have content in fact. The legal order they support must be effective; it must be generally obeyed and enforceable.

The norms of the international legal order are actual and not merely hypothetical because they support an effective legal order. By 'effective', Kelsen means that in practice an international delict is followed by the imposition of a sanction. In domestic law, the state alone enforces sanctions. In international society the imposition of sanctions upon malefactors is decentralised: it may be carried out by the aggrieved states, by the international community acting in support of the victim or by the procedures of collective legal enforcement, such as the UN security system. Sanctions may range in severity from economic boycotts to war. The key point is that whilst sanctions in international law are a matter of self-help rather than the exclusive provenance of a universally acknowledged authority, they are nonetheless sanctions because states have both in principle and in practice, says Kelsen, the right to enforce them. More than the right, indeed, they have the duty, in that all 'police' actions are carried out ultimately on behalf of the international community whose common interest is served by international law. Decentralised sanctions also preserve the principle that all use of force which is not directed towards the imposition of sanctions is itself an international delict, and thereby itself liable to sanction.

International legal norms do more than support an effective legal system; they serve not merely as the analogues of domestic legal norms, but as higher norms in relation to domestic norms. Kelsen rejects pluralistic and dualistic theories of international law. International norms are 'completed' by national legal norms, but international law also regulates areas which would otherwise be controlled by the state. Ultimately, the conduct of states is reducible to the conduct of individuals. In consequence, every article of domestic law (including economic and commercial articles) can in principle become the subject of international treaties:

> In a sense national law is determined by international law. If national law is considered alone, the original authority of a sovereign power in the state is a hypothetical norm; but if considered in the context of international law, the validity of the national order comes from a positive norm within that law: that of effectiveness. ...It is according to this principle that international law empowers the 'Fathers of the Constitution' to function as the first legislators of a State. The historically first constitution is valid because the coercive order erected on its basis is efficacious as a whole. Thus, the international legal order, by means of the principle of effectiveness, determines not only the sphere of validity, but also the reason of validity of the national legal orders. Since the basic norms of the national legal orders are determined by a norm of international law, they are basic norms only in a relative sense. It is the basic norm of the international legal order which is the ultimate reason of validity of the national legal orders, too.[46]

To support his rejection of a dualistic conception of the relationship between domestic and international law, Kelsen cites the fact that positive law within a state may prevent the enactment of a law where this would conflict with the state's international legal obligations. Therefore, the pluralist or dualist theory comes into conflict with the facts of positive law:

> the basic norm of international law is that its precepts be obeyed..., that the principle of efficacy makes this more than a hypothetical norm, and that the sphere of competence of domestic legal orders is determined by the higher norms of international law. This evidently goes beyond the more cautious view of many international lawyers that some principle such as *pacta sunt servanda* is the most that might be considered as a higher norm. In fact...the very idea of the state presupposes that the dependent relationship of domestic to international law is acknowledged. Thus it is by reference to international legal conventions that the continuity of a state

which has undergone a revolutionary or constitutional transformation is recognised.[47]

Finally, whilst Kelsen recognises the absence of international judicial autonomy in matters of jurisdiction or review, other similarities between domestic and international law are stressed:

> Both methods of creating law, the customary and the statutory one, occur in international as well as in national law. General international law, it is true, does not recognise legislation and law making by the judiciary, the two most important aspects of norm-creation in the modern State. But courts and legislative organs can be created by international treaty, which is itself a method of creating statutory law. The decisions of an international court are norms of international law....[48]

Difficulties With Kelsen's Theory

A problem for this theory arises when a domestic court rejects international law where it contradicts a national statute. To distinguish between a national legal order and international law, it is necessary to demarcate separate areas of juridical competence, and it is generally the case that international law takes priority over domestic law only when the state specifically undertakes to abridge the validity of certain domestic laws. This is usually the result of an accession to an instrument creating supranational legal powers, such as the Treaty of Rome, to which states are bound only by a voluntary and revocable sovereign act.

If the holistic conception of international law runs foul of the facts of the self-abridgement of domestic law, its value lies in elucidating the fact that states come into being in a world of international law which they have neither created nor consented to, but to which their adherence will crucially determine the perception other states have of them. The rights of sovereignty, including, for example, ownership of natural resources, access to resources whose ownership is largely non-territorial, such as the sea bed, and so on, are there as given from the point of view of the new state. Though it may seek to reform international law, or extend its sovereign rights, there is not much historical precedent for new states rejecting the rights already assigned to them.

There are problems with Kelsen's account of international sanctions. No international consensus on the rights and wrongs of an alleged delict may exist, nor on the form and desirability of sanctions. What international law has to say on the principles of self-determination and non-intervention may be especially weakened in practice by lack of international consensus. The enforcement of sanctions may also conflict with the requirements of the balance of power, and of narrower *raison d'état* generally, as in the failure of the League of Nations to respond to the Italian conquest of Abyssinia, or of the Allies to respond to the Soviet seizure of the Baltic Republics and part of Finland in 1940–1. The demand for international sanctions where little or no consensus exists has seemed to critics of this conception of international law so much to overstep the limits of international law as a partial principle of international order, complementary to other mechanisms, as to make it a serious threat to that order.

Whilst the use of sanctions in the form of military intervention engenders risks of escalation to the point where the force employed becomes wholly disproportionate to the ends it was intended to achieve, the use of lesser forms of sanction, such as economic boycotts, has been notoriously ineffective, as in the case of UDI Rhodesia or the Soviet Union after its invasion of Afghanistan. It may even be that the discord and resentment generated by recriminations over 'sanctions busting' by some states is itself a consequence of too high expectations of international consensus, and that there is a substitution of moralism for a more pragmatic recognition of the competitive and opportunistic nature of international relations.

Most international law is the law of treaty, often bilateral and usually binding only a few states. Violations of such law may only directly affect the interests of the party states. The likelihood of sanctions being imposed by the international community generally, or by a significant number of its members, when their immediate interests are not at stake, and when the possible costs of international sanctions are so high, is as a rule remote. Whatever the objective interests of the international community in the observance of international law generally, the performance of a disinterested police function is discouraged by immediate and potential costs. Indeed, the positing of the validity of international law upon the possibility of sanction raises acute problems of the 'viability' of many small and newly independent states as members of international society. The chances of these states acting in concert, let alone independently, being able to bring effective sanctions to bear against a major power or superpower violating international law are very slim.

Here, Kelsen's theory of international law appears still more con-
servatively oriented towards the status quo than is implied even in the
recognition that it contains a volitional element of more damaging
effect to the weak than to the strong. The idea of sanction found in
this theory makes the will of the major powers not only the condition
of the implementation of international law, it makes the exercise of
this will a condition of the efficacy and therefore the validity of the
system of international law as a whole. Although it makes the legal
aspect of the sovereignty of states itself subject to a higher norm of
international law, it offers little hope of international law serving as a
vehicle of international justice when the requirements of this conflict
with the political facts of sovereignty.

In a world of sovereign states, the imposition of sanctions can only
be a matter for the judgement of those states acting singly or as a
group. *Raison d'état*, and not an abstract commitment to the integrity
of international law *per se* will motivate states in this regard. Yet from
the standpoint of Kelsen's theory, the question of motivation is not
necessarily of importance. It is enough that a sanction should follow a
delict of international law, no matter that the practical origin of the
sanction should have a more sectarian origin in the threat posed by
the violation to the concrete interests of the states that impose the
sanction. Motive is only important where intervention against a state
which has committed no delict occurs, for then that use of force itself
constitutes a delict and becomes the legitimate grounds for the use of
force by the international community to rectify it. Whilst it may be
that the consistency with which the sanction is applied to violators of
international law is diminished by the decentralised and largely self-
interested way in which it is imposed, this does not vitiate the efficacy
of the international legal system as compared with domestic law since
it is not the case in the latter either that all delicts are in practice
followed by a sanction. Criminals sometimes get away.

This seems, however, to miss the point. In domestic law, the principle of a mandatory sanction in the event of a delict is contained
within the legal system. The form sanction takes and the nature of the
authority that will impose it are also specified. It is in this prescriptive
aspect of domestic law, and not in the practical effectiveness of the
enforcing agencies in detecting violations of law and imposing
sanctions, that domestic law differs from international law. There is
no equivalent principle in the latter. The system of self-help, the
mixed-motive nature of imposition of sanctions, and the incapacity
of many states to use the mechanisms of enforcement available to

more powerful states preclude even those minimum concepts of formal equality and impartiality of consideration which are incorporated in our ideas of domestic law. At this point the analogy of the two sorts of law breaks down.

Much too little has been written about the Hart–Kelsen debate. Whilst of inestimable value in itself, it nonetheless seems, at least to the present author, as the last gasp of the twentieth-century neopositivist, international legal debates. Its fundamental rejection of the natural law tradition represents a severe limitation to its scope of argument.

Sovereignty and the 'Volitional' Nature of International Law

We now come to the third apparent dissimilarity between domestic and international law. The former is binding irrespective of the consent of those subject to it. This remains true as a legal fact whatever grounds are argued for the political legitimacy of the state. From the point of view of those who reject international law as law in any sense analogous to domestic law, the sovereignty of the state is absolute in that neither the law which proceeds from it nor its own nature as the source of law is derivative of any authority above the state. The state is a self-subsistent legal order. Law comes only from sovereign power, of which there is none above the state. The state, as absolutely sovereign, can never be bound by international law except in so far as it voluntarily binds itself to a treaty or convention. This decision is always revocable. Kelsen's conception of international law as embodying a 'higher norm' is, on this view, rejected. There is no self-subsistent international legal order, only the aggregate of the volitional acts of sovereign states. The absence of sanctions in international law merely testifies to this fact.

This 'command theory of law' is associated in its modern (late nineteenth-century) form with John Austin, but it is in Jean Bodin's *Six Books of the Commonwealth* that the absolute theory of sovereignty is first developed.[49] In Bodin's theory, as John Plamenatz notes,

> Sovereignty is defined as the 'absolute and perpetual power in a republic'. It is 'perpetual' because, whoever has it, though he acts through agents, does not lose it; it is perpetual in the sense of inalienable. It is absolute because whoever has it 'holds it, after God, only by the sword'; it is absolute in the sense of unconditional.

The sovereign makes the law, which is his mere command, and himself is not subject to the law which he makes. Law is defined as 'the command of the sovereign touching all his subjects'....[50]

It is in Hegel that we find the most uncompromising rejection of the idea that a sovereign power can be bound by the precepts of international law against its will:

> International law springs from the relations between autonomous states. It is for this reason that what is absolute in it retains the form of an ought-to-be, since its actuality depends on different wills each of which is sovereign. The fundamental proposition of international law ... is that treaties, as the grounds of obligation between states, ought to be kept. But since the sovereignty of the state is the principle of its relations to others, states are to that extent in a state of nature in relation to each other. Their rights are actualised only in their particular wills and not in a universal will with constitutional powers over them.... It follows that if states disagree and their particular wills cannot be harmonised, the matter can only be settled by war.[51]

The view that there is an inescapable contradiction between international law understood as a non-contingently binding order and the fact of sovereignty has been attacked, notably by Oppenheim in his 'International Law'. His view also deserves quotation at some length:

> The very notion of International Law as a body of rules of conduct binding upon States irrespective of their Municipal Law and legislation implies the idea of their subjection to International Law and makes it impossible to accept their claim to absolute sovereignty in the international sphere. Their mutual independence is indeed a fundamental rule of International Law; but it is only by reference to a higher legal order that the mutual independence of States, viewed as a rule of law, is conceivable. On the other hand, owing to the weakness of International Law, its supremacy over the States composing the international community is limited to the duty which it imposes upon them to observe and, within a restricted sphere, to submit to the enforcement of the existing rules created by custom or treaty or flowing from the very existence of the society of States. It does not as yet include a competence on the part of the international community to impose fresh obligations upon an unwilling State, or to interfere with its rights in cases in which changed

conditions require the adaptation of International Law to the requirements of international peace and progress. Neither does it yet include the duty to submit international disputes to judicial determination.[52]

Despite these practical limitations, the binding nature of international law as a system is stressed:

> New States which came into existence and were through express or tacit recognition admitted to the Family of Nations thereby consented to the body of rules for international conduct in force at the time of their admittance. It is therefore not necessary to prove for every single rule of International Law that every single member of the Family of Nations consented to it.... The admittance included the duty to submit to all the rules in force, with the sole exception of those which, as, for instance, the rules of the Geneva Convention, are specially stipulated for such States only as have concluded, or later on acceded to, a certain international treaty creating the rules concerned.[53]

Self-interest is the 'unifying factor' which ensures states' ultimate respect for international law. Though 'economic nationalism, political intolerance and the pursuit of self-sufficiency' create barriers among nations and may serve temporarily to weaken the effectiveness of international law, this 'retrogression' is a temporary phenomenon, and does not challenge the continued existence of the international community.

The very concept of sovereignty which has given rise to its purported contradiction with international law, and to the 'auto-limitation' theory of the latter, that is, the view that its validity can both logically and in fact come only from the voluntary accession of states to its precepts, has also been challenged. As Benn and Peters note,

> The problem arises... only because 'sovereignty' is ambiguous. It comes from treating the word as if it means the same thing both in the context of municipal and of international law. In the first context, it means that the state system is self-subsistent, i.e., that the basic norm or criterion of validity applied by its courts is within the system, not outside it. But in the second context, it means that a state is self-governing in respect of other states (as distinct, for example, from a colony subject to the municipal law of a parent state); but this does not mean that it is not a partial order in relation to international law.[54]

There is a clear sense in which international law is as much a self-subsistent legal order as is domestic law: the enforcement of a statute in violation of a principle of international law constitutes a delict within the terms of that system, and it is not a priori certain that domestic law assumes priority over international. To argue that the sovereignty of states 'means' that they cannot be bound by international law is more to reassert the supremacy of the state than to argue why this assertion should be accepted, either legally or philosophically. As Hart notes,

> For the word 'sovereign' means here no more than 'independent'; and, like the latter, is negative in force: a sovereign state is one not subject to certain forms of control, and its sovereignty is that area of its conduct in which it is autonomous. Some measure of autonomy is imported, as we have seen, by the very meaning of the word state but the contention that this 'must' be unlimited or 'can' only be limited by certain types of obligation is at best the assertion of a claim that states ought to be free of all other restraints, and at worst is an unreasoned dogma. For if in fact we find that there exists among states a given form of international authority, the sovereignty of states is to that extent limited, and it has just that extent which the rules allow.[55]

The Dual Meaning of Sovereignty

The importance of the seeming contradiction explored here has justified presenting the arguments in some detail. There are good reasons beyond this conflation of the two meanings of sovereignty to suspect that the contradiction is more apparent than real. For one thing, sovereignty is itself a matter of degree.[56] Principalities such as Monaco or Andorra have only a quasi-sovereign status, but are not thereby entirely denied international personality. Former colonial dominions, notably those of Britain, were recognised in international organisations, including the League of Nations, before they attained sovereign independence.

The idea of promise undermines the assertion of sovereignty as absolute. It is on the willingness of a state to acknowledge the principle of *pacta sunt servanda* as a mutually binding principle that its accession to treaties is accepted as significant and becomes the basis for legitimate future expectations. States decide their agreement to particular articles of international law, not to the terms of reference within which that agreement has significance. Treaty as law is expected to be respected. This includes treaties imposed on defeated powers, that is, under conditions of duress. The justice of such treaties was defended by Grotius and his successors both on the grounds that its denial would make conflict practically interminable, and because a defeated power still remained a member of international society and therefore subject to the obligations of international law.

Most important is the concept of the sovereign state as only a partial legal order with reference to international law. This has a very practical dimension. We noted that new states come into existence bound by principles of customary international law, and by a whole system of law conferring rights and duties on states qua sovereign entities. The law gives rights to states, such as to pursue their objectives through a recognised legal process. Even those states long considered as international pariahs have argued vigorously for the rights that international law confers on them.

States do not only acquire prescribed rights and duties on coming into existence: the acquisition of new territory entails the legal responsibilities attaching to the ownership of such territory, which might include, for example, the acceptance of the jurisdiction of the international law of the sea. What is important to note is that sovereign consent to particular articles of international law is not equivalent to consent to the system as a whole. This latter consent is neither asked for nor required. It is implied by statehood. However seriously some states violate international law, it is rare for any state to effectively renounce all its responsibilities.

So international law does not depend for its significance upon sovereign acts only. The form and the content of sovereignty are themselves partly determined by international law. The limited efficiency of the implementation of that law creates in practice a wide sphere of sovereign action, and this at times obscures the derivative aspects of sovereignty with respect to the international context as much as to the state's relation with the individuals who compose it.

Hart's approach goes a long way to explaining why the above should be the case, though in the end he fails to address the fact that the idea of sanction is inextricably bound up with the idea of law. Kelsen offers an inadequate account of sanction, however, and offers a conception of international law whose practical consequences do not evidently go far beyond the facts of power politics. Neither approach bridges the gap between domestic and international law which lies above all in the decentralised nature of the latter and the contingency of its sanction, but they do demonstrate the important areas of analogy between the two types of law.

If the reef of sovereignty is sailed over, there is no reason to deny international law the status of law. We can now assess whether it serves as a constituency of international justice.

4.4 INTERNATIONAL LAW AND INTERNATIONAL JUSTICE

Domestic law is more than a mechanism of social regulation. In modern society it comes to embody principles of social justice, however imperfectly. In developed societies, both socialist and market-capitalist, law provides for progressive taxation, social insurance and welfare provision, and for a range of other continuous state interventions in society. It is therefore important to ask whether international law is capable of providing a constituency of international justice to complement, or even to displace, the function of the state in effecting conditions of justice. At both a philosophical and a practical level we have challenged the claims of the state to represent an exclusive or unique justice-constituency, and have allowed international, individual and, to a lesser degree, global justice-claims against the state. The question is whether international society provides, through the medium of international law, for the satisfaction of these claims and rights. If it has no means of so doing, the idea of justice beyond the state will be at best a very restricted one.

The Competence of International Law in Political Disputes

This view has been attacked by Sir Hersch Lauterpacht in the name of a reasserted modern tradition of natural law as a counter to legal positivism.[57] International law has conventionally determined its competence, as between justiciable and non-justiciable disputes, to use Lauterpacht's terms, according to a distinction between legal and political questions. Justiciable disputes, the province of international law, can be settled by existing, ascertainable rules of international law. They concern existing legal rights, as opposed to any purported rights to have the law changed, and are of 'secondary importance' in the sense that they do not affect the 'vital interests' of states such as territorial integrity, sovereignty, and honour.[58]

International law is not, on this view, something separate from or above international politics. For this reason its competence is restricted by the sphere of the political. Whereas justiciability within the state is merely a question of the competence and jurisdiction of the courts, in international law states circumscribe the responsibilities into which they enter by the concept of justiciability as described above. Lauterpacht sees the distinction between political and legal as the definition of international legal competence as bogus. More precisely, the theory of the absolute sovereignty of states which began with Vattel is now said to be obsolete. Once it served to express first

> the right of the State to determine what shall be for the future the content of international law by which it will be bound; [second] the right to determine what is the content of existing international law in a given case.[59]

The concept of non-justiciability as a limiting factor was further used to lend weight to international law by preserving its status as law, despite the differences with domestic law. Its nature and import are made 'objective' by this restriction, and by its equation with matters of independence and vital interests.

Lauterpacht argues that this is no longer valid, and argues further for the complete competence of courts to decide on disputes. His discussion focuses on the history of arbitration courts and tribunals, and particularly the Hague Convention for Pacific Settlement and the Covenant of the League of Nations, which are seen to testify to this competence. More recent examples of the competence of legal agencies in matters once viewed as exclusively political are Chapter 6 of the UN Charter concerning the Pacific Settlement of Disputes, the reference of legal disputes understood in a broader sense than given above to the International Court of Justice, or the power of the Security Council to intervene where international security is threatened under the Articles of Chapter 7 of the Charter. There no longer appears to be an objective distinction between justiciable and non-justiciable disputes. The distinction serves only as an obstacle to progress in international relations, and to undermine the purpose served by international arbitration:

> As the conception of justiciable and non-justiciable disputes is wide enough to include any of the restrictive clauses, even those of a most sweeping character, there is a danger of the progress achieved being in many instances altogether illusory. Even where it is not so, the confusion and doubts which it is bound to create tend to defeat to a large extent the essential object of

arbitration treaties, whose practical reason of existence lies not so much in the frequency of their application as in their effect in fostering a sense of security and recognition of the ultimate arbitrament of law. The doctrine of sovereignty even becomes the negation of the idea of law.[60]

International Consensus and the Settlement of Disputes

It may be that what is distinct about international law is lost if the areas of consensus among states are exaggerated. As the sheer scope of international law grows, as the range of international conventions and agreements on subjects ranging from trade to respect for human rights expands, and as these elements of international law come to represent new moral norms of international conduct, thus far international consensus is extended. We have distinguished between sovereign consent to particular articles of international law and consent to the legal system as a whole. The former should not, however, be understated. With respect to current disputes, it is clear that not all are to be considered as justiciable irrespective of the consent of the protagonists. The impasse reached by both the Security Council and the General Assembly over the mutual non-recognition of Israel and her neighbours (excepting Egypt), and over the international status of the Palestine Liberation Organisation, are examples of this. The doctrine of automatic justiciability might itself become a source of international conflict if pushed beyond the limits of international consensus.

The 'Common Law of Mankind'

Such a view of the extended competence of international law is a necessary condition of its serving as a vehicle of international justice, in that violations of justice become in principle subject to an authority which does not derive entirely from voluntary concession or self-abridgement of sovereignty. But it is not sufficient to show that the content of international law serves to cover more than merely the relations of sovereign states, and thereby functions as a law of an emerging world community and as a defence of individual justice and rights. This scope is, however, attributed to international law by C. Wilfred Jenks.[61] It now derives from more than a single, European legal system. Jenks sees the beginnings of a common law of the world community, in which the regulation of inter-state relations is only one component:

> By the common law of mankind is meant the law of an organized world community, constituted on the basis of states but discharging its community functions increasingly through a complex of international and regional institutions, guaranteeing rights to, and placing obligations upon, the individual citizen, and confronted with a wide range of economic, social, and technological problems calling for uniform regulation on an international basis which represents a growing proportion of the subject matter of the law. The imperfect development and precarious state of the organized world community is reflected in the early stage of development of the law, but does not invalidate the basic conception.[62]

The role of the UN and its specialised agencies in the creation of a common law of mankind is stressed, although natural law analogies are not pushed so far as to disguise the fact that states remain the primary constituents of the international legal order.[63]

Jenks argues that the confrontation of the equality of states doctrine with the facts of international interdependence and common interest both requires and impels this transformation of international law:

> The concept of sovereignty, though frequently reasserted, especially by new and newly influential members of the international community, has already clearly evolved from one of freedom from external control to one of full status in, but subject to, the law, and this new conception has received an increasing measure of recognition in the judgments and opinions of the International Court. The concept of the equality of States, while still variously interpreted and widely entertained in its most extreme and comprehensive form, continues to evolve towards one of equal protection of the law rather than of an equality of rights and functions which would make impossible any progress in international organisation.[64]

International law increasingly embodies human rights. This fact is a consequence partly of the development of nineteenth century laws concerning the prohibition of slavery, the practice of plebiscites and mandates and the protection of minorities, but must also be viewed as a reaction to the experience of totalitarianism in the mid-twentieth century. The provisions of the Universal Declaration of Human Rights, including the responsibility for aliens undertaken by signatory states, affect the working of internal legal systems, at least in principle.

There remains, though, the main obstacle to the emergence of a common law of mankind. States are responsible for the implementation of those rights that international law ascribes to individuals, and unless these rights are recognised in the domestic legal systems of those states their legal implementation is impossible. Whilst Jenks recognises that such rights

> are by their very nature of a different legal character and are not susceptible of enforcement by legal proceeding at the instance of an interested party until implemented by specific legislation.

This is in practice no great problem,

> because in the case of many of these rights... including the right to just and favourable conditions of work, the right to rest and leisure, the right to equal pay for equal work, the right to protection against unemployment, the right to social security, and the right to form and join trade unions, the necessary specific legislation already exists, internationally and nationally, in the form of the relevant labour conventions, some of which have been widely ratified, and the national legislation implementing these conventions.... The common law of mankind towards which the international legal system has already evolved so far is increasingly a law with a developed social content.[65]

Nevertheless, there remain problems in the development of an international law of human rights. For one thing, the Universal Declaration of Human Rights of December 1948 was passed by the General Assembly only with the abstention of the Soviet bloc. Ideology still creates a gulf between the legal enactment of rights and the political question of their enforcement. But Jenks remains optimistic about the development of a universal legal order from the common elements of the various legal systems. Whilst observance of rights internationally depends on the conditions of political freedom within nations, conversely the international guarantee of rights and civil liberties reinforces the observance of rights within the state.

The Limits of International Law as a Vehicle of International Justice

Each of these claims about the evolving nature of international law contains some truth, but they require qualification. The growth of the international community, the concomitant expansion of international law to a global sphere of operation, and the 'export' of European doctrines of the state and sovereignty have led to a greater formal and legal equality of the world's people. But this equality has not been parallelled by equality of condition; and there remain disaffected and persecuted minorities denied self-determination, and thereby effect-ively excluded from international society.

We have argued that from an ethical and philosophical point of view individuals must be considered as the ultimate members of international society, but we are at a very early stage of the global implementation of human rights and the securing of minimum welfare which alone will make this essential truth a reality. In addition, the formal inequality of states has not, as we have noted, brought equality in representation and decision making in international economic or security organisations.

The range of human rights conventions now existent has not, despite the admixture of 'genuine' ideological dissent and cold war politicking which has beset much of their implementation, presented the threat to international order which the limited consensus on such topics was thought by sceptics to make inevitable. But aside from the welcome salience and encouragement of positive expectations which the International Conventions and the Helsinki accords gave to human rights, problems of their implementation in domestic legal orders remain. Whilst the incorporation of the provisions of the European Convention on Human Rights into the national law of certain EU states is welcome, the agreement of other states to inter-national rights conventions continues to be practically worthless.

Julius Stone has explored the conflict between the conception of international law as one encompassing states only and as a fledgling common law of mankind in which individuals are the ultimate bearers of rights and duties, even though their states may be the immediate subjects of international law.[66] He is less sanguine than Jenks in foreseeing how this conflict may be reconciled. He is concerned with the problems of removing those 'gross defaults' that are no longer tolerated domestically from international relations. He rejects the analogy of states' rights and human rights:

> whatever human claims are assumed to lie behind such 'fundamental', 'basic', or 'natural' rights of a state under interna-tional law, these cannot, even if we regard them as demands justi-fied by higher law, necessarily be co-ordinated with existing legal rights.[67]

Stone's emphasis is upon

> [those] obstacles... presented by the compartmentalized system of territorial states to the framing of a conception of justice on a humanity-wide basis. For the aggregate of state entities cannot as such constitute a meaningful justice-constituency, and their existence also blocks that access to the demands of men and women of all nations which is pre-required for bringing them into a single justice-constituency.[68]

The problems of an emerging justice-constituency extend beyond the conflict between sovereignty and humanity-wide justice. There is a clear sense in which knowledge of one's own society, particularly the deeper cultural and ideological beliefs which structure that knowledge, influences perceptions of justice and injustice. At its simplest, whether an individual's economic, social and political relationship to others or to the state's authority appears just or unjust will depend upon beliefs about the inevitability or necessity of hierarchy and deference, upon the perception of the individual as a solitary being or as part of a class, upon the prevalence of social taboos concerning class and status, and so on. The perspectives of established 'domestic' societies are bound to seem more real and immediate to their members than those of a world society of a more abstract nature, and at a relatively earlier stage of development.

Further Difficulties for the Implementation of Principles of International Justice Through International Law

One critic of the idea of international society has argued that the European ideas of nationhood and self-determination that were adopted by the former colonies rather than demands for a 'simple restoration of the traditional status quo ante' have had a radically destabilising effect on the international system as these 'various societies have been brought, however precariously and artificially, into the orthodox system of diplomacy and statehood'.[69] Others excoriate the 'nationalism and bigotry' of the new states, and contend that the extension of the topics of international law to include a whole spectrum of economic and other human rights has overstretched the concept of legality. An increase in the quantity of international law does not, on such a view, imply more sophistication in the perennial problems of the management of conflict in international relations, or any alteration of the fact that international legal agreement is purchased by political bargain. The structural problems of international relations remain, the only difference now being that there are now more states with more divergent interests and greater disposition to dissent from the customs and conventions of international law.

The claim that the introduction of questions of human rights overstretches the competence of international law can be understood in a number of ways. If it is taken as the positivist claim that only states are members of international society, and thereby subjects of the law of that society, we have already rejected this. There is no reason to accept the implication that there is a sphere of 'private conduct' (that is, the internal affairs of the state) in which the state 'ought' to be free from external scrutiny once the crude analogy of states and persons is rejected. If the sovereignty of states has been compromised by human rights agreements, it is a fragile and immature sovereignty that needs to be guarded from its own indiscretions. Governments have chosen to sign those conventions. If the claim means merely that the implementation of such conventions has been less than adequate, that must be conceded.

Whilst the point that international law is subject continuously to the deeper currents of international politics is a sharp counter to more utopian hopes for a 'law of the community of mankind', the view that the admission of the new, subversive states to international society has undermined respect for international law seems premature.[70] For example, Iran appealed to the United Nations to recognise its plea that Iraq was the initial aggressor in the Gulf War, and that Iran's conduct was legal under the right of self-defence guaranteed by the UN Charter. Whilst it is the case that Iran, Syria and Libya have each sponsored terrorist actions against the citizens and diplomatic representatives of other states, it is surely excessive to claim that the post-imperial Arab world in general has failed to abide by the principles of international law.

More specifically, the status in international law of principles of self-determination, non-intervention and economic justice, central to our concerns in this study, has been challenged by many authorities. In the case of self-determination, Article 1 of the 1949 Draft Declaration on the Rights and Duties of States declares that 'Every State has the right to independence and hence the right to exercise freely, without dictation from any other State, all its legal powers, including the choice of its own form of government', whilst General Assembly Resolution 2131 of December 1965 maintains that 'No State has the right to intervene, directly or indirectly, for any reason whatever, in the internal or external affairs of any other State.'

Leo Gross has argued that self-determination is merely a principle of the UN Charter, and not a right.[71] Questions of legal right are resolved by investigating the practice of the United Nations' member states, not its organs such as the General Assembly. There is, claims Gross, no evidence that this right has been conceded in the general practice of states, nor that self-determination is a principle of customary international law. Whilst

> self-determination has been granted or conceded to an impressively large number of peoples or nations... it would not be possible to supply the missing element, namely that practice was based on a sense of legal obligation. On the contrary, the practice of decolonisation is a perfect illustration of a usage dictated by political expediency or necessity or sheer convenience.[72]

Thus such devices as UN Resolutions are not seen to represent a shift from individualistic to collectivistic origins of customary international law; nor do they represent an alternative means of expression of the collective will of the nations through international fora and organisations rather than through the traditional processes. It is maintained that UN Resolutions and the like are not legally binding on states, and may only become effective as customary international law where the regular compliance of states which have not formally consented to them becomes the established norm.

There is some force in this argument. Whatever normative arguments can be made for the right of self-determination, these have come from former metropolitan powers in the form of ex post facto rationalisations. One might argue against the above view that, whilst decolonisation was certainly not carried out in response to acknowledged legal obligations, nonetheless the de facto granting of political independence established a legitimate expectation that nations' aspirations to independent statehood would be met, and that in this way self-determination has become a right guaranteed by customary international law. Be that as it may, it is clear that if the recent practice of many post-colonial states which now find themselves facing secessionist struggles is considered, the undoubted success enjoyed by self-determination in the three decades after 1945 as a political, if not as a legal, principle has now largely come to an end.

The standing of the principle of non-intervention in international law has also been questioned. The principle ultimately derives from the rights of international recognition that sovereignty entails: indeed, the fact of recognition might even be taken as a definition of what sovereignty is.[73] *Pro tanto* non-recognition might be considered a form of intervention. And yet, as Rosalyn Higgins points out,[74] this is quite a regular occurrence in international relations, and may be undertaken by states individually or collectively, as in the case of South African Bantustans or Rhodesia after UDI. The same may be said of trade boycotts. Under the terms of the UN Charter, or the European Conventions on human rights, states acquire the legal right to challenge the internal rights policies of others even where their own nationals are not involved, although this remains a most politically sensitive area of 'interference'. Nor has the non-intervention Article of the UN Charter prevented a plethora of Resolutions directed against the internal policies of states. This raises the question whether anything short of direct military action is to be considered as intervention.

Intervention continues to be a political reality, whatever international law or the United Nations says about it. Political influence and clientelism encourage intervention in all its varieties. In times of rebellion and civil war, the principle of non-intervention conflicts with that of self-determination as rebels demand the latter and governments demand outside help as a sovereign right. Since there are usually more benefits for external powers in supporting existing governments, self-determination usually takes the lower priority. Given these political facts,

> the task of the international lawyer over the next few years is surely not to go on repeating the rhetoric of dead events which no longer accord with reality, but to try to assist the political leaders to identify what is the new consensus about acceptable and unacceptable levels of intrusion.[75]

Intervention on humanitarian grounds, even when the possibility of major violations of rights are very real, has evoked mixed responses, as in the hostile response of the General Assembly to the interventions by the United States in Iran and by Israel in the Entebbe Airport hijacking. States which intervene at such times often use different pretexts to justify their action.[76] Thus, India at first justified intervention in Bangladesh in 1971 on humanitarian grounds, and then played this down in favour of the claim that Pakistan had attacked India first. Similarly, Vietnam claimed in 1979 that the Cambodian people not it had overthrown the Khmer Rouge regime in Cambodia. The UN Security Council debate polarised around this question, with no support coming from either side for the principle of humanitarian intervention.

The future of international economic law as a vehicle for international distributive justice has also come into question. It has been denied[77] that customary international economic law, or multilateral economic arrangements falling short of economic law, amounts to an economic world order, although such order, showing a high degree of legally (and effectively) binding rules, is more likely to be found in sectional or regional organisations such as the EEC, COMECON, or the specialised agencies of the UN (though these latter are partial legal orders). International economic law is conditioned by the political order as much as is other international law. Moreover, international economic law does not amount to *jus cogens*, that is, 'law binding irrespective of the will of the parties'.[78] For example, economic sanctions are seen as symbolic and ineffective, as when France, Germany and Japan took the opportunity of UN sanctions against Rhodesia to increase trade with that 'illegal' state; or flukes, as when UN sanctions were applied to North Korea and China during the Korean War at a time when the Soviet Union was absent from the Security Council.

Schwarzenberger is most sceptical about economic human rights, and about the changes in their specification from the Universal Declaration of Human Rights to the 1966 International Covenant on Economic, Social and Cultural Rights. Whilst many provisions are retained, gone are the

> rights to a free choice of employment, to protection against unemployment and to protection against arbitrary deprivation of property. Besides this, developing countries, although enjoined to pay 'due regard to human rights and their national economy' – the one is likely to cancel out the other – are expressly authorised to discriminate against non-nationals.[79]

The Covenant assumes that all signatory states are, or are becoming, democratic. In consequence, the objects of the Articles are often incompatible with the type of states that actually exist:

> These objectives presuppose a minimum of homogeneity which is absent in the United Nations. Thus one of two results is almost predestined: degradation of such community ideals to ideologies or their reduction to irrelevant utopias. What is impossible in so heterogeneous an environment is to transform such economic human rights into rules of a living international economic order.[80]

Here, then, are three main forms of scepticism about the rights of international distributive justice: that they are without specific meaning; that the policies of most developing states rule out their implementation (and that this, by extension, legitimates developed countries contributing little or nothing to assist the securing of those rights); and that these rights are securable only in political democracies. We shall turn to these questions in the next chapter. But it does appear that the international economic order is far from having the nature of *jus cogens*, despite the hopes of writers such as Jenks, or the aspirations of advocates of 'solidarity' rights to growth and development.

The Value of International Law in Furthering International Justice

Despite the ambiguities of international law in these areas of international and individual justice, it would be excessive to conclude that international conventions have had little effect on the climate of international expectations of just conduct by states.[81] The Universal Declaration of Human Rights, the UN Charter, the Geneva Conventions, the International Covenants, various conventions on the treatment of refugees, the Charter of Economic Rights and Duties of States, the Helsinki Accords: all create interrelated norms which are not rendered valueless by being of a declarative nature and dependent for their actualisation upon the domestic legal systems of states. Governments refusing formal consent to such conventions are at least confronted with the need to justify their position in political terms, whatever their assertions of inviolable sovereignty.

The norms of international society are part of the political climate within which states compete for influence – and for security. As Max Weber noted, national power and national security are inseparably connected with prestige and reputation.[82] In an era in which the costs of war have become practically limitless, observation of basic human rights and norms of just domestic and international conduct (however imprecise) may secure for a state some of the *gloire* formerly associated with the use of violence.

International competition by the aggressive assertion of the superiority of one social system over another has been a feature of the ersatz violence of the Cold War. Realist writers point to this when asserting that agreements on the specifics of international justice, and above all on the nature of human rights, are counterproductive. Such agreements are said to promote ideological conflict and the threat of disorder rather than moral consensus. Yet more than this can be said for attempts through international law (albeit 'soft' law) to promote international justice than this negative assessment of their value. For one thing, states' adherence to conventions, as much as the conformity of their conduct with their declarations, influences the perception other states have of them. Rights-violating practices within states may be of considerable concern to the governments of other states, and influence expectations of external aggression.[83] Those who are held especially fast by the realist straitjacket, and who are bent on following the narrowest interpretation of *raison d'état*, may become quite desensitised to such indications.

5 Human Rights, the State and Global Justice

We favoured a conception of the state and international justice which appears as a viable response to the realist and cosmopolitan traditions. We have termed this a 'complex instrumentalist' conception. We still need to show why it is that the amendments proposed in a complex instrumentalist theory of the state to the basic premises of the natural law tradition are necessary in securing a more comprehensive range of types of international justice-claims than could be specified within the terms of classical natural law theory alone.

Questions of both the justice-claims and correlative responsibilities of political communities in respect of self-determination and the practice of intervention have already been raised. We have certainly not finished with them yet. I only wish that space allowed us to treat these issues more fully and separately at this stage. But it sadly does not. Anyway, to add anything of real significance to the existing literature would probably require another book.[1] Instead, our focus is on rights – individual and collective – as grounds for at least sketching an outline of principles of world justice.

5.1 HUMAN RIGHTS

We can best see what can be said positively about human rights and about the role of the state in upholding them if we first consider some of the more important arguments against introducing human rights discourse into international relations.

The first of these arguments proceeds from the denial that rights have any meaning except in relation to specific governmental and legal systems. Thus Jeremy Bentham ridicules the idea of natural or 'imprescriptible' rights; that is, rights that are said to be 'anterior to the establishment of governments' and that 'cannot be abrogated by government'.[2] Laws alone confer rights; the obscurantist belief in natural rights, says Bentham, encourages 'a spirit of resistance to all laws'.

If Bentham were arguing that individuals only have rights when they form themselves into a state, because (following Rousseau) they only become moral beings at this point, then the state becomes in effect the source of rights, and as such ethically prior to the individual. The question of where the capacity for holding rights derives from is, for Bentham, a meaningless one. Any attempt to answer the question, 'Why do we have the rights that we do?' is bound to end up in metaphysical or naturalistic 'nonsense upon stilts'.

The natural law which is said to exist in the state of nature gives 'to each man a right to everything, which is, in effect, another way of saying, nature has given no such right to anybody: for in regard to most rights . . . what is every man's right is no man's right'.[3] This is only a 'nominal universality and real nonentity of right, set up provisionally by nature in default of laws'. Worst of all, on this view, the supposed indefeasibility of such rights implies more than that positive law is not required for their validity. Law is itself 'proscribed' from all interference with such rights.

Bentham insists that the rights that natural law is supposed to prescribe are contradictory. Laws take away liberty; but, at the same time, 'all rights are made at the expense of liberty'.[4] All rights have corresponding obligations attached to them. And, whilst laws limit liberty, the enjoyment of liberty in the sense of protection from coercion by other persons as opposed to the state requires laws: 'no liberty can be given to one man but in proportion as it is taken from another.'[5] Again, the right of property is said to be imprescriptible; but the right to property implies the further restriction of liberty, for it involves the prevention of others from making use of that property. This right is valueless unless its object is specified, and this is not possible within the unlimited sphere of natural rights. Bentham's objection is not simply that the actual rights guaranteed by government and law are the only ones with more than a fictive meaning; the assertion of natural rights as constraints on laws seems to him to subvert all positive rights.

This position may be compared with that of T.H. Green, who allows the idea of rights against the state, but not of rights against society:

> The sovereign, and the state itself as distinguished by the existence of a sovereign power, presupposes rights and is an institution for their maintenance. But these rights do not belong to individuals as they might be in a state of nature, or as they might be if each acted irrespectively of the others. They belong to them as members of a society in which each recognises the other as an originator of action in the same sense in which he is conscious of being so himself.[6]

Green says that the idea that rights proceed only from the sovereign power 'conflicts with the primary demands of human consciousness'. People may have rights as members of social groups, such as families, without the state existing. In the modern state, however, Green typically wants it both ways:

> it may still be true to say that the members of a state derive their rights from the state and have no rights against it. We have already seen that a right against society, as such, is an impossibility; that every right is derived from some social relation; that a right against any group of associated men depends on association.... Now for the member of a state to say that his rights are derived from his social relations, and to say that they are derived from his position as member of a state, are the same thing. *The state is for him the complex of those social relations out of which rights arise....* [My italics][7]

In the end, this position is much like Bentham's, although it is derived from different premises. Green's position might seem less hostile to the idea of rights outside the state, because he locates rights within social relations, and we have argued for the existence of an international society. But he really means that society reaches its highest form in the state.

Positive Rights and Natural Rights

The rights that are secured exclusively by the state are not, then, the only ones we need to consider. If we confine our attention to these rights alone, there will be nothing to say about the justification of the state outside its own self-defining terms, and nothing whatever to say about its external rights and obligations. If the state is in effect the means by which rights are brought into the world, then each state is unique in this respect vis-à-vis its own population, and we have no comparative criteria by which to judge one state to be better or worse than another in terms of the defence of justice and rights.

The natural law tradition makes individuals the ultimate bearers of all rights and duties. Because the state in practice guarantees many of the (inherent) rights of its people, it is assigned a potent, though never an absolute, moral status. This respect for the state as an institution which makes rights effective leads Grotius to deny that citizens have, at least in most circumstances, a right to rebel against unjust rulers, although outsiders may intervene on their behalf. In the end, states are bound by natural law in the same way as individuals are, and have rights and duties under natural law only because they are made up of persons, the only self-subsistent moral ends that exist.

A defence of the natural law epistemology of rights thus serves as a response to the deficiencies of the views we have just examined. We saw also that the natural law tradition has postulated a much richer and deeper set of obligations among states than the narrow, egoistic sort of natural right against which Bentham turned his scorn and derision.

But if natural rights are superior to legal-positive rights in defining the state as a constituency of justice and in accounting for its external obligations, they are not in themselves sufficient. In the form in which the classical natural law tradition developed them, they do not define the content of rights held by individuals against their states; nor do they offer other principles concerning the legitimacy of political authority. Whilst natural law tradition before Vattel made much of the obligations among states, it did little to place individuals' needs and welfare at the basis of those obligations. We are given no means of passing from the theoretical identification of the individual as the bearer of rights to the practical consequences of the existence of inherent, universal rights as the basis of rights and obligations existing not just between states, but between members of different societies.

If none of the arguments we have examined has succeeded in refuting the idea of inherent rights, or prevented us from seeking their philosophical justification, we still need to make a positive defence of the origin of extra-legal rights. To do so requires more than the natural law tradition as we have reviewed it can offer. We need an answer to the question, Why do we have the rights that we do? We need to show epistemologically significant characteristics of human beings in virtue of which we can assign authentically moral – in the sense of universalisable – rights to them.

Rights and Agency

A highly promising construction of a first-order theory of rights and why we possess them has been put forward by Alan Gewirth.[8]

Gewirth criticises both classical and modern versions of natural rights as being purely intuitionistic, and as not constituting an argument for rights, whilst the derivation of rights from interests undermines (since 'interests' vary greatly from one person to another) the minimum egalitarian content of rights which enables them to be

ascribed to all persons equally. In addition, attempts to ground rights
in the inherent capacities of human beings, or to define rights as
equivalent to justified claims for the fulfilment of crucial needs, raise
the familiar problem of the derivation of an 'ought' from an 'is'.
Instead we are offered a theory of human rights based upon the
capacity of human beings for rational action:

> the concept of a right, as a justified claim or entitlement, is logically
> involved in all action as a concept that signifies for every agent his
> claim and requirement that he have, and at least not be prevented
> from having, the necessary conditions that enable him to act in
> pursuit of his purposes.[9]

Moreover, 'the agent logically must accept that all other prospective
purposive agents have the same rights to freedom and well-being as he
claims for himself.'[10] Agency is a feature, one might say the defining
feature, of all human beings. Therefore, the rights to enjoy those
conditions that make purposive action possible are generic rights,
and not merely attached to the individual because of some peculiar
feature that he or she displays. It follows that:

> since the predicate of having the generic rights belongs to the
> original agent because he is a prospective purposive agent, he
> logically must admit that every purposive agent has the generic
> rights.[11]

The individual cannot deny that he has a right to the conditions of
action, either in a 'positive', material sense, or in the sense of being
protected against the outside restriction of his freedom, without
denying his own agency – a denial which would be meaningless as
well as impossible. All human beings have the capacity to act intentionally and voluntarily, which does not of course means that they
always do so. In consequence, no agent can rationally deny to another
those conditions that he is unable rationally to deny to himself. The
argument for rights is now moral in Gewirth's sense of being 'cat-
egorically obligatory', and in relating of necessity to the interests of
others.

The necessary conditions of action must include material provision
for the prospective agent, as well as the absence of outside interference. Therefore, the need for an account of positive rights is implied.
As a further consequence of this, the specific capacities and needs of
individuals must determine what kinds of resources are requisites of
agency for each actual (and unique) person. If we nonetheless assume

that there are conditions of agency common to all persons, then the task that remains is to describe a set of universal, basic rights. But we can see that basic rights must be permissive as well as protective. They are rights *to* as well as rights *against*.

The main virtue of Gewirth's argument is that it suggests a way of overcoming the standard objection to Kant's moral philosophy, which is that it is purely abstract and formal, and that it does not lend itself to the specification of what actions in particular circumstances can be translated into categorical maxims. The introduction of the concept of agency, and of the necessary conditions for realising it, provide for a theory of human rights in which the recognition of the other as an end in himself, as a rational and purposive being bound by the moral law, requires the provision of opportunities and resources whose content is specifiable. Such an argument goes some way towards refuting the claim that human rights are 'essentially contestable' from an ethical and cultural perfective, and gives to them a first order, or categorical, basis.

Rights and Culture

Let us look again at some arguments against human rights from the standpoint of cultural relativism.

One of these is that the West, in general, has stressed civil and political rights (especially the right to ownership of property) above economic and social rights, whilst in communist states economic and social rights have been secured, where they have been secured, at the supposed cost of the suppression of civil and political rights.[12] The latter are respected only so far as they do not imply limitation of the powers of government or of the 'working class'.

Another problem of relativism is said to be that in the Third World, collective rights, including self-determination, have been viewed as democratic rights to self-government rather than as 'organic' rights inherent in the nation as such. Such collective rights are usually asserted, claim the sceptics, as primary in the sense that individual rights have no meaning in their absence. They are also asserted unconditionally; the right of self-determination comes to be considered independently of the practical capacity for self-government. Thus,

> To those who argue that freedom from colonial rule has led not to an increase but to a decline in respect for civil and political rights,

that transfer of wealth from rich countries to poor has merely benefited the rich in the poor countries at the expense of the poor in the rich, or that the economic conditions of the blacks in South Africa are the best in the African continent, it can be replied that racial and national dignity represent a more vital human right than any of these things, even if those who have always taken them for granted find this hard to grasp.[13]

Not only are rights in the Western understanding not universally enjoyed; they are not accepted as morally valid in many societies: 'The idea that the universal validity of rights is self-evident in the light of reason is an eighteenth-century illusion.'[14]

These arguments are not convincing. In the first instance, the meaningfulness of the dichotomy between the classical liberal or 'negative' rights on one side and 'positive' rights in the form of resource entitlements on the other has already been questioned. In addition, the exclusive association of different 'bundles' of rights with antagonistic political systems is historically misleading. It suggests a very benign process of economic accumulation in Western societies, ignoring such inconvenient events as the Enclosure Acts or the repression of trades union activity in nineteenth-century Britain. Nor is there reason to believe that governments that suppress civil and political rights are better at guaranteeing economic and social ones.

This dichotomy implies that the polarisation of rights discourse is static. In fact, the recent history of Western countries has seen the transformation of the 'nightwatchman' state of classical liberalism, the guarantor of 'negative' freedoms, into the modern, interventionary state, which is expected to secure economic and social rights through collectivist provision. (Perhaps this process is now being put in reverse.) And evidence of increasing toleration of cultural, religious and even (to a lesser extent) political diversity certainly preceded the explosive events of 1989 in the communist world. Such evidence was there when the cynical manipulation of human rights rhetoric for cold war purposes reached its apogee in the years immediately after the Helsinki Accords.

The 'illusion' of the eighteenth century was not that rights existed in all societies in the sense of being actually secured, but that morally significant features of human beings *per se* gave rise to their having certain rights.

The understanding of emergent global norms of respect for human rights displayed by governments in their justifications of internal policies, in their general reluctance to denounce human rights as significant, and in their efforts to interpret such so as to appear in conformity with them, suggests that there is at least an emergent common conception of rights. This does not entail the absurd claim that all governments, or all societies, are equal in their respect of human rights. It only entails that they are not always talking past one another when rights are under discussion.

The Practical Necessity of Both Positive and Negative Rights

Aside from the philosophical question of what respect for persons requires in terms of the assignation of rights, the dichotomy of economic and social rights on one side and civil and political ones on the other is practically specious. A certain minimum degree of economic provision is a condition of being able to enjoy the 'negative' rights of civil and political freedoms or legal protection and redress. None of these matters if I am starving. The right to equality before the law is denied to those who cannot afford legal representation, and to whom free or subsidised legal services are denied. Organisation by groups or separate individuals on behalf of an economic interest or a political, social or religious cause also requires access to resources. Classical pluralism does not assume an egalitarian distribution of resources – money, education, articulacy, contacts – between interest groups, but it does assume that no-one is denied access to them entirely.

The enjoyment of political and civil rights is also usually necessary for the protection of one's economic and social rights. The black migrant worker had no redress against sudden deprivation of his 'livelihood' in the cities if the apartheid South African government forcibly removed him under the terms of the Group Areas Act, or even sought to 'denationalise' him by forced removal to a 'homeland'. The former-Soviet bloc dissident found himself, after a prolonged period of unemployment owing to the fact that no agency of the state – the sole employer – would take him on, being prosecuted under 'parasite' laws for refusing to work.

The Universality of Rights

There is a double sense in which the ascription of rights is universal. One is that such ascription, if it is seriously intended to carry the moral weight involved in the concept of a right, must imply the satisfaction of the other, minimal conditions that must obtain for the enjoyment of that right to be possible. The other is that the ascription of rights in a moral, as opposed to a legal, sense must relate to all human beings generally, since rights in this sense describe some intrinsic, equal moral worth and not one that is wholly culture-specific.

To some, it seems ridiculous to speak of rights except in the context of a particular society, state or era. It seems to them dangerously presumptuous to attack or displace the religious, social and cultural conventions of societies by abstract accounts of rights. On this view, the idea of the emancipation and equality of women has no place in traditional Moslem or Hindu society, intermarriage between the races may be prohibited if social mores oppose it, people may be denied the right to vote unless they are property owners or have attained a certain degree of education, whilst in other societies intellectuals who express independent views may be deprived of civil rights or imprisoned because the 'security of society' is said to warrant it.

The satisfaction of basic rights involves at the very least sufficient provision of the conditions both of security and of subsistence to allow a secure and worthwhile existence for individuals and for the groups of which they are members. Basic rights do not in themselves challenge the validity or importance of other substantive legal, cultural, civil, political, economic or social rights in societies, but specify a minimum content for such rights. They represent limits on moral relativism. Total rights enjoyed by people will extend beyond basic core rights in a just society. Justice as a maximal concept is certainly not coextensive with a minimum definition of rights.

Another consequence of dismissing basic rights is that it has the effect of shielding certain cultures and states from criticism. China has consistently refused to support international rights conventions on the grounds that rights attach firstly to states and nations, and then to classes, and lastly, and only derivatively, to individuals. China's legal system in the Mao era defined individuals in terms of their class backgrounds and, at least until the overthrow of the 'Gang of Four', conducted open trials, grimly named 'struggles', in which 'counter-revolutionary' and other 'bad elements' were subjected to humiliation and self-abasement at the hands of the 'masses'. The 1978 Amnesty International Report on the Chinese penal system, for instance, is most disturbing to read because the idea of the individual as a bearer of rights and with a moral, not to say a human, personality of his or her own becomes in that system completely submerged in the doctrine of class war.[15] It is a graphic example of a familiar historical process by which the idea of class or nation serves not to express an aspect of the individual identity, nor to safeguard a part of individual autonomy and dignity, but to eclipse and even annihilate that personality.

The Philosophical Defence of Economic and Social Rights

It has been argued many times by conservative commentators on both domestic and international politics that economic and social rights are conceptually as well as empirically quite distinct from civil and political rights, in addition to being differently understood in different societies. The argument runs that because rights imply duties, only the latter sort of rights are truly universal. Both duties and rights must be possible to perform, whereas, argues Maurice Cranston, many economic and social claims, especially as put forward in poor countries, are impracticable of realisation, unlike political and civil rights.[16]

Sceptics about social and economic rights, and about redistributive principles intended to support those rights, have argued that rights need to be related to a given community, that demands for economic justice should depend on minimum welfare and social justice within recipient states. For now, we shall only consider the claim that positive rights lack the imperative form that negative rights possess. This claim can be understood in two senses: that the ascription of negative rights of security of property, civil liberties, and so on, to a person does not entail that he need be provided with the resources to enjoy the activities and opportunities which his negative rights exist to protect; and that positive rights, unlike the universal obligations of forbearance to which negative rights give rise, do not give rise to obligations on anyone's part to satisfy them.[17]

The 'Compossibility' of Rights

It is often argued that negative rights are 'compossible' in a sense in which positive rights are not. Their universal satisfaction (that is, the protection of 'individual domains' against coercion) is taken to impose no costs on finite resources, merely to require mutual forbearance, whereas in a world of scarcity, the fulfilment of one person's positive rights at a particular level of available social resources can only be at the disregard of another's. Furthermore, government intervention and redistribution of resources which the satisfaction of positive rights requires, are said to violate negative rights to property and other economic freedoms.[18]

But this argument fails. It is by no means certain that positive and negative rights can be sufficiently distinguished in practice to permit the establishment of an order of priority between them. The violation of negative rights through outside interference, whether from domestic or foreign governments or from powerful interest groups, is one chief reason why many of the world's people are deprived of a livelihood. Therefore, what appear as demands for positive rights are often in fact demands for rights of non-coercion as the first condition of self-help and subsistence.

The truth is that to search for the origins of both sorts of rights will lead us in the same direction. The idea of negative rights, the claim that certain violations of this integrity should never be inflicted on people, is an assertion of people's abstract, equal moral value. But we have also noted that the introduction of the idea of agency lends a categorical element to rights, and that the respect of agency requires material resources, the substance of positive rights. This is itself a consequence of the equal moral value of individuals.

Yet the protection of property, for example, requires additional resources which, in times of mass privation or when there is otherwise a deep sense of injustice, may be great. It is not at all clear that the abstract negative right to security of property justifies indefinite claims on scarce resources for the protection of property, if only for the reason that it is unclear whom this right is being asserted against. It is presumably asserted against the potential thief; but not all members of society are thieves. So why should the opportunity costs incurred by the diversion of resources to protect a particular individual's property be borne by others who may neither benefit from his possession of it, nor pose a threat to his continued possession of his property?

F.A. Hayek attempts the witticism that the right of paid, regular holidays asserted in the Universal Declaration of Human Rights might as well be extended to Abominable Snowmen, such are its chances of being realised. Yet it does not seem prima facie unreasonable to draw up a set of 'basic rights' which could be generally satisfied without requiring limitless resources.[19]

Legitimate claims to economic and social resources can arise in other ways. Negative rights to non-interference may, as we noted, be violated in such a way as to prevent people helping themselves in creating their own means of subsistence. This may take the form of coercive deprivation of resources – such as paramilitary thugs destroying peasant smallholdings to obstruct land reform or to encourage collectivisation – or denial of the fundamental negative right of initial equality of opportunity in creating the means of subsistence and in fulfilling personal projects in life. This denial takes many forms. In developing countries, production for consumption by privileged elites may effectively deprive the subsistence part of the economy of even minimum agricultural resources, whilst grossly unequal distribution of income generates a chronic inflationary momentum which leaves those on the margins of economic life in a hopelessly disadvantaged position. In developed societies, the translation of economic inequalities into social inequalities often creates effective barriers to equal access to opportunities and rewards. As a result, the lack of those resources that are the substance of positive rights comes to constitute a denial of negative rights also, at least assuming that the right to benefit from opportunities entails the right to be able to take them up.

Fundamental Needs and Rights

The nature of positive rights as such is clearer where absence of resources is not a consequence of external abridgement of the right of self-help. Children, the elderly, the disabled, or the majority of the world's population who live in countries without the resources to provide a minimally adequate diet, health provision or basic education, are examples of people who are not only being prevented from exercising their capacity for self-help, but who lack such a capacity, or possess it only in a limited way. The existence of fundamental need, where self-provision is not possible, gives rise to a right in respect of the object of that need.

To show this, we may again consider H.L.A. Hart's conception of 'special rights', which arise either from explicit contract or implicitly from the 'mutuality of restrictions' which is the necessary condition of civil society. All the people mentioned above may have special rights against others because of some special relation in which they stand to them. But the view that all persons derive the same kinds of rights, which are binding with the same kind of imperative force, from similar kinds of situations, is one that needs to be defended.[20] That defence must, in turn, depend on some deeper argument for the equality of all persons as potential bearers of rights. Since it is a familiar proposition that there are few if any empirical senses in which human beings are equal, agency provides the most satisfactory criterion of human equality. Indeed, without the concept of agency as the essential condition for the ascription of rights, it is not clear why identical personal attributes would in any case lead to the requirement that persons be treated equally.

If needs are to be the criteria for the distribution of at least the most important social resources (let us for now say those that are indispensable to life, and to unstunted physical and social development), then the right to have one's needs provided for, where resources exist but where self-help is insufficient to meet those needs, is grounded in that same assumption of equality of persons-as-prospective-agents which is needed to make sense of the concept of special rights, as well as the broader range of negative rights with which classical liberal theory has been concerned. We cannot compartmentalise rights into negative as opposed to positive, or formal as opposed to substantial categories because the conditions of agency are either met or not met, and these conditions are always both protective and permissive.

Distribution and Relevant Reasons

In circumstances, then, where the individual is incapable of self-help, his fundamental needs ought to be the first condition met by the distribution of economic and social resources. The pattern of distribution of resources in a society must, of course, meet many other conditions, and satisfy other sorts of rights than basic ones. But with respect to that increment of distributable resources which is required to satisfy those basic rights whose objects are the satisfaction of fundamental needs, such needs are a sufficient and not merely a necessary condition of a just distribution. A corollary of this is that it is irrational as well as wrong to introduce other distributive criteria in respect of fundamental needs. Thus, Bernard Williams has argued that the provision of medical care, for instance, on the grounds of capacity to pay rather than of illness must be ruled out.[21]

This principle of the 'operativeness of reasons' has been disdained by libertarian thinkers and others who reject the notion of positive rights. For example, Robert Nozick denies that equality of treatment which is said by supporters of positive rights to require the distribution of (essential) resources according to need, can be argued for, as opposed to being merely asserted as desirable.[22] But this denial is unwarranted. The abstract equality which underpins negative rights and special rights becomes concrete in the equal capacity of all persons to actually exercise those rights. Equality before the law is meaningless if some people by virtue of their superior wealth can 'purchase' a favourable legal verdict.[23] Equality requires that criteria for access to the particular good be relevant to the good itself.

Basic rights are operative in that sphere of needs which the principle of agency transforms into rights, and distinguishes from the sphere of 'wants' understood as claims on resources that are not primary conditions of agency as such, though they may be for particular sorts of activity. We have noted that basic rights thus understood establish priorities for the social distribution of resources up to the level at which basic rights are generally met. To maintain this is not to discount the importance of special rights as such above that level of provision. The idea that human needs generate rights is not in itself a principle of substantive equality; special rights may exist which legitimately give rise to unequal distributions of social goods.

The justification of those inequalities that are needed to provide incentives for economic growth and for the overall expansion of available social goods will depend on those additional resources being used to satisfy basic rights. If short-term incentives are resourced at the cost of anyone's basic rights, then that individual is thereby being sacrificed to the future welfare of others.

All positive rights are conditional in the sense that they cannot give title to resources that are non-existent. The abstract equality of which they are an expression serves only to guarantee the material conditions of agency to the extent that this is possible without further denial of another's basic rights, and the point at which this occurs is always defined by the level of available resources. But the question of availability must not be restricted to the particular state alone.

It has been our position that the moral authority of the state and of its external claims depends on its protection of justice and rights at home. This is so because all the justice-claims of the state are valid only to the extent that the state mediates the legitimate justice-claims of its members, and translates them into demands that may be made against the international community. There is nothing in the nature of the state that permits us to construe it as an autonomous or independent bearer of rights or entitlements to just treatment.

But 'ought' implies 'can': the obligation of the state to secure the basic rights of its people, for example, depends on its being materially able to do so. If it is not so able, then this obligation, being universal in its nature though falling initially on the state whose people are in need, passes on to other states. Again it does so only mediately, that is, in so far as states are the representations of societies. It is between societies as groups of actual, living people, and not between states as political abstractions, that obligations ultimately exist. We may say that all individuals, wherever they may be, have obligations to provide resources to secure the basic rights of others, provided only that their own basic rights remain secured. The special rights enjoyed by people as members of particular societies and legal orders only become independently morally operative at this point.

The Primacy of Rights

Rights are not coextensive with morality as applied to the treatment of others, but they are primary concepts in the morality of politics, because other moral criteria for treatment, such as merit, or love, are of diminished importance in determining the just distribution of social goods amongst strangers. It is not necessary, or relevant, to have intimate or subjective feelings about another to recognise him as a prospective agent, with all that that entails. But it does entail making it possible for him to act when he cannot do so alone. That is why, whatever the independent value of negative rights or special rights, it is simply an insult to deny a person in such a situation the material conditions of a meaningful existence. There is an ascending scale of seriousness of such insults.

In a society in which education is sold as a commodity, so that material wealth, and not intelligence, motivation or other determinants of the capacity to benefit from education become the sole criterion for its distribution, the essential moral equality that the ascription to persons of all types of rights assumes and the degree of material equality that the concept of agency requires are mocked.[24] They are mocked still further when claims for food or primary health care are denied the status of rights. Negative rights do not strictly entail the satisfaction of positive rights; but when their assertion is associated with the denial that there are such things as positive rights, then they become worse than valueless.

5.2 THE STRUCTURE OF INTERNATIONAL ECONOMIC RELATIONS

The economic and social aspects of basic rights are quite evidently denied to untold millions of the world's population. We have constructed a theoretical defence of rights; we now need to answer the practical question: how far is the denial of these rights and justice-claims a consequence of the structure of international economic relations?

Interdependence and International Relations

In the realist perspective, national security is top of the agenda; its military, strategic and economic dimensions are the principal concerns of governments. International integration and co-operation are limited, voluntary, and exist only where tangible benefits to governments can be realised. In contrast, the theory of interdependence stresses the growth in salience of the 'low politics' of economic welfare and protection of resources and markets through international co-operation. Whilst national power is still accepted to be important, the hierarchy of issues is no longer inflexible.[25] It is the nature of the new global linkages that the 'power' of states is not uniform across all levels of interaction with other states and sub-state groups. For example, the representation of small states in international political and economic forums may enable them to extract concessions (economic or military aid, 'most favoured nation' status) from more powerful, developed states, in return for their support of the latter on issues of 'high politics'. The usually strong support of Caribbean states (Cuba obviously excepted) for the United States provides an example of this.

In general, interdependence theorists concur in regarding the conception of international politics as a 'zero-sum game' as being a dangerous anachronism. Whilst there is disagreement as to how far realist paradigms are able to incorporate the facts of interdependence, interdependence theory makes much greater use of the idea of reliance; there are mutual costs if relationships fail.[26] But there need be no presumption that the benefits or the costs of interdependence are shared evenly. Interdependence is still competitive; marginal relative advantage is sought between parties. Interdependence can be 'vulnerable' as well as merely 'sensitive'.[27]

Genuine interdependencies of ecological protection and scarce resources are stressed, without the rather affected pessimism of the World Order Models Project school that nothing short of system transformation will permit much to be done about these questions. Most of all, the synergistic nature of the international system of production is emphasised, along with the diminished significance of the nation-state as the basis of the global organisation of production.

This is not enough to make the state irrelevant as a sphere of distributive justice; but where the economic product available within a state is no longer the equivalent of the labour expended and the value added therein, distributive justice evidently no longer comes to an end at its borders.[28]

Interdependence and Inequality

Interdependence theory gives us a richer understanding of the dynamics of international power. We cannot always simply affix magnitudes of power and dominance to the relationships between particular states. These values will change across different areas of interaction, and over time, being negative in some areas and positive in others. Patterns of sensitivity and vulnerability are often subject to quite frequent and rapid change.

There is a real danger that interdependence theory can be used to obscure critical areas of international inequality and subordination which are of a persistent nature. The growing importance of 'low' politics does not alter the fact that the politics of security and military power still serve to reinforce international hierarchy. The idea of the 'relativity' of power relations in the new 'low' politics may come to serve as the ideological justification of this state of affairs. The rewards of sponsorship and 'most favoured nation' status for those developing or otherwise weak states that pursue compliant policies towards developed states and the economic interests based within them offer the former circumscribed possibilities of advancement on the coat-tails of the powerful.

The Brandt Report stresses the mutuality of benefits to be derived from an explicit recognition of interdependence as the organising principle of North–South relations.[29] Where asymmetries are compounded, however, and where economic inequality is translated into still greater discrepancies in political influence, and where interdependent 'growth for all' increases the gap between rich and poor and leads to the further immiseration in absolute terms of the already marginalised classes in poor societies – then interdependence comes to serve as an ideological disguise of pervasive structural inequalities.[30]

The theory of interdependence has been attacked as 'the new ideology of the development establishment',[31] implying a non-existent mutuality and equality in relationships between North and South, whereas in fact the relationships that exist embody systemic inequality. Supposed interdependence is seen as a means of buying off the radical demands of the Group of 77 states and, more importantly, as a means of discouraging cartelisation by Southern commodity suppliers in a manner similar to OPEC.[32] The discourse of international economic relations is shifted away from justice towards 'mutual advantage', without any conclusive demonstration that fundamental interests can be reconciled within the existing economic and political order.

The Nature of Economic Dependence

The background to demands for a New International Economic Order in the 1970s was a growing rejection by the leaderships of underdeveloped and developing countries of a sort of growth that served only to widen inequalities between North and South. This was combined with hostility, expressed by governments of the Group of 77 states who were increasingly frustrated by the effective stalemate of the UNCTAD process, towards the operation of 'market forces' and the idea of comparative advantage where these embodied grossly unequal bargaining strengths.

The combination of inflation and recession in the developed world led to a worsening of the terms of trade experienced by the South even where commodity prices were rising, as happened in the mid-1970s and early 1980s. The economies of the South were subjected to the combined effects of sharp price increases in imported manufactured goods, a decline in relative export earnings of particularly grave concern to export-oriented economies, and, after the loans free-for-all in the years of highly inflationary petrodollar surpluses, chronic and increasing indebtedness.

As already noted, a main feature of contemporary political economy is the shift from international trade towards the internationalisation of production. The value product of multinational corporations now exceeds the entire value of trade in the non-communist world, and even then the figures for international trade include intra-firm transfers. As Ankie Hoogvelt has persuasively argued, severe technological dependence has followed from this, with parent companies overcharging their wholly or partly owned subsidiaries in developing states for maintenance, sales and royalties, and thus replacing the old expropriation of dividends with hidden transfers.[33] She notes that this amounts to a new form of surplus extraction, based on a new separation of ownership and control. Technological dependence has replaced first political and then economic dependence. The effect of the internationalisation of production on Southern states has been to open up a divide between those that have mineral and fuel resources and industrialising markets which enable exchange in world markets, and those that do not.[34]

Against this background, it is unsurprising that political efforts to restructure North–South economic relations have been hampered by differing and ultimately incompatible motivations. The principle of 'trade not aid' was adopted at the first UNCTAD meeting; in subsequent meetings and in the GATT rounds demands have centred on positive discrimination in favour of exports from developing countries. These demands have largely been rejected, especially by the United States, on the grounds that discriminatory preferences contravene the free trade principles from which all are supposed to benefit.

The question of how North–South economic relations are to be interpreted is of crucial importance for understanding the normative issues that the larger question of international distributive justice raises. We may distinguish 'liberal', 'structuralist' and 'Marxist' interpretations.

The Liberal View of North–South Economic Relations

The liberal interpretation informs the orthodox attitude of most governments of developed states towards Third World development. The importance of unrestricted economic contacts is stressed and developing countries are encouraged to adopt 'open door' policies on trade, investment and the movement of labour, which are seen as the only way to avoid both capital and labour shortages. In this dominant view, the principle of comparative advantage ultimately leads to growth on both sides, whilst the international specialisation it produces is also mutually beneficial. The South benefits from trade according to factor endowment. Trade facilitates higher levels of national savings and consequently of investment, encourages the production of material goods which in turn provide further incentives, encourages entrepreneurship, and serves to develop technical and management skills which are essential to future growth.

In addition to the assumption that contacts between the developed and the developing world are mutually beneficial, three further propositions may be taken to be generally typical of the liberal outlook. Firstly, the condition of most Third World economies is at least comparable to earlier stages of development in economically advanced countries. Questions of natural factor endowment and cultural attitudes will be crucial for future development in poor countries, just as they have been in rich ones. The developed world can only offer assistance, such as through selective aid and non-discrimination against processed exports from developing countries (often more the exception than the rule), to encourage a process of growth which ultimately can come only from within developing societies themselves. Secondly, the wealth of the rich is not seen as in any way the cause of the poverty of others. On the contrary, global inequalities as well as those within developing societies are seen as indispensable to economic growth. The process of development in the Third World can only be assisted by access both to the capital and to the markets of the developed, industrial world. Thirdly, there is an assumption that private enterprise and free markets, both within states and internationally, are most conducive to growth, and there is a related suspicion of socialism and planning.

To take these arguments in turn, the idea of mutual benefit in international economic relations is a highly questionable one. Thomas Weisskopf has argued that capitalist forms of economic 'development' in the Third World tend even to worsen underdevelopment, political subordination and inequality in the distribution of income, both within developing societies and internationally. The structure of demand becomes biased in favour of elites, and against unskilled labour, which becomes increasingly economically marginalised.[35] Growing concentrations of wealth, the 'demonstration effect' of Western-style consumerism, the consequent increase in imported goods, and the influence of capital-intensive production techniques lead to persistent foreign exchange crises and the diversion of precious resources away from development. At the same time, the urgent need of developing countries for aid leads to political subordination by institutions like the IMF or the World Bank, and further compromises national autonomy when this has already come to mean little to elites, more concerned with safeguarding their privileged relations with foreign patrons than with the overall interests of their societies.

In addition to creating problems of technological dependence, multinational corporations may also come to erode the political authority and economic capacities of host governments in Third World states. Transfer pricing between different branches of corporations diminishes the tax-raising capacity of such governments, and thus deprives them of resources needed for infrastructure, education and health provision, and other objectives in improving social welfare and labour productivity, objectives which are themselves requisites for future, self-sustaining growth. The effect of such corporate activity has often been to increase the metropolitan dependency of the 'middle class' of developing states and simultaneously to exclude them from strategic levels of management, so that domestic business elites remain at the level of 'branch plant managers', excluded from those decisions that vitally affect their countries' interests. At the same time, governments become overwhelmingly dependent on these corporations to provide funding through exports for imported capital goods, to avert foreign exchange crises, and to finance through their taxes government expenditure on infrastructure and training.

None of these effects is anticipated by the equation of conditions in the now developing world with earlier stages of progress in the developed world. Too many features of the situation of the modern South were never experienced by the economically advanced states. These include the absence of comparative advantage with respect to the already-developed world across most of the spectrum of manufactured goods, and the consequent reliance of most Southern countries upon food commodities, raw materials and mineral exports for most of their earnings.

The developed states of Europe and North America never experienced a phase of development where investment capital was almost wholly controlled by economic centres outside their ambit, which were able to control the supply of development finance principally to suit their own economic interests rather than those of the developing states.

The once-developing states of the Western world were never historically burdened with huge external debts which declining terms of trade and export revenues made it impossible even to effectively service, or as a consequence of which international financial institutions offering little help beyond the recycling of credit were able to insist that development resources be used to service debt, that export dependency be further increased, and that welfare and training programmes be curtailed: 'In summary, the developed states of the West never passed through the conditions which beset the developing world today.'[36]

In a world of fundamentally unequal exchange, and still more unequal ability to command development resources, it is unreal to suggest that patterns of consumption have no appreciable effect on the scale of these inequalities. This fact undermines the credibility of reliance upon 'market forces' for economic development. Production is only undertaken where demand exists. Aside from the difficulties of import substitution confronting developing states, the unequal concentrations of wealth in their societies and the consequent predominance of consumption by elites in the total composition of demand promise to skew unplanned production accordingly. The opportunity costs imposed by such production in terms of diversion of resources from agricultural development and the provision of other basic societal needs are evident.

The Structuralist Approach

Structuralist theorists, such as Gunnar Myrdal, have responded to the inadequacies of liberal theories of development by focusing on terms of trade as the crux of global inequalities.[37] Trade, so far from promoting growth, is seen to have widened the North–South divide. Inelasticity of demand for primary exports and a competitive international market lead to declining prices for commodities from developing states, whilst monopoly in the markets of the developing world leads to higher prices for developing countries' necessary imports. Income thus gets transferred from poor to rich.

Other structuralists stress disparities in power as a feature of transactions generally. Johann Galtung has focused on problems of structurally unequal exchange between 'centre' and 'periphery' states at many levels: economic, political, cultural, military, and so on.[38] These structural inequalities exist within societies as much as between them. The advanced export sectors of Southern economies created by trade have little effect on the rest of the economy in growth terms; indeed, they drain resources from it. Externally, unequal power relations are reflected in the limited opportunities for capital investment in supposedly developing states in the face of more lucrative Northern market opportunities. As a result, investment comes to be concentrated in export sectors. The modern sector in post-independence states has often been

> very small and narrow in its base, catering mainly to the consumption needs of a fraction of the people and unable to provide employment to a fast-growing population. The result [has been] that an increasing proportion of this population [has been] thrown on the backward sector of an economy based on subsistence farming and other primitive occupations, thus giving rise to the phenomenon of growing under-employment and poverty in these regions – as a result of being drawn into a common world economy.[39]

One major problem is the irrelevance of much of the technology which Southern states have imported to the real needs of their societies. A small and mechanised industrial sector absorbs a lower and lower increment of the expanding labour force, increasing under-employment where lack of investment in technology causes continuing low levels of productivity. The effects are to reduce the savings-potential of these countries and to shift resources and priorities to production to favour the rich, leading to a distorted form of economic development which is out of line with the real needs of the community.

This form of partial development has created an educated and urbanised middle class separate from and hostile to the rest of society in underdeveloped states. The elite/mass separation in these societies, based upon growing economic differences, is seen as the central problem of growth.[40]

Marxism and Dependency Theory

Marxist theorists have been critical of structuralist theory for not focusing on exploitation as the inevitable condition of international capitalist production, and for being too concerned with matters of unequal exchange. The absence or proscription of trades unions and the willing compliance of the repressive mechanisms of states with capitalist enterprise in the developing world have led to depressed wages and poor conditions of labour, and in consequence high rates of extraction of surplus value and profitability. The Marxist-Leninist perspective views trade between North and South as inherently exploitative, and not merely as unequal.

The theory of imperialism developed by Lenin and J.A. Hobson explained its motivations in terms of foreign investment opportunities for surplus capital unable to find profitable investment domestically, the search for new markets, and the need for cheap, new resources.[41] This position is open to a number of familiar objections, of which the most serious is that instead of an outflow of capital, an actual movement of capital back to the metropolises has characterised recent North–South relations, whilst the chronic debt burden of developing states has further transferred capital to the North. In addition, Marxist-Leninist arguments rely on underconsumption and export of surplus theories, and on the existence of dependence by advanced economies on Southern raw materials. But developed states may absorb surplus structurally, by means of Keynesian economic policies, state welfare provision and other forms of public expenditure. Moreover, dependence on the supply of resources from the South, whilst important, is by no means total, since both substitutes and other sources often exist.

The modern, neo-Marxist school of dependency theorists have confronted the problems with the 'classical' approach, and incorporated a number of assumptions similar to those of the structuralists into their analysis.[42] Trade encourages backward forms of production in the South, whilst economic monopoly leads to declining terms of trade for Southern exports and still sharper increases in the prices of manufactured imports. The 'periphery' is seen to be integrated into a world capitalist system in which the division of labour denies possibilities for development. International economic relations are considered as a system within which surplus value is expropriated by the units of capital based in the developed states.[43] The poor countries are needed as reservoirs of cheap labour and materials. What development there is within them is uneven and unequal. Underdevelopment is seen as the underside of capitalist development.[44]

In dependency theory, capitalism is seen as a system of monopolistic exchanges whose effect is to transfer surplus from the peripheral to the centre. Within periphery states, this takes the form of monopolistic trade between provincial centres and the countryside, and the decapitalisation of the latter. Relations of production as such are no longer the exclusive or even the primary forms of exploitation.

It is not evident that dependency theory adds a great deal to the structuralist approach. In fact, it suffers from major problems. One is that the idea of exploitation has a very specific connotation in the Marxist corpus: the extraction of surplus value is the absolute condition of capitalist production. The unequal standing in terms of subsequent economic exchange (the distribution of income and commodities) between capitalist and worker is the consequence of this primary relation of exploitation in the process of accumulation. When it is unequal terms of exchange in themselves that are under consideration, 'exploitation' loses this exact meaning, and the structuralists' conception of 'unequal exchange' is more appropriate.

This sounds like a quibble in comparison with the fact that it is not exploitation that appears as the dominant characteristic of North–South relations. It is rather the marginalisation of most of the world's population by the global system of production, partly in consequence of the forms of development that have occurred. It is true that the profitability of foreign capital and the position of domestic elites may depend on the prevention or limitation of real development in the South, but such development would itself provide future and greater rewards, at least domestically. It would be unwarranted to maintain that governments of developing states generally have been forced into pursuing anti-development strategies in response to such interests. Against the fact that exploitation remains a central feature of international economic relations must be set the still darker question of the irrelevance of the needs of the majority of the populations of the world's (supposedly) developing societies to the motives and objectives of international production.

In summary, the value of interdependence theory as a critique of the realist conception of the state is eclipsed when it is used to disguise deep, structural inequalities of power. Few relationships of interdependence produce equal benefits on all sides, or equal freedom in choice and availability of alternatives. North and South do not have an equal interest in not rocking the common lifeboat. The glib use of the rhetoric of interdependence does not justify the assumption that one party can be made better off without making the other worse off, nor the assumption that the costs imposed on the better off by improving the position of the worse off are to be felt only in the short term, before a new, higher plateau of benefits can be reached for all. The optimistic promise of mutual benefits contained in the Brandt report are belied by the fact that the reform of an international system in which inequalities are not self-correcting, and in which growth is far from guaranteed for the poorest, seems likely to require more radical proposals than those proposed.

5.3 GLOBAL INEQUALITIES AND RESOURCE TRANSFERS

Foreign aid, in the form of bilateral economic assistance and multilateral contributions to UN agencies and to world financial institutions such as the World Bank offering discounted loans and other facilities, has been roundly criticised by both left and right. From the left it has been argued that economic aid has been intended to serve the interests of the rich rather than the poor, either by being tied (in the case of bilateral aid) to the future purchase of imports from the donor states, or more generally by being made available only for those forms of economic development that are compatible with the interests of developed countries and of the corporations based within them. The corollary of this is that aid may be used by the developed countries (particularly by the United States) to discourage the governments of developing ones from adopting socialist or collectivist approaches to economic development.[45] The Hickenlooper Amendment, providing for the suspension of US aid to any country in which US-owned assets have been nationalised without 'prompt and effective' compensation, is an example of such an approach.

The application of the economic theories of industrialised states to the economies of developing ones leads, it is argued, to wholly inappropriate policies, such as the diversion of funds away from desperately needed agricultural development to industrial projects of questionable efficiency. These are more than technical questions: aid is used as a lever to alter the social priorities of governments. The significance of the commitment of Northern donor states to liberal economic principles such as free markets, trade security and effective debt servicing is, in the view of many left-inclined critics of present aid policy, that first international monetary stability, then growth, then (if at all) questions of social welfare and distributive justice are the descending order of priorities for donor states. In practice, stability remains elusive, whilst growth exacerbates inequalities, and expenditure on social welfare programmes comes to be actively discouraged by donor governments and international organisations alike.

In sum, the radical critique of aid is that it serves to increase the trade and investment dependence of developing states, strengthens the position of elites within them, stunts agricultural development, and reinforces economic linkages which are already disadvantageous for developing and underdeveloped countries. In addition, the weighted voting system of the IMF and other organisations in favour of the major donor powers both enshrines and protects an international hierarchy in which the South plays a subordinate role.

It is important to identify the counterproductive and damaging features of particular aid policies, but to do so should be to support a plea for forms of aid which avoid these consequences and not to make a case against resource transfers per se. Nor does it seem consistent to describe aid as imperialism when it is simultaneously asserted that the level of aid globally is too small to have any significant effect on disparities of economic power between North and South.

Whilst aid intended primarily to serve the self-interest of donors has in some circumstances served to increase inequalities and protect elite privilege in recipient societies, this harmful interference by donor governments and organisations does not serve to establish the converse case, that questions of distributive justice and efficiency of usage of resources are illegitimate criteria for the supply of aid, and that no attempts to influence the policies of recipient governments are ever justified. To argue against these assertions is certainly not to justify aid as a means of ensuring ideological conformity and the maintenance of international hierarchy. But nor does the rhetoric of 'aid as imperialism' justify the assertion of an absolute doctrine of economic sovereignty as a counter-principle to this hierarchy.

A Right-Wing Offensive Against Aid

Criticism of aid from the right has stressed market forces and trade as the basis of growth, and rejected the idea that there is a prior need for infrastructure or 'nation building'. Aid is said to have encouraged anti-market and *dirigiste* outlooks on the part of the governments of developing states. In this vein, P.T. Bauer has argued that planning leads to the 'over-politicisation' of economics and social life, and also hampers growth.[46] Resources are wasted on grandiose projects when even the provision of that basic infrastructure and functions that market incentives do not exist to provide would be enough to stretch the capacity of most developing states. Aid has only served to foster resentment in developing societies as a result of a false belief, inculcated by ideologically motivated elites in both Northern and Southern countries, that the societies of the former owe a debt to the latter. The redistributive effect of aid is said to be from the poor in the developed states to the wealthy in the Third World.[47]

What is important is the whole web of social and cultural attitudes within societies. The ceteris paribus assumptions of macroeconomics are rejected. Instead, certain social and cultural traits are associated with growth prospects. Asiatic authoritarianism, contemplative attitudes, lack of personal curiosity, and beliefs in the 'organic unity' of nature are seen as inimical to development. The remarkable economic success of certain Far Eastern states is rather problematic for such a hypothesis.

Aid, finally, is seen both to exacerbate economic dependence and to stifle growth by discouraging the free market conditions necessary for it. It thereby creates a self-perpetuating need for further aid, and may even widen the gap between rich and poor countries. As the benefits of aid tend to accrue to the better-off, it may also exacerbate inequalities within recipient societies. It may serve to feather-bed incompetent and anti-Western elites, and to underwrite domestic repression of productive groups.

Not all of these criticisms are without value, but we should have serious reservations about the self-righteous tone of conservative commentators. It is disingenuous for arch defenders of the international status quo, such as Bauer and Robert W. Tucker, to excoriate wastage on 'show projects', such as multi-terminal international airports in developing countries, when the association of power and prestige with ostentatious wealth in the developed countries produces a quite inevitable example effect on the attitudes of elites in the developing world. Nothing is a surer butt of jokes at a country's expense than an international airport with a pitted runway and a corrugated-iron terminal building. However, the private consumption of elites, whilst frowned upon as wastage by the wise and virtuous men of international development agencies, is usually on a much lower scale than is regarded as the just reward for people of equivalent seniority and responsibility in the developed world. Such lifestyles may still consume resources unjustifiably when primary social needs are unmet; but ideas of status and merit are globally contagious and hard to overcome.

The claim that inequality and maldistribution within recipient states lessen the responsibility of the developed world to transfer resources is far from obvious. Once again, blame is transferred to the victims. Domestic injustice, wastage, governmental incompetence, and even persecution of the most productively advanced groups are major problems with which the administration of aid and other forms of resource transfer must contend. They are constraints on the degree of global distributive justice that can be achieved, not reasons to abandon all efforts in that direction.

Needs or Rights?

We have so far spoken about basic rights at quite a high level of generality. We need now to be more specific, but let us begin with the idea of 'basic needs'.

Such an approach is developed by Paul Streeten,[48] who views the diminution of inequality as much less important than meeting needs. More particularly, the redistribution of increments of income which the fulfilment of basic needs necessitates is seen as more practicable in political terms than is the redistribution of total wealth. 'Equality' is said to be an abstract and as such a divisive concept, compared with the real and tangible benefits which the basic needs approach promises to the most deprived groups in a community, and which can be more easily measured as an index of economic success. Equality as such 'is probably not an objective of great importance to most people other than utilitarian philosophers and ideologues'.[49] The moral priority of the relief of poverty, as opposed to the pursuit of wealth as a goal in itself, is also thought likely to be more germane to the cultures of most developing societies. Social equality is not a primary objective for the further reason that inequalities are said to be justified, following Rawls,[50] where they improve the position of the worst-off members of society, as compared to a wholly egalitarian distribution of resources:

> A development strategy guided by the goal of meeting the basic needs of the poor points to a different composition of products and choice of techniques. A strategy to make income distribution more egalitarian is likely to encourage more labor-intensive methods of production and thereby generate jobs and primary sources of income for the poor.[51]

The value-assumption here is that the provision of basic needs has a claim on resources when these are not met which is always greater than that of non-basic goods. Where there is a gap between available resources and what is needed to meet basic needs, a policy to fulfil the latter is still to be preferred.

On the credit side, the basic needs approach places the satisfaction of primary needs as prior to more extensive rights, including in the most general sense 'special' rights as understood in the first section of this chapter. However, the emphasis placed upon social knowledge as a condition of response to needs may be taken to imply that a philosophical defence of certain types of need as giving rise to rights is impossible or irrelevant, whilst we have argued the contrary. The securing of the minimum resources for a secure physical existence is an imperative which takes precedence over (but does not invalidate) questions of historical responsibility for the creation or perpetuation of need. This latter factor is not to be dismissed, but its exclusive assertion as a source of obligation can be, and has been, used as a device by the governments of communist states and the more advanced developing states to place the responsibility for resource transfers solely with the former colonial powers. Whilst these continue to have special obligations, the recognition that the provision of basic needs is a general imperative extends the scope of international responsibility way beyond what many states would wish to countenance.

Basic Needs, Distributive Justice and Paternalism

Unfortunately, the concern of the basic needs approach with equality and justice is narrowly circumscribed beyond this point. The relationship between needs and the specific benefits accruing to developed states and their commercial interests from unequal economic exchange is understated or ignored. There is a convenient consequence of this for the developed world. The double-edged effect of making basic needs primary is that, whilst the provision of minimum conditions of existence is valued more highly than non-essential consumption, the narrow definition of basic needs may be compatible with a fixed or only slightly increasing total supply of resources. Scarcity becomes less of a problem, and claims on the resources of the rich are thereby diminished. A recognition of historical and contemporary responsibility as a factor in the obligations to which poverty gives rise must produce a conception of distributive justice which exceeds the minimalistic criteria of basic needs.

Concern seems to be shifted from national economic growth to an exclusive attention to the needs of the poorest. International measures of redistribution come to be dependent upon internal redistribution in recipient states, yet no adequate conception of the nature of social justice within those states, nor of the legitimacy of the external claims of their members, is offered. On one view, the basic needs approach is a step towards an international social policy designed to complement the global management of an increasingly internationalised system of world production[52] and a means of avoiding the main questions of international distributive justice which confront that system.

Basic Rights

One particularly valuable conception of basic rights as the grounds for international resource transfers has been put forward by Henry Shue.[53]

The first thing to note is that basic rights are conceptually and practically broader than basic needs as we have described them. The complementarity between rights to shelter, food, education, and so on and civil and political rights is stressed; together these constitute 'integrity rights'. In rejecting the view, which we earlier associated with Maurice Cranston[54] and others, that economic and social rights are not absolutely binding in the way that 'negative' rights are, Shue argues that those economic rights that are subsistence rights have the highest priority. They are to be considered at least as important as those political rights concerned with the integrity of the person:

> three particular substances – subsistence, security, and liberty – are basic rights. The main conclusion is that subsistence rights are basic, but a valuable part of the case for taking subsistence to be the substance of a basic right is the demonstration that the same reasoning that justifies treating security and liberty as the substances of basic rights also supports treating subsistence as a basic right.[55]

These rights are complementary and basic because respect for people as agents requires respect for their autonomy and their capacity to act in fulfilment of their projects. If basic rights are not secured, this capacity for agency is denied. Basic rights, then, are everyone's minimum reasonable demands upon humanity. They are the rational basis for justified demands the denial of which no self-respecting person can reasonably be expected to accept. Why should anything be so important? The reason is that rights are basic in the sense used here only if enjoyment of them is essential to the enjoyment of all other rights.[56]

Subsistence rights are not to be considered as coextensive with minimum economic rights generally, nor do they imply an equality of condition. Rather, they specify a minimum level of provision below which no-one should be allowed to fall, a level below which the possibility of enjoying an active or fulfilled life disappears. And rights always imply correlative duties.

Basic rights are 'a restraint upon economic and political forces that would otherwise be too strong to be resisted, and they are social guarantees against actual and threatened deprivations of at least some basic needs'.[57] Within the category of basic rights, security and subsistence rights cannot always be sharply differentiated. Security rights must also be guaranteed by society, which itself imposes costs:

> Rights to physical subsistence often can be completely satisfied without the provision by others of any commodities to those whose rights are in question. All that is sometimes necessary is to protect the persons whose subsistence is threatened from the individuals and institutions that will otherwise intentionally or unintentionally harm them. A demand for the fulfilment of rights to subsistence

may involve not a demand to be provided with grants of commodities, but merely a demand to be provided with some opportunity for supporting oneself.[58]

The extension of this theory has important implications for the relationship between Western policies towards Third World and satellite states, and rights observance within those states. The sphere of moral responsibility includes more than support for politically repressive and barbaric regimes. For the West, it would include denying support for economically exploitative regimes, refusal to back multinational corporations whose operations have dire effects on rural underemployment and poverty and which predominantly service elites and comprador groups, as well as stopping aid and development policies that encourage dislocated and harmful economic growth.[59] Drawing on the history of communist and other authoritarian states, the list would include support for governing parties that impoverish their people through brutal and incompetent planning strategies and 'class warfare', or that waste vital resources on military expenditure which their own internal policies of repression necessitate.

Denials of negative or 'liberty' rights may come to constitute denials of positive rights also. There is more to be said for positive rights than the right not to be deprived of one's capacity for self-help, but those who assert the primacy of negative rights often ignore their violation as a factor leading to material deprivation and to consequent claims by and on behalf of the afflicted, claims which they then dismiss as spurious. When people are already deprived of the means of subsistence by external agency, strictures against further interventions and the 'threat to liberty' which they pose add insult to injury.

Basic rights, then, are premised on the insistence that the integrity of the person requires, along with a range of basic liberties, the recognition of entitlements to resources where self-help is insufficient to provide them, as well as rights to security of person and property. This complementarity of rights is seen to be necessary at a practical level. Once we supplement the idea of basic rights with the philosophical conception of agency we have a deeper understanding of them, one that is grounded in the essential attributes of personality and not merely in external contingency. The concept of basic rights arises from a recognition that the characteristics of human beings that produce the idea of rights in the first instance point to the necessity of both permissive and protective conditions of action.

The securing of basic rights is the minimum responsibility of any government towards its people, where this is materially possible for a government acting on its own. Where it is not, the imperative nature of basic rights imposes obligations on other states to provide assistance towards securing these rights, where this can be done without compromising the basic rights of the citizens of donor states. These mutual rights and obligations, however, exist ultimately between *societies*. States are the immediate mechanisms of their satisfaction, but only actual persons can be the subjects of moral rights.

Basic rights are in many respects akin to natural rights as Grotius and the other classical natural law theorists conceived them. The idea of agency and the conditions of its effectiveness give a specific content to those rights which was previously lacking. In so doing, it also gives specific content to international obligations between states and societies in respect of their fulfilment.

Basic rights are also basic in the sense of being restrictive: they cannot be arbitrarily substituted for the full range of other operative rights. They are also basic in the more important sense that their fulfilment takes priority over that range of rights – legal, civil, political, and cultural as well as to welfare beyond the basic rights minimum – that people enjoy by virtue of belonging to a particular society or living in a particular state. The securing of basic rights is itself the condition of their enjoyment. These more extensive rights come into effect with independently binding moral force only when basic rights are universally met. Put another way, basic rights define the demarcation of *droits nécessaires* and *droits volontaires*. They separate that area in which political communities may legitimately look to the rights and the broader welfare of their own from that other area in which global rights and welfare take precedence over the interests of the particular community. This is, perhaps, the crux of our whole argument. The state becomes legitimate as a constituency of justice when, and only when, it works its hardest to ensure that basic rights are met globally. That it require the co-operation of other states is no argument against this.

5.4   PROBLEMS OF INTERNATIONAL DISTRIBUTIVE JUSTICE

Two recent approaches to distributive justice differ markedly in their international implications. If neither entirely works, they do at least shed light on the subject.

John Rawls and International Justice

In Rawls' theory of justice, the circumstance in which the need for principles of justice for economic and political institutions arises is a self-sufficient society which is 'a cooperative venture for mutual advantage', but in which there is both 'an identity of interests since cooperation makes possible a better life for all than any would have if each were to live solely by his own efforts' and 'a conflict of interests since persons are not indifferent as to how the greater benefits produced by their collaboration are to be distributed, for in order to pursue their ends they each prefer a larger to a lesser share'.[60]

To decide upon the principles regulating the distribution of the advantages and costs of social co-operation, the persons who will constitute the society enter into a hypothetical Original Position in order to choose principles of social justice. These persons do not know what positions they will occupy in society, what economic, social, educational or other advantages or disadvantages they will enjoy. Indeed they know nothing about their own personal and social identities beyond the 'veil of ignorance'. They are, however, assumed to be rationally self-interested and mutually disinterested.

The Original Position is not meant to be a literal account of the formation of societies and states, but an abstract and hypothetical version of the social contract, the results of which permit the assessment of how close institutions and distributive arrangements in a society come to an ideal of free, rational and voluntary social co-operation. The principles of justice Rawls believes would emerge from the Original Position are:

> First: each person is to have an equal right to the most extensive basic liberty compatible with a similar liberty for others. Second: social and economic inequalities are to be arranged so that they are both (a) reasonably expected to be to everyone's advantage, and (b) attached to positions and offices open to all.[61]

These principles are serially ranked: equal liberty is prior to greater social and economic advantages, and must not be sacrificed to it. It is, however, recognised that the full enjoyment of personal, civil and political liberties requires at least that level of economic and social provision to allow a life of minimum dignity and security. What is to be shared out in society is given in Rawls' account of primary social goods, including such things as 'rights and liberties, powers and opportunities, income and wealth'. The principles of distribution are part of a larger and more basic conception of 'justice as fairness':

> All social values – liberty and opportunity, income and wealth, and the bases of self-respect – are to be distributed equally unless an unequal distribution of any, or all, of these values is to everyone's advantage.[62]

Rawls assumes a 'conception of justice for the basic structure of society conceived for the time being as a closed system',[63] and devotes only a few paragraphs to its extension to international relations. At various points he describes the society he has in mind as 'self-sufficient' or 'more or less self-sufficient', although this supposition is relaxed for the derivation of principles of international law.[64] Here, the Original Position is extended in such a way that the parties become representative of different nations, ignorant both of the relative position of their own nation with respect to other nations, and of their own position within their national societies. Rawls' suggested principles are, in his own words, familiar:

> The basic principle of the law of nations is a principle of equality. Independent peoples organised as states have certain fundamental equal rights. This principle is analogous to the equal rights of citizens in a constitutional regime. One consequence of this equality of nations is the principle of self-determination, the right of a people to settle its own affairs without the intervention of foreign powers. Another consequence is the right of self-defense against foreign attack, including the right to form defensive alliances to protect this right. A further principle is that treaties are to be kept, provided they are consistent with the other principles governing the relations of states.[65]

It should be noted that no international difference principle operates in Rawls' extension of his theory. There is consequently nothing about global redistribution of wealth. The state is seen as the appropriate constituency of justice. However, as we have often noted, states are not closed systems; the facts of trade and interdependence prevent the idea of a 'co-operative venture for mutual advantage' being restricted only to domestic society. Therefore, an international difference principle must apply.[66] If principles chosen in the Original Position are to protect the worst-off, it would be important to insure against being born into a poor society. As Robert Amdur has noted,

Global application of the difference principle is thus likely to push Rawls' theory in a more radical direction. It is almost certain to require a far more egalitarian distribution of wealth than that which presently prevails. Under this principle, an affluent state that is perfectly just internally (whose inequalities all work to the benefit of the worst-off group) may still be unjust vis-à-vis other nations. Justice is likely to require monetary and trade reforms, debt cancellation, and, more important, massive development aid; in short, a substantial redistribution of wealth from the rich nations to the poor.[67]

Such a principle might be thought even more important to the participants in the Original Position. By and large, both the minimum resources available and the chances of improving one's position are greater in richer societies, whereas in societies with an acute shortage of resources, both may be effectively non-existent. Disadvantage may be absolute as well as relative. Therefore, the need to compensate for the mishap of finding oneself in a poverty-stricken society would be pressing. It should be noted that the difference principle has no relation to past exploitation or deprivation of resources; such arguments are irrelevant to the Rawlsian justification of initial principles.

The major problem of Rawls' theory is with respect to the role of the state in global distributive justice. He assumes the state as the appropriate constituency, but does not specify why those in the Original Position, knowing that co-operation extended beyond the boundaries of the state, should nonetheless choose it as the sphere of operation of the principles of justice to be chosen. Even if they did, unless there were a necessary reason for confining questions of distributive justice to the state, or unless there were an international difference principle in operation, it is unclear how Rawls could defend the view that a 'war for economic gain' would necessarily be unjust. There is no requirement for the poor to respect the advantages and possessions of the rich, unless the rights of both are incorporated in a difference principle to which both could have consented.

Independent states are also assumed for the negative reason that the idea of a world government conflicts with Rawls' belief in individual participation in decision-making. As a result, redistribution where an international difference principle requires it is still to be mediated by sovereign governments, who may not use it to benefit the worst off in their societies. International redistribution is not internal redistribution writ large. But since states are, considered morally, fictive entities without the capacity of a unitary and rational being for choice, individuals and not states remain the ultimate beneficiaries of international justice. In consequence, donor organisations (including governments) must be considered to have a right to tie the transfer of resources to the adoption of fair distributive policies (as specified by the difference principle operating domestically) on the part of recipient governments. The claim of the latter that sovereignty is thereby infringed is not to be allowed. Intervention might even be chosen in the Original Position as an automatic means of implementing the difference principle whether it is violated internationally by states refusing to deliver up the resources to which others are entitled, or domestically by conditions of social injustice.

We have noted the dangers of intervention as an overt (and usually of necessity) military activity, despite the existence in relations between certain states of what amounts to 'structural intervention'. There are excellent reasons not to choose intervention as an imperative principle. And an obvious question is, 'Wouldn't people value the autonomy of their states more than to allow for regular interventions, with all their attendant dangers, and risks of escalation?'

These ambiguities about the state arise because Rawls' theory of the value of the state as a constituency of rights and justice is too thin. The same may be said about Beitz's extension of the Rawlsian argument,[68] in which the facts of mutual benefit through global co-operation extend the difference principle to international relations. The interpretation of this as a principle of international justice is both too permissive – it ignores the rights and justice-claims individuals and groups may hold against their states, and against one another within their states – and too restrictive: there are rights that do not arise through co-operation or interdependence, and basic rights as we have understood them are among these.

It is also interesting to note that whilst Rawls' justification for self-determination is grounded in the assumption that societies are self-sufficient, the granting of such an assumption would not make it clear why the facts of internal co-operation and self-sufficiency should give rise to external rights of autonomy. A source of ambiguity in Rawls' position on self-determination is that whilst the value of collective goods (including the right to autonomy and respect as a member of a group) is defended in Rawls' theory, individual choice places constraints on collective claims whenever these pose a threat to individual autonomy, and there is the at least latent danger of this in most claims for self-determination.

Radical Global Egalitarianism

From a different perspective, Peter Singer takes an uncompromising view of the extent of the obligations of private individuals as well as of states in overcoming global poverty. He contends that

> neither our distance from a preventable evil nor the number of people who, in respect to that evil, are in the same situation as we are, lessens our obligation to mitigate or prevent that evil...: if it is in our power to prevent something very bad from happening, without thereby sacrificing anything else morally significant, we ought, morally, to do it.[69]

If it is the case that in a time of famine, for example, few other people are likely to donate the amount to relief which would, if that amount were donated by everyone, prevent the famine, then this fact serves to increase rather than diminish my moral obligation; so that

> it follows that I and everyone else in similar circumstances ought to give as much as possible, that is, at least up to the point at which by giving more one would begin to cause serious suffering for oneself and one's dependants – perhaps even beyond this point to the point of marginal utility, at which by giving more one would cause oneself and one's dependants as much suffering as one would prevent...[70]

Whilst Singer does not go along with Bauer in claiming that

> The moral obligation to help the less fortunate cannot be discharged by entities such as governments. It can be discharged only by persons who are prepared to impoverish themselves and weaken their material position relative to others in order to help their poorer fellow men[71]

he sees no reason to assume that the responsibilities of individuals are subsumed in those of governments.

The basic rights approach, indeed the whole argument for justifying positive social and economic rights, requires equality only in the sense of equality of treatment in the satisfaction of those rights. Arguments could be made to show that a fuller conception of rights requires a more substantive social and economic equality, but equality in this sense has not been our concern. Basic rights certainly do not require an absolute equality of condition among persons, according to a principle of comparing marginal utilities of donors and recipients. It is not in any case clear how such utilities could be measured. Material wealth has different significance, and leads to different opportunities, in different societies. A cross-cultural comparison of the utility derived from the possession of material resources would be, in practice, impossible to make. Social opportunities, respect and autonomy are also rights of agency, and the relationship of these rights to physical resources are also cross-cultural variables.

Causality as a source of obligation to redistribute resources is a vital element left out by Singer. It is surely warranted to assume that those societies, and those individuals and groups within them, that most benefit from an unequal system of economic exchange thereby incur the greatest obligations of redistribution. Causality is not a necessary part of the obligations to which primary need gives rise, but the distribution of those obligations across donor societies is as important as it is where rights exist because people have been deprived of resources through unequal exchange. Singer offers no account of how the burdens of redistribution are themselves to be subject to a principle of distributive justice across society.

The rights to resources to which deprivation gives rise have at no stage been argued to be coextensive with rights to resources or opportunities in general. Special rights arising from contract, promise, family and kinship relations, and, in a general sense, membership of a society are also to be considered. It has only been remarked that the idea of agency as the ultimate source of all rights requires that basic rights be assigned priority over the satisfaction of other rights, since otherwise the minimum conditions of agency are denied. One of the values of providing for people's basic rights is that a range of personal opportunities is opened to them, and these include opportunities to enter into relations with others from which special rights arise. Instead of these distinctions, Singer offers an account of undifferentiated, and unexplained, obligations to redistribute resources which avoids all discussion of rights and the circumstances which create them.

Distribution to the point of equalisation of conditions may even undermine the agency of the recipient. The most poignant feature of global poverty is that it is for want of the most basic resources for self-help that so many suffer it. Charity is at the whim of the giver; once the permissive conditions of self-help are created, the autonomy of the recipient is restored. Everyone has the right to have his or her fundamental needs provided for, but beyond this point it is common experience that people's enjoyment of resources depends on their being able to proffer reasons relating the possession of those resources to their own actions (even if these reasons are sometimes unsound).

Basic Rights and International Obligations

The weaknesses and omissions of the approaches we have been considering further encourage us to believe that basic rights should be the most important criteria of international distributive justice. They are not of course the only criteria: questions of unequal and coercive economic exchange and compensation for past exploitation and subjection are of great importance also. But the conception of basic rights that we have defended here, and the specification of the circumstances which cause those rights to be denied, takes some account of those other conditions of injustice, as we have seen. We begin with a fundamental problem which we have not yet tackled. We have spoken a great deal about obligations existing between states and societies, in respect of past exploitation, political and economic subjection, or currently unequal or even coercive economic relations, as well as in respect of basic rights. But what exactly does it mean to say that collectivities like states or societies have mutual responsibilities? How do group obligations differ from individual ones, and how do these obligations devolve upon private individuals or sub-state groups?[72]

The Problem of Collective Responsibility

Evidently states vary greatly in their promotion of the common good. States often act to uphold powerful sectional interests or classes, and thereby incur moral responsibilities which correctly pertain to those interests and classes alone. Most historical variants of imperialism have generated such responsibilities. The potential of the state to represent the common social interest is no ground for holding that all classes of society bear common responsibility for all externally directed actions of the state. Nor, by the same token, does popular support for imperialistic policies, or for any other rights-violating policies, imply popular responsibility where that support has not been a necessary condition of such a policy's being adopted or maintained.

Claims made in terms of international distributive justice may be considered as restitutive where they have their basis in former exploitation, or as claims for the satisfaction of basic rights where primary human needs exist unmet. The distributive principles of the obligations to which the different rights embodied in these claims give rise will also be different. In the case of restitutive claims, those social groups whose economic position has benefited most from the past exploitation of others will have the greatest responsibility to make good that exploitation. The fulfilment of this responsibility can be at least approximately secured through progressive taxation as a means of funding overseas aid and other resource transfers.

In this instance, the responsibilities of states and societies are not coextensive. What about instances where the violation of the rights of people outside a particular state benefits all or most groups within that state? Above all, what about the distribution of obligations to meet basic rights when the circumstances in which those rights are not secured cannot be said to be caused (at least not directly caused) by external action?

A relevant concept here is that of 'moral proximity'.[73] An agent is responsible for the outcome of his action to the extent that the action was a sufficient and not merely a necessary cause of that outcome or that the action constrained the choice of others whose actions were necessary conditions of the outcome, and in either case that the action was intentionally directed towards the outcome produced. Such a concept is not without pitfalls, not least in that the people who most benefit from policies and actions are not always the ones who instigate them. This consideration aside, there are at least three levels of practical application of the concept of moral proximity.

Firstly, it determines how far rights violations are caused as a direct result of state policy, whether it be support for depredatory multinational corporations, or diplomatic resistance to changes in international economic agreements that benefit domestically based corporations operating abroad.

Secondly, it determines to what extent various social groups have benefited from a rights-violating policy, where this is unequal between groups. Once again, it appears unacceptable to hold collectivities responsible in an undifferentiated way. Lastly, in the case of the obligations to which the existence of the basic rights of members of other societies give rise, the distribution of those obligations should not be such as to increase inequalities within donor societies. Any regressive element to the funding of resource transfers is morally arbitrary if all the members of the donor society are equally innocent of causing deprivation. In fact, a stronger supporting case for progressive taxation is that there is often a causal relation between economic policies that benefit aid donors and the condition of poverty of the aid recipients. Again, a principle of proportionality between the distribution of benefits received and the distribution of obligations of restitution is required.

Where the moral proximity argument becomes most obscure is in its application over time. Firstly, where distributive justice requires restitution, the determination with any degree of precision of how obligations should be distributed may be difficult. The institution of inherited private wealth in capitalist societies does permit the identification of which contemporary individuals and social groups have most benefited historically from rights-violating policies, but the way in which benefits have accrued to different social groups over decades or centuries may be visible only in outline. Robert Nozick, for one, offers no real evidence that it may be visible at all.[74]

It can be argued, for example, that the more privileged sections (at least) of the British working class benefited in absolute economic terms from the access to markets and resources provided by the Empire, even as they were themselves victims of high rates of economic exploitation.

Secondly, the estimation of the extent of the effect of imperialism on the retardation of economic development in former colonies is beset with counterfactual arguments, even though that effect was certainly not zero. Historical responsibilities cannot be evaded; but they are unlikely to be as clear as is the evidence we have seen that contemporary economic relations between rich and poor countries severely damage the development prospects of the latter.

Lastly, an initial inflow of resources obtained in an exploitative manner may be a necessary but not a sufficient condition of economic growth. Members of societies have rights as a result of their co-operative efforts, and on the basis of what are best termed 'settled expectations'. By the latter is meant rights to those resources that sustain a pattern of social life and provide the basis for provision for future generations, even where those resources were initially obtained unfairly. It is not claimed that such rights are any more absolute for societies than for individuals. The obligation to make good a theft is never completely avoided, whatever subsequently was done with the loot. Nor does it follow that any of these possible sources of collective responsibility for previous harm is beyond all determination. What is clear is that the calculation of economic benefits and therefore of the degree of restitution required between societies that have historically stood in a relationship of exploitation and subjection is difficult and often ambiguous.

For this reason, and not because the historical determinants of current patterns of distribution within and between states and societies are either morally or politically unimportant, in questions of international distributive justice greater weight will in practice have to be given to the current identification of clear causal links between policies of benefit to the developed world or to elites in developing and underdeveloped countries, and the denial or erosion of rights in the latter.

But distributive questions where such a link is tenuous or uncertain are often equally pressing. Severe need and deprivation themselves necessitate the international transfer of resources. Of course, where 'historical' determinants of global inequalities consist of policies which are very recent, or are continuing, many or all of the problems of historical attribution of distributive obligations become much less vexed. Beyond such policies and relationships, international distributive justice requires the satisfaction of basic rights, which exist without the support of arguments concerning the apportioning of blame for current circumstances. One of the reasons why underdeveloped states insist on the historical, restitutive aspects of justice-claims is that without these considerations, aid and resource transfers have the quality of mere charity.

Natural Resources and Distributive Justice

The examination of the distributive obligations existing between states inevitably raises the question of entitlement to natural resources. Distributive justice involves more than historical and present relations of production and trade. The question of how a society or a state can be said to have a moral right to the resources on or under its territory leads to further questions. One of these is how redress for past exploitation of resources essential to the wellbeing of communities (past and present) by colonial or otherwise predatory states is to be made. Another question is whether states whose territories contain natural resources inadequate to sustain even the basic conditions of social and economic life for a people can be said to have a right to resource transfers by virtue of their plight alone, and not in respect of past depredations.

A possible approach to the international distribution of resources that would tend towards similar consequences rests on the Lockean theory of property rights.[75] A community can be said, on such a view, to have a right to that with which it has mixed its collective labour.

The difficulty is that the usual proviso that 'enough and as good' be left for others to appropriate is belied by the exclusion of outsiders practised by communities (this being, indeed, a condition of their self-identity as such) to which legal and political expression is given by the sovereign state. The modification of the proviso to one in which it is enough that those excluded from appropriation should benefit, in some general sense, from the economic and social benefits generated by a system based on restricted access to resources is hardly one that finds expression in the reality of the international economic system.

It might be argued that the aim of global redistribution of resources should be to compensate for those deprived of resources in accordance with the modified proviso. But aside from the loss of autonomy and opportunities for self-sufficiency which such a redistribution would view with equanimity, the practical problems of such an approach, not least that of whether ownership and control of resources can ever be separated in the real world from distributive outcomes, should dissuade us from placing much faith in it.

One response to this line of argument has been that the distribution of physical resources presents a quite different problem for international as opposed to domestic justice, because in the latter case (at least assuming a self-sufficient society) unequal access to resources by individuals within a community can be compensated for by redistribution by governments of the total social benefits accruing from the exploitation of those resources. Evidently, this is not so readily achieved among states. Since resources are not, like natural talents, merely a morally arbitrary question of luck whether one is born with them or not, global principles of distribution must apply to them.

It is possible here only to sketch out some of the relevant considerations in developing principles for the (re)distribution of physical resources. The key point is that the question of entitlements to (at least) those resources essential to some minimum level of economic security and the possibility of a shared social existence is related to the supposed distinction between positive and negative rights. The securing of both sorts of rights was seen to be required as a moral consequence of the recognition of human beings as sentient beings, capable of purposive action.

To argue that someone has only 'special' or negative rights to security of property or the person, when this is intended as more than a statement of legal fact, is indeed to attribute to him an inviolable moral character by virtue of which he has the capacity to bear such rights. But the concept of agency which gives real ethical substance to that character is only hypothetically recognised, since it is denied that anyone has any positive (resource) entitlements against others, even where provision through self-help is not possible.

The relevance to the question of entitlement to natural resources becomes evident. The conditions of agency permit and require the special rights, including those to resources, to which particular instances of contract or promise give rise. The equal capacity, and equal freedom, of individuals to acquire special rights is generally, perhaps necessarily, assumed by rights theorists as diverse as Locke, Nozick and Hart. But this assumption requires a deeper theory of moral equality. Given the unequal capacities of human beings in almost all respects, agency has emerged as the best way of understanding this deeper equality.

To recognise agency as a moral idea involves the imperative, as we saw, that the conditions for agency be met. To recognise agency, but not the imperative nature of the conditions of its realisation amounts in fact to self-contradiction. If people have the capacity to acquire rights to property, it cannot be morally irrelevant that there simply are no resources for them to acquire. The normative importance to be attached to the empirical rights and obligations which individuals acquire in their common existence proceeds from their capacity as agents; but the very recognition of this fact must lead to an acknowledgement that the justice of the content, and distribution, of property rights within a society cannot depend alone on the special rights attached to individuals in that society.

The conditions of agency mean that the initial distribution of natural resources cannot be considered as morally arbitrary. The redistribution of natural resources *per se* poses extraordinary practical problems. Firstly, the above arguments suggest that a distinction be made between that component of any society's wealth derived from the exploitation of natural resources through co-operative endeavour, and to portions of which special rights are held by individuals, and the remaining component to be donated to some international scheme of redistribution. The guiding principles for such a 'division' of national wealth would inevitably be speculative and open to endless counterfactual objections. Moreover, whilst territory as a basis for statehood does not carry with it unconditional rights to the resources under the territory, there is no practical way of sharing out resources by means of land transfer, or even by means of multiple sovereignty over particular areas of territory, which does not challenge the integrity of established communities, and the basis of security and settled expectations which gives particular value to the idea of community.

Since the actual transfer of physical resources is often impractical, not least since the technology for the efficient exploitation of resources has obviously developed and become most concentrated in those countries with the greatest resource assets, principles of distributive justice must address the problem of resource entitlements indirectly by relating national shares of global wealth to their relative endowments of resources. The problem of resource entitlements becomes in large part one of compensation for certain communities' lack of access to resources. The basic rights approach to international distributive justice must lead to principles of compensation.

The qualification to this requirement must be to avoid paternalism by compensating relatively resource-deprived societies in such a way as to make self-reliance possible. It would be particularly appropriate to do this by transferring to them the technological means of exploiting what resources they do possess more effectively. In fact, the questions of historical exploitation in terms of the overall relations of production, and the coercive historical expropriation of resources, are unlikely to be separable.

Resource entitlements, then, enter more indirectly into the general context of global redistribution, but only because of the practical difficulties to which their implementation gives rise, and not because they are intrinsically any less important than redress for historical exploitation. For one thing, inappropriate aid may serve to undermine the essential self-subsistence of agricultural economies by reducing local market prices.

Basic Rights, Society and Equality

We saw in the first part of this chapter that a standard objection against the idea of rights that specify resource entitlements is that it is impossible to say against which group of people those rights are held. Related to this is a further objection that we must confront at this stage: why should membership of a particular society confer special entitlements which are denied to outsiders? Surely accidents of birth should be discounted as morally irrelevant to questions of rights and distributive justice. Indeed, it might be objected that concepts like 'membership' – and even 'society' – are tendentious in that they disguise pure contingency with ill-defined implications about special duties and rights among individuals of a sort that need to be argued for rather than to be surreptitiously introduced by the use of such terms.

This objection might be countered by following Rawls in defining society normatively as a sphere of co-operation for mutual benefit. We have already argued that the international sphere can be said (at least to a degree) to resemble a society in this sense also: in terms of economic interdependence to a still greater degree than in the realms of international law and other forms of social and cultural co-operation. What then is so special about belonging to one society rather than another as the criterion for determining what sort of rights one possesses?

Critics of the idea of positive rights pose this problem in the belief that it has no solution and that it reveals the absurdity of claiming such rights for non-members. In their view, we should either dispense with positive rights altogether, or accept that the rights enjoyed by individuals in a particular society, and guaranteed by the state, are arbitrary from a moral point of view and must give way to a more or less infinite set of rival claims for the global redistribution of wealth, freedoms and opportunities.

The conception of basic rights that we have developed avoids this crude and simplistic choice of alternatives. The rights and correlative duties which arise only through participation in civil society and which are enforced only by the state are recognised. Equal political obligation and the equal rights to liberty to which it gives rise, as much as the contractual relations between individuals upheld by civil law, produce a pattern of entitlements, opportunities and resources peculiar to each society. But beyond these rights and duties lie basic rights as we have described them. It is because people are agents, autonomous moral beings pursuing their separate ends in a context of mutual dependence, that they are capable of holding the general and special rights distinctive of civil society. Before these rights can be meaningfully exercised, basic rights, the indispensable minimum conditions of individual action and social participation, must be secured.

Pace the legal positivists, all rights derive their ultimate meaning from the fact of human agency. It seems impossible that any truly determinist theory of human behaviour could lead to a theory of rights in either the permissive or protective senses, when the enjoyment of such rights is always optative in its nature. That is to say, rights are valued as means of securing particular ends. Basic rights are logically as well as empirically prior to other rights because they are the prerequisites of the exercise of agency. The consequence of this is that the universal, global fulfilment of basic rights takes precedence over the satisfaction of the fuller range of rights peculiar to the particular state and society. 'Takes precedence' – but in no way refutes or undermines such rights, which are themselves the product and consequence of agency.

The satisfaction of basic rights, the provision of resources to satisfy needs without whose satisfaction purposive human action is impossible, becomes the first task of global distributive justice. But basic rights are by no means the only source of distributive justice-claims. They are not commutative or restorative in their nature; that is, they apply independently of any previous action or inaction by others. Agency leads first to basic rights, and then on to the fuller range of political and social, public and personal, rights and obligations. The material substance of these latter of course depends on the stage of social and economic development achieved by a society, and this is at least in part the result of the effectiveness of individual and social action in achieving their goals. There is a didectical relationship between agency and the preconditions of its realisation. The synthetic resolution manifests itself in the practical impossibility of conceiving abstract agency as something wholly separate from the concrete conditions of its self-realisation.

Strict egalitarianism may, in the end, overturn the consequences of agency. Now, to secure the condition of purposive human action is in itself pointless if that action, and its consequences for good or ill, is not allowed to be free and self-determining.

Though it is no ultimate test of the viability of an argument that it conforms to popular prejudices, the arguments we have adduced in favour of basic rights are at least implicitly recognised in many powerful and important social beliefs. It seems to many to be intolerable to assert the abstract, moral equality of individuals and simultaneously to argue that there is no responsibility placed upon any individual or group to provide urgently needed resources for a poor or destitute person without other access to them. It seems equally unacceptable that individual property rights should be made the cardinal tenet and assumption of liberal political philosophy in a world in which mass starvation persists. Hayek believes that these responses are merely 'atavistic'.[76] On the contrary, the philosophical premises of the basic rights argument lend to them a powerful justification beyond the sphere of the purely emotive.

Basic Rights and Distributive Justice

That social life generates special rights of reciprocity in consequence of the self-limitation which co-operative existence requires is more perspicuous than more grandiloquent notions of social contracts. A climate of reasonably settled expectations as a condition of enjoying such special rights may itself be understood as a corollary right. But the content of these special rights is not a matter of indifference from the standpoint of distributive justice. There is an important sense in which respect for individuals gives rise to justice-claims against society.

A central weakness of modern libertarian and neo-liberal political theory is that, in their denial that there is such a thing as social justice or positive rights, they fail to perceive that people do take the level of their incomes as an indicator of the social esteem in which they stand, and as an implied recognition of their value. The context in which such recognition occurs includes a distribution of resources according to some widely if approximately understood (though not necessarily accepted) 'index' of values attached to various occupations. Being thus recognised, in addition to having one's basic rights respected, is an important part of the sense of belonging to a society, and of being thus acknowledged. This is another facet of the fact that the meaning and value of social goods are largely specific to societies in the way that basic rights are not.[77]

The protection of these rights, and the preservation of conditions of social justice in which rights of agency and social respect are secured, is the heart of the moral justification of the state. Where social justice addresses basic rights it is categorical in its nature, but it is also highly particular in its relation to cultural understanding and the assignment of values within each society. It is the corresponding particularity of the state, in most instances formed by long interaction with its society, which is the origin of the special relation of the state to justice. It is, however, the universal element of moral propositions that prevents the sphere of justice being exclusively defined by states' boundaries, and prevents the rights of the individual being ascribed to him solely as a member of his society. Cultural pluralism is limited by basic rights.

A consequence of this is that intervention in a society in which basic rights are violated has a different moral character from other intervention defended on grounds of prohibiting unjustifiable practices. The latter kind of intervention is paternalistic, and threatens cultural autonomy. In practice it may be difficult to distinguish one kind of intervention from another, and consequentialist arguments against intervention still apply, but to deny such a difference is to assign an absolute moral character to the state, and to make cultural integrity subordinate to this.

The persistence of injustice within developing states is repeatedly urged as a reason for denying aid. Where such aid is essential to the securing of basic rights, the stipulation that it be linked to domestic reforms does not amount to illegitimate intervention. It addresses the claims of the individual and the society to just treatment, and no absolute value can be attached to sovereignty as a counter to those claims, nor as a means of defining every external attempt to influence state policy as paternalistic.

Where attempts to induce governments to introduce social reform meet with limited success, the obligation to transfer resources is not absolutely terminated, as long as there is at least a possibility of some of the resources reaching those who are currently deprived of basic rights. To deny all forms of aid because of the self-interested stance of ruling elites is to bring further punishment on the victims of their policies, and to deny the validity of their independent claims for justice. The primacy of the state itself, as represented by its rulers, as the source of claims is asserted by such a denial.

The tying of aid to increases in improvements in social justice no more destroys the practical exercise of sovereignty, and its role as the organising principle of international relations, than does the recurrence of military intervention, or the existence of customary international law. Instead, it provides a new determinant of the environment in which sovereignty is effective. It is when 'absolute' sovereignty is asserted as the indispensable condition of the state's guarantee of justice and rights that what is essentially a means becomes an end. Intervention automatically constitutes unjust interference only when it is not aimed at securing the most basic of those rights, but at protecting an economic or political hierarchy that embodies injustice. Intervention is not to be condemned simply because it trespasses in the inner sanctum of the deity known as 'sovereignty'.

5.5 THE COMPLEX INSTRUMENTALITY OF THE STATE

There are now sufficient grounds on which to make a full defence of a complex instrumentalist theory, and to show the validity of the additions we have made to the specification of our revised and expanded paradigm beyond the basic premises of the classical natural law tradition. We can see in particular how important the concept of agency as the primary source of rights has become in the development of our theory of the state and international justice. In this summary of our argument, it will be necessary to restate the initial premises from which we have drawn our conclusions thus far, as well as to see what further conclusions can be reached.

The Continuing Relevance of Natural Law Tradition

Our first proposition in Chapter 1 was that natural law tradition continues to offer the most appropriate conception of the state and international justice. The difficulties in the natural law prescription of individual rights are met by the idea of agency as the ground of rights.

The insights of natural law theory, at least prior to Vattel, and the tradition of the 'society of states' to which they led, have been defended, albeit selectively and not without criticism, as continuing to offer the most satisfactory background ethical theory of international relations. The ethical self-subsistence of the state is denied, whilst a moral theory respecting the rights of individuals as ultimate, but which at the same time transcends their purely egoistic nature, is offered. What natural law theory by itself has lacked is a deeper theory of rights and of the central place of rights in defining the conditions of the legitimacy of a particular state. The strong conception of human rights offered in the present study, and their location at the centre both of the justification of the state and of principles of international justice, helps at least to supply this omission.

Natural law theory does not of itself set out to bring about an international society; its relevance depends on the existence of sufficient mutual understanding and respect to allow international relations to be conducted on a basis of at least a minimum set of shared values. Positive law is a practical index of international society; natural law specifies its ideally binding principles. We have seen that the present international system merits the description of a society, albeit one in which international law only imperfectly reflects ideal justice. Nonetheless, it is a society to which the principles of natural law remain highly relevant.

The metaphysical status of natural law and the difficulties in specifying those features of human personality and the 'greatest good' for man are well recognised. These difficulties are perhaps less relevant in the tradition of natural law as it relates to international society than in its application to domestic society. In its international application, it does not set out to determine the conditions of social existence *ab initio*, but to provide ultimate standards of conduct in the relations of existent social and legal entities, that is, sovereign states. We have seen enough evidence to sustain the argument that it is precisely because the natural law tradition does not specify immutable and precise principles applicable to each and every circumstance of conflict over issues of international justice, but rather retains the character of a flexible yet comprehensive moral outlook on international relations, that it gains its strength. It seeks to provide an effective framework for international moral theory, one that recognises both the diversity and the flawed nature of existing political institutions and practices.

The conceptual and practical distinction between natural law and positive, international law or the Law of Nations – higher and lower law, we may say – is more apposite than the essentially unstable ethical dualism of the realists. The natural law tradition recognises at once the inevitability of cultural and political diversity, the perilous nature of intervention in support of any transcendent conception of the good, and the critical tension which exists between the undoubtedly universal element in our conceptions of rights and justice and the dangers of 'cultural imperialism'. Charges of the latter are usually brought where critiques of justice and rights-practices come to reflect and to exacerbate inequalities of international power.

At the same time, the natural law tradition avoids outright moral scepticism or solipsism. It embodies ultimate principles as ideal criteria of just conduct and relations, but insists that the translation of such principles into political action should occur in a context of tolerance and restraint. It is recognised that intervention and force, even – or especially – when employed in the service of high moral principles, are often the causes of other moral evils of equal or greater magnitude.

If the natural law tradition recognises the persistence of conflict, it also stresses the possibilities and advantages of co-operation. It is based on the conviction that historical experience and human reason lead to deductive principles concerning how states and societies can best coexist. In a world of vast nuclear stockpiles, of a growing global ecological crisis, and of resurgent nationalistic and ethnic aspirations, it is ill-advised to sneer at the idea that we might have something to learn from the moral aspirations – or even the practices – of theorists and statesmen of distant centuries.

The natural law or 'society of states' conception of world politics nevertheless faces up squarely to the conflict of the real and the ideal. If pure natural law is an image of the moral ideal, the best to be hoped for from positive domestic and international law is that it should embody a code of behaviour that men and states can actually live up to. The natural law tradition accepts the distance between the good and the possible. It embraces an authentic moral realism against the seemingly sophisticated but often facile and unwarranted scepticism of many authors of the realist school. It accepts the universal element of international moral principles insisted upon by Kant and his successors in the cosmopolitan tradition, but does not ignore the costs or dilemmas of implementing such principles. In short, it rejects the stark choice offered by other traditions between a discounting, or even rejection, of international moral imperatives and an impossible doctrine of moral perfection.

If natural law tradition has been seen to offer a more appropriate description of the ethical context of international relations than either of the other main traditions with which we have been concerned, it still does not adequately describe the most significant moral features of the state in relation to justice and the individual. This is because it lacks an adequate theory of the individual as a bearer of particular rights. Individuals are seen as the ultimate subjects of natural law, but the rights ascribed to them by that law are formalistic; in the end, it is left up to the state to determine their content. The state's legitimacy rests only ambiguously on its upholding of the natural rights of its subjects. Thus, Grotius will not allow subjects the right to rebel against a tyrant, although other states may have the duty to overthrow him.

We saw too that there is a bifurcation in the naturalist tradition on the question of the necessary or voluntary status of obligations between states. A theory of basic rights premised upon the concept of agency sets minimum substantive conditions concerning the relationship of the state to the individual. In the event of the non-fulfilment of these conditions, neither the political authority of the state nor its external justice-claims can be considered to be legitimate. Furthermore, such a theory is necessary to give substance to principles of international distributive justice. *Basic agency rights fill the essential lacuna in natural law theory.*

Justice, the State and Ends in Themselves

The second and third propositions we put forward in Chapter 1 are related, and derive much of their force from natural law premises. They are, however, often associated with liberal, and more especially contractarian, political theories which may dispense entirely with natural rights assumptions.

Our second proposition was that the state can never constitute an absolute, an ethical end in itself. The state can never rise above being a means for the realisation of individual and collective values. These values change over time and across societies, but possess a universal and irreducible content in the form of basic rights. For this reason, there can never be an a priori defence of the state. The value of the state is derivative; it comes from its securing of other, first order values.

Our third proposition concerned the content of those values. It was that the securing of individual and collective rights forms the basis of the state's legitimacy, and the legitimacy of its own mediated justice-claims. At the same time, we have seen that neither natural rights in the classical formulation nor legal-positivist accounts of rights are sufficient for our justificatory purposes. Rights based on agency, which point in their positive content to the universal provision of at least minimum conditions of subsistence, must be satisfied.

Since human action also takes place, and finds its meanings, within a social and cultural context, collective rights also follow from the same capacity for agency to which we ascribe basic rights. Indeed, we have argued that 'collective' rights from a formal, ontological point of view are properties of individuals, but of individuals in their capacities as parts of a whole.

One of the greatest and most lasting values of the classical natural law tradition is in its dispelling of the idea that the rights and other justice-claims of states can be considered as self-subsistent, arising directly from the state's supposedly autonomous moral personality. All organicist or constitutive conceptions of the state as in some way existing on a different, higher ethical plane than that of mere individuals are rejected. They are, in fact, no more than insidiously misleading metaphors.

The most important premise we have drawn from the natural law tradition, and for which we have argued most strongly, is that states have rights and obligations only because individuals do, and the same moral laws ultimately specify what these are in either case. The state is the guarantor, not the progenitor, of rights and justice.

The role of the state in securing particular forms of international justice has been analysed from a viewpoint of the individual as ethically prior to the state, and from the view that the interests and welfare of the individual provide the criteria of legitimacy of the external claims of the state. These and all other ethical features of the state are wholly derivative of those of its members. Rights are not reified in the state. The very idea of an international society, as understood in its moral sense by the natural law theorists, depends for its coherence on the supposition that individuals are its ultimate constituents, even though their interests are represented mediately by states.

The legitimacy of the state and of its external justice-claims, then, lies in its relationship to the rights of its people *qua* people and not merely *qua* citizens. This means, as we have already indicated, that we must look beyond the particular rights embodied in a given legal and particular order if we are to determine the conditions of that legitimacy. Otherwise, we shall remained trapped in a circular, even tautologous argument, unable to ask meaningful questions about the nature of the state from outside, as it were. We should have to abandon any serious enquiry into the forms of international justice or the state's relationship towards them. We should have to accept that rights and all other justice-claims are essentially statist terms of discourse, which serve at best as rhetorical devices when translated into the language and the practice of international relations.

Individual Rights, Collective Rights, and the State

Fourthly, there is a sense in which all forms of justice are primarily both individualist and distributive in their form. Justice is concerned with the way rights, resources, opportunities, privileges and obligations are assigned to particular people. It points to particular, distinguishing features of individuals as appropriate criteria for distributing these benefits and burdens. However, 'social justice' is often used as a synonym for 'distributive justice' in its more usual and narrower sense, that which concerns the allocation of wealth – the whole range of economic and social resources – among members of a society. Social justice in this sense recognises the mutual obligations of members of society in respect of material provision, and usually specifies further criteria such as equality of opportunity, rights of political participation and representation, and other goods held to be important for the equal respect of persons. But it remains, when defined in this way, essentially individualistic in its assignments. Only when social justice is defined in a broader sense, one that recognises the fully social aspect of the individual's existence and stresses the rights of individuals as participants in the social whole, does it become remotely adequate as a condition of the legitimacy of the state's internal standing or of its international claims.

Social justice understood in the latter, broader sense involves more than the satisfaction of the claims of individuals, and embraces the fact that collective rights are more than the sum of the rights of all the individuals who make up the group. The presupposition here is that whilst the purely abstract individual is a source of ends from a formal point of view, no substance can be given to his claims for justice unless he is considered as a member of society. Justice is above all a relational idea, and social relations do not have an 'objective' existence independent of the meanings attributed to them by human beings.

We might seem about to fall into a contradiction. If collective rights are in some sense qualitatively different from the claims of individuals, it might seem that the state, which has been accepted as a necessary but not a sufficient or exclusive condition for the realisation of justice and rights, attains by the same token a moral standing which is different from, and perhaps greater than, the aggregate of the morally legitimate claims of the people who compose it.

Fortunately, it is not necessary to accept an individualistic account of justice, nor to deny any distinct meaning to collective claims, in order to avoid this apparent contradiction. The nature of the rights of states and of nations can be understood as conceptually independent (though related in terms of the reasons for their assignation) of those rights we normally think of as belonging to individuals as such, without conceding that the former have in any sense a life of their own. Groups, including states, would not have any rights if their citizens had none. But it does not follow from this that the individual's needs or rights can readily be met irrespective of conditions pertaining to the group as a whole, if the social identity of the individual and his own deeper sense of well-being depends closely on his affiliation with the social group.

The state acts too as a protective sphere of distinct cultural, ethnic and social traditions; it is a sphere, properly understood, of mores, rather than an independent and self-subsistent ethical order. Self-determination as a justice-claim may be spuriously made, may in certain cases express political demands that can be met at a level below full political independence, and certainly may serve as an internationally disruptive principle with significant moral costs. There is ultimately no answer to the question why nations as opposed to other collective identities should alone have the 'right' to political independence. It seems that in a world of other nation-states, the chronic hunger some nations feel to give concrete expression and reinforcement to their self-identity can be satisfied by nothing less than sovereign statehood. This satisfaction becomes for them the condition of the realisation of most, or even all, other values.

Cosmopolitan theorists might respond by saying that the individual's legitimate interest in the wider social good may simply be counted as the grounds of one of his rights. This would be a recognition of the fact that it is a feature of certain rights or justice-claims that they cannot be enjoyed by the individual unless they are enjoyed by others. This in itself, the argument might continue, does not give rise to collective claims or rights which are understandable only in themselves.

An important distinction must be made here. Certain forms of justice or rights can only be enjoyed in common with others; but other sorts of justice or rights can only be understood in relation to the group. My enjoyment of material wealth may be diminished by the mass poverty with which I am surrounded; how much it will be diminished depends upon my psychological traits and not upon ethical principles as such. But I cannot be said to enjoy a right of self-determination whilst other members of my nation are living in political subjection, for the very obvious but important reason that such a right is indivisible, and this defines the nature of a collective right.

We can understand justificatory doctrines of the state based on claims of self-determination, or on some other corporate aspect of the state's relationship to society – doctrines which cosmopolitan theorists disallow – without either reifying the state or regarding it as a source of ends in itself, just as we can understand the qualitatively distinct nature of collective rights without losing sight of the fact that individuals, and not collectivities of any kind, are the only ends in themselves.

The Values Secured by the State Point Beyond It

Our fifth proposition was that, however great the role of the state in securing justice and rights, the nature of those values points beyond the state as an exclusive sphere for their satisfaction. To understand this more clearly, we have emphasised the quite separate logics of what we have termed 'special rights' and 'basic rights', to which we shall turn in a moment.

The insights of the natural law tradition have supplied this element of universality of rights and justice, at least up until the point in the historical development of that tradition where the direct analogy of states and persons led to the displacement of individuals as the ultimate members of international society and the ultimate subjects of international morality.

The state is indeed 'porous' in terms of international distributive justice, but the content and extent of such claims must be accommodated with the legal-customary rights to resources and to specific forms of treatment by the institutions of the state and by other members of the political community which have their origin in the legal, political and cultural structures of civil society. This accommodation preserves the *droits nécessaires* of natural law theory against the belief common to Vattel and his successors as well as to 'realists' of all historical ages that all other-regarding actions by states are voluntary in their nature.

Such an accommodation is often not easy; but the theory of agency as the basis of rights provides a direct answer to the question, why do we have the rights that we do? and provides, too, a means of reconciling intra-societal rights with obligations existing between states and societies. Most importantly, it gives specific content to those mutual obligations of states to which natural law theory addresses itself, but for which it fails to provide an independent justification. Finally, and in accord with natural law, the concept of agency places the individual firmly at the centre of all justice-claims.

The international securing of basic rights in a world where sufficient resources exist for this to be possible must be the minimum stage at which the special rights of groups and individuals within independent civil societies begin to give rise to obligations of equal or greater concern.

To deny that justice and rights are inescapably statist forms of discourse, that they must assume the political order of the state, is to hold that justice and rights have a continuing existence beyond the state. Basic or subsistence rights create responsibilities elsewhere than for the governments of states in which those rights exist unmet. The location of these rights, not within a particular political or legal order, but within a philosophical conception of individuals-as-agents, means that the above holds true even, indeed especially, when the governments of potential-recipient societies are indifferent to or engaged in the suppression of those rights.

It has emerged from our criticism of cosmopolitan theories that the practical effectiveness of the state in securing justice and rights lends to it a high (though conditional) value as a political institution. We can acknowledge this without holding for one minute to the view that the continuing dominance of the state in the modern world means that the justice found within it, where it is found, is the only sort that matters. We can also acknowledge that there may be relatively few unvarying and precise principles enabling us to apportion rights, resources and other goods between the province of the state and the universal human interest. But however high the level of generality of such principles, and however broad and non-specific their scope may seem to be, to discover them is of the highest importance.

What has been offered here is a set of first principles and conditions which require specific and concrete application to be of value in terms of practical policy. All political action begins with a 'world view' of some kind. There never has been nor can be action without values. Such action would best be guided by the recognition, at the very least, that justice does not stop at the water's edge.

Ideal Theory in the Real World

This leads us on to consider our final proposition. Noting that, whilst the values secured by the state do indeed point beyond it, the state remains the principal or only means of securing justice and rights for most of the world's people, we have emphasised that to make any sense of the problem of the state and international justice, the conflict between claims of sovereignty and of justice and rights must be considered at its empirical and normative levels. The analysis offered so far permits us to draw a number of conclusions concerning this conflict.

We have dealt at length with one of the central disputes in the political theory of international relations, a dispute that extends beyond the cosmopolitan versus realist terms of debate. It is between those who see nothing distinctive about the state in its capacity to promote human values (a position held by those who base the defence of the state on a 'narrow' reductionist criterion such as social justice in the restricted sense we discussed above, as well as by more thorough-going cosmopolitans) and those who maintain that the sorts of justice-claims with which we have been concerned all point in their 'inner logic' to the state as the condition of their meaning as well as their realisation.

A complex instrumentalist characterisation of the state and international justice offers an alternative to these persistently opposed views, the ultimate sterility of which is indicated by the seeming impossibility of any discourse between them.

Just as we have rejected the view that all claims for justice find their meaning only within the state, and just as we have rejected the deprecation or denial of the state as a necessary arena of justice, so we should reject the view that the relevance of the state in the promotion of human justice is no more than a practical misfortune of contemporary world politics (or perhaps of human nature). There are classes of interests and rights which it is difficult if not impossible to imagine being upheld if the sovereign state were to disappear. We must repeat that no narrowly reductionist, and certainly no exclusively individualistic, justificatory theory of the state can be allowed to follow from the denial, already made, of its moral autonomy. The state as an independent political order may serve as the only effective means of protecting the rights and welfare of collectivities, and of safeguarding and expressing the self-identity and cultural integrity of a people. The emphasis is on the word may: such claims are often made quite spuriously by the leaders of states and of majority groups within them in an attempt to draw a veil across injustice and oppression.

We have insisted on two conditions for the admissibility of the securing of collective rights as an argument for the legitimacy of the external claims of the state. The first is that collective rights are to be understood as ultimately being assigned to the individuals who make up the collectivities, not to mythical corporate entities called 'the people' or whatever. They differ from what we usually think of as individual rights in that they refer to individuals in their aspect of participants in a collectivity, individuals whose welfare cannot be secured or even understood outside this context.

The second condition is that justice-claims made by states by virtue of their securing collective justice must be demonstrably valid in the particular instance; there can be no appeal to any general principle of the inviolability of sovereignty to set aside the facts of the particular state's case.

It is evident that the tension between prescriptive – let alone ideal – political philosophy and the reality of international practice is most acute at this point. After all, states are generally regarded as sovereign, and their rights as such respected, whatever the degree of domestic observation of individual and collective justice and rights.

Yet no philosophically coherent theory of the state and international justice can draw back from this practical conflict. We cannot now allow, at this late stage, the state to present itself as an absolute, as a self-subsistent ethical being, or let its leaders plead immunity from moral censure. If a state does nothing to secure the rights and other valid justice-claims of its people, if it is instead indifferent to those claims or deliberately violates them, its claims of sovereignty and associated rights deserve no moral respect whatever. There can never be a presumptive claim of sovereignty because the state can never be considered as a morally independent entity.

There are good pragmatic grounds for respecting the principle of state sovereignty in international relations as a general rule, and sometimes even in the case of a state that evidently violates the principles of legitimacy we have described. We have noted that individual and collective intervention against offenders in this respect may do greater damage in respect of justice and rights than it succeeds in preventing. A high value must be placed on peace and security. But none of this is an argument against insisting on a prescriptive theory of the state, or against denying it ethical self-subsistence. It is only to say that in the real world the moral and material costs and benefits of alternative courses of action must be considered. Whatever the dictates of the prudential arguments, they can never render the existing state of affairs less reprehensible or regrettable. Those who maintain that practical politics must set aside moral evaluations have no way of explaining how moral dilemmas come about, and come about constantly. If there were no moral principles, there could be no moral dilemmas. We could never understand Max Weber's distinction between an ethic of pure intentionality and an ethic of responsibility if we ever believed that moral principles were optional in their binding effect.[78]

Once again, natural law theory has shown us the way. It distinguishes a sphere of positive law, or the Law of Nations, from the sphere of natural law not merely out of a recognition of the incorrigibility of human conduct, but because it insists that man's highest duty is to seek justice in the world of the possible and the actual. At the same time, it never allows conduct, whether at the individual or international level, to be excused from judgement before the higher court of natural law. If there were not rules of justice that transcended what is commonly, or for that matter ever, attained in international relations, then there would be no standards by which to judge one type of action as better than another. This is more than most realists can swallow. The conflict between the just and the practically attainable is not something to be conjured away by the equivocal semantics of the realist school; it is part of the fabric of the world we are all obliged to live in.

Conclusion

The defence of the state as the means by which most rights for most people are secured must always depend on the global securing of basic human rights. This is the starting-off point for any theory of international justice, and it follows from our treatment of the priority question between special rights, or those rights peculiar to a particular political society, and basic rights. The conditions for the domestic legitimacy of the state, and therefore of the range of its external justice-claims, only become fully operative in a world where all basic human rights are met. Then the realm of special rights as we have defined them provides a defence of the state as a distinct ethical order, though the continuing priority of basic rights must always deny to the state any pretence to moral autonomy.

The above is a straightforward and uncompromising statement of our general conception of the role of the state in securing the values of justice in domestic society and in international relations. Its simplicity as a condition of the defence of the state belies the stark fact that what it asks for in world politics has so far never been achieved. Nor does it seem likely that such conditions as we have specified will be achieved in the imaginable future. We have no choice but to make do with a very poor second-best.

It is absurd to deny the validity of the state as a constituency of justice or of political obligation because we live in a world where basic rights are in fact not secured. Here, the ideal confronts the real most acutely, and inevitably leaves us feeling uncomfortable. But we should not fail to insist that the philosophical defence of the state in the context of international justice depends precisely on the securing of basic rights globally. What our analysis has revealed to us is that the fundamental principles of international obligation and the fundamental principles of the legitimacy of the state are one and the same.

Justice in international relations both transcends the state and in its various forms is constrained to accept it as the practical means of its implementation. Claims for justice must in the largest part be secured by the state and in the relations of states, through, for example, international resource transfers and international law. Increasingly, as the economic and therefore the political independence of states is diminished by the emergence of a truly global economy, it is at the inter-state level that all justice-claims must be put forward.

242

This is only a counsel of despair if we believe that the moral content, and capacity for improvement, of international relations is both fixed and very limited. We saw, particularly in our discussions of international law as a vehicle of global justice and of the conditions permitting a greater degree of international distributive justice, that the pessimism of the realists in these respects is both unwarranted and self-fulfilling.

The instrumentalist conception recognises and even insists on the recognition of the conflict between sovereignty and the imperatives of justice and rights as a paradigm conflict of ideal and empirical political theory. At the same time, our approach also insists that it is insufficient simply to expose the fact of this conflict. The arguments of those writers who have considered it as an ineluctable fact of international life have borne perhaps the main brunt of our criticism. The necessity of justifying the state in moral terms must doubtless require the ultimate resolution of this conflict. Such a resolution cannot come about at the level of theory; it can only come about through practical action to increase the degree of justice in international relations.

Yet we have said that the resolution of the conflict seems to lie far off. Instead, the ideal must often be subordinated to the empirical, and the truer correspondence of the cosmopolitan ideal to the universal nature of moral values be admitted in principle, and partly ignored in practice. The best justification for the state is probably that it is better now and for the foreseeable future at upholding rights and justice than any alternative political institution. It is understandable if a large part of the world's population responds to this conclusion with little enthusiasm.

It is also understandable if the reader feels disappointed inasmuch as I have failed to answer all of the questions which he or she might have hoped to have seen more light shed upon. I mainly set out to frame these questions as clearly as I possibly could. I am happy to leave the rest for others.

Notes

INTRODUCTION

1. See in the area of justice, especially Robert Nozick, *Anarchy, State and Utopia* (Oxford, 1974) and John Rawls, *A Theory of Justice* (Oxford, 1972); of rights, Ronald Dworkin, *Taking Rights Seriously* (London, 1978) and Alan Gewirth, *Human Rights* (Chicago and London, 1982); and of civil association and the nature of law, F.A. Hayek, *Law, Legislation and Liberty*, vol. I (London, 1976) and Michael Oakeshott, *On Human Conduct* (Oxford, 1975).

2. See, especially, Charles Beitz, *Political Theory and International Relations* (Princeton, 1979); Christopher Brewin, 'Justice in International Relations', in Michael Donelan, ed., *The Reason of States* (London, 1978); Mervyn Frost, *Towards a Normative Theory of International Relations* (Cambridge, 1986); Terry Nardin, *Law, Morality and the Relations of States* (Princeton, 1983); and W.H. Smith, 'Justice: National, International or Global?', in Ralph Pettman ed., *Moral Claims in World Affairs* (London, 1979).

3. See S.I. Benn and R.S. Peters, *Social Principles and the Democratic State* (London, 1959), pp. 63–71; John Gray, *Liberalism* (Milton Keynes, 1986), pp. 45–50.

4. See our later discussion of Alan Gewirth, *Human Rights* (Chicago and London, 1982) and Henry Shue, *Basic Rights: Subsistence, Affluence and US Foreign Policy* (Princeton, 1980).

1 JUSTICE IN INTERNATIONAL RELATIONS

1. See Werner Levi, 'The Relative Irrelevance of Moral Norms in International Politics', in Richard C. Snyder, H.W. Bruck and Burton Sapin, eds, *Foreign Policy Decision-Making* (New York, 1963). An excellent survey of counter-arguments is given in W.H. Smith, 'Justice: National, International or Global?', in Ralph Pettman, ed., *Moral Claims in World Affairs* (London, 1979). On the historical evolution of conceptions of the relationship between justice, politics and the state, see R.J. Vincent, 'Western Conceptions of a Universal Moral Order', in *British Journal of International Studies*, vol. 4, no. 1, April 1978. A word about our approach generally is in order here: it falls broadly within the 'classical' tradition of understanding international relations. This tradition views moral and philosophical questions as among the most important in the study of world politics. The behaviouristic-scientific (or 'scientistic', depending on one's prejudices) approach to international relations not only fails to address these questions, but often intentionally depreciates their importance or suppresses them altogether. For an excellent review

of the debate between these two schools of analysis in international relations, see Klaus Knorr and James N. Rosenau, eds, *Contending Approaches to International Politics* (Princeton, 1969). See especially the chapters by Morton A. Kaplan, 'The New Great Debate: Traditionalism vs. Science in International Relations', and Hedley Bull, 'International Theory: The Case for a Classical Approach', in that collection. Our position is closest to Bull's. It is also broadly a reductionist position; international relations are explained largely (though not wholly) in terms of the interaction between the domestic economic, political, cultural and ideological structures of states and the institutional framework of the international system. For a contrary view emphasising systemic constraints on states' behaviour, see Kenneth N. Waltz, *Theory of International Politics* (Reading, Mass., 1979). Cf. Kenneth Boulding, 'Theoretical Systems and Political Realities', in *Journal of Conflict Resolution*, vol. 2, 1958; and Richard Rosecrance, 'International Theory Revisited', in International Organization, vol. 35, no. 4, 1981.

2.   Hugo Grotius, *De Jure Belli ac Pacis Libri Tres* (Oxford, 1925); Samuel Pufendorf, *De Jure Naturae et Gentium, Libri Octo* (Oxford, 1934); also, *On the Duty of Man and Citizen* (Cambridge, 1991). See, too, Richard Tuck, *Natural Rights Theories* (Cambridge, 1979). Above all, see Andrew Linklater, *Men and Citizens in the Theory of International Relations* (London, 1982, 1990).

3.   Of the many books that have influenced my thinking about the concept of justice, those I have found especially valuable include: J.R. Lucas, *On Justice* (Oxford, 1980); David Miller, *Social Justice* (Oxford, 1976); John Rawls, *A Theory of Justice* (Oxford, 1972); Nicholas Rescher, *Distributive Justice* (Indianapolis, 1966); Michael Walzer, *Spheres of Justice* (Oxford, 1983); and the collection of essays in *Nomos VI: Justice*, eds Carl J. Friedrich and John W. Chapman (New York, 1963). Above all, see Hans Kelsen's superb *What Is Justice?* (California, 1967). There is a difference, and often a conflict, between what is 'just' in respect of needs, rights or merits, and what is 'justified' as being conducive to some other, valued social purpose: for example, economic growth. See Brian Barry, 'Reflections on Justice as Fairness', in Hugo A. Bedau, ed., *Justice and Equality* (Englewood Cliffs, 1971).

4.   On the meaning of equality of treatment, see Gregory Vlastos, 'Human Worth, Merit, and Equality', in Joel Feinberg, ed., *Moral Concepts* (Oxford, 1969), and Richard McKeon, 'Justice and Equality', in Carl J. Friedrich and John W. Chapman, eds, *Nomos VI: Justice* (New York, 1963). See also T.M. Scanlon, 'Rights, Goals and Fairness', in Stuart Hampshire, ed., *Private and Public Morality* (Cambridge, 1978). The classic statement remains that of R.H. Tawney, *Equality* (London, 1952).

5.   Aristotle, *The Ethics* (Harmondsworth, 1976), V, pp. 177–8.

6.   H.L.A. Hart, *The Concept of Law* (Oxford, 1961), p. 158.

7.   See Amy Gutmann, *Liberal Equality* (Cambridge, 1980), esp. ch. 1. For a vigorous defence of the idea of equality, see Philip Green, *The Pursuit of Inequality* (Oxford, 1981); cf. J.R. Lucas, 'Against Equality', in *Justice and Equality*, ed. Hugo A. Bedau (Englewood Cliffs, 1971); and Nozick, *Anarchy, State, and Utopia*, pp. 232–8.

8. Aristotle, *Ethics*, pp. 176–7.
9. David Miller, *Social Justice* (Oxford, 1976).
10. Ibid., pp. 151–2.
11. H.L.A. Hart, 'Are There Any Natural Rights?', in Jeremy Waldron, ed., *Theories of Rights* (Oxford, 1984), p. 83.
12. Ibid., p. 84.
13. Ibid., p. 85.
14. See also W.N. Nelson, 'Special Rights, General Rights and Social Justice', in *Philosophy and Public Affairs*, vol. 3, Summer 1974.
15. For the argument that rights to resources are both primary and incompatible with distribution according to any principle of aggregate utility or other socially derived maximand, see Nozick, *Anarchy, State, and Utopia*, pp. 167–74; see also E. Mack, 'Distributionism Versus Justice', in *Ethics*, vol. 86, no. 2, 1976.
16. Miller, *Social Justice*, p. 148. For a discussion of rights and needs as species of interests, see Lucas, *On Justice*, ch. 2.
17. Such an equality of respect is the foundational assumption of Rawls' *A Theory of Justice*. See discussion of this in Ronald Dworkin, *Taking Rights Seriously* (London, 1978), ch. 6. On the Rawlsian derivation of principles of justice, and possible alternatives, see D.W. Rae, 'A Principle of Simple Justice', in Peter Laslett and James Fishkin, eds, *Philosophy, Politics and Society* (Oxford, 1979).
18. See Henry Shue, *Basic Rights: Subsistence, Affluence and US Foreign Policy* (Princeton, 1980), ch. 5, §5.
19. On the inter-connectedness of these justice-claims, and their historical development, see Julius Stone, 'Approaches to the Notion of International Justice', in Richard A. Falk and Cyril E. Black, eds, *The Future of the International Legal Order* (Princeton, 1969). It may be that an economic or welfare conception of a 'world interest' is easier to define than is such an interest in social and political terms. See Kenneth Boulding, 'The Concept of a World Interest', in Bert F. Hoselitz, ed., *Economics and the Idea of Mankind* (New York, 1965).
20. See Hersch Lauterpacht, 'The Grotian Tradition in International Law', *British Yearbook of International Law*, vol. XXIII, 1946, pp. 1–53.
21. Emile Durkheim, *The Division of Labor in Society* (New York, 1933), part 1, chs 2–4.
22. See Karl Marx, 'Contribution to the Critique of Political Economy', in Lewis S. Feuer, ed., *Basic Writings on Politics and Philosophy* (London and Glasgow, 1969), pp. 84–5. Marx famously refused to define capitalism as unjust, because for him there could be no meaning assigned to such a term other than the juridical and political meanings corresponding to existing social and economic relations in a given society, at a particular state of historical development; see *Capital*, vol. I (New York, 1967), p. 194. Marx's view stands in absolute opposition to the conceptions of justice to be defended in the present study, but there is no space to pursue the matter here. See Robert C. Tucker, 'Marx and Distributive Justice', in Friedrich and Chapman, eds, *Nomos VI:*

Justice, op. cit.; Steven Lukes, *Marxism and Morality* (Oxford, 1985); and Alan W. Wood, 'The Marxian Critique of Justice', in *Philosophy and Public Affairs*, vol. 1, Spring 1972.

23. Hedley Bull, *The Anarchical Society* (London, 1977), p. 83.
24. Charles Beitz, *Political Theory and International Relations* (Princeton, 1979).
25. Ibid., pp. 76–9.
26. This is a common feature of the realist tradition discussed in Chapter 2.5. See Bull, *Anarchical Society*, pp. 93–8.
27. See discussion in Ali Mazrui, *Towards a Pax Africana* (London, 1967), ch. 8.
28. A view strongly maintained by Levi, 'The Relative Irrelevance of Moral Norms in International Politics', op. cit.
29. Hans J. Morgenthau, *Politics Among Nations* (New York, 1985), pp. 349–52.
30. See discussion of Vattel in Chapter 2.3, and Peter F. Butler, 'Legitimacy in a States System: Vattel's Law of Nations', *The Reason of States*, ed. Michael Donelan (London, 1978).
31. Ian Brownlie, 'The Expansion of International Society: Consequences for the Law of Nations', in Hedley Bull and Adam Watson, eds, *The Expansion of International Society* (Oxford, 1984), p. 361.
32. Ibid., pp. 361–2.
33. James Turner Johnson, *Just War Tradition and the Restraint of War* (Princeton, 1981), pp. 76–7; and Francisco de Vitoria, *Political Writings* (Cambridge, 1991) ch. 6.
34. Hersch Lauterpacht, 'The Grotian Tradition in International Law', in *British Yearbook of International Law*, vol. XXIII, 1946, p. 27.
35. See John Stuart Mill, 'A Few Words on Non-Intervention', in *Dissertations and Discussions*, vol. III. (London, 2nd ed., 1875); and F.S. Northedge, *The International Political System* (London, 1976), chs 2, 3.
36. See Walter Schiffer, *The Legal Community of Mankind* (New York, 1954, 1972), part 1, ch. 1.
37. As Beitz titles part II of his *Political Theory and International Relations*.
38. Ibid., part II, §6.
39. Again, the essence of Beitz's final view.
40. See Mervyn Frost, *Towards a Normative Theory of International Relations* (Cambridge, 1986).
41. Ibid., ch. 6 passim.
42. See Terry Nardin, *Law, Morality and the Relations of States* (Princeton, 1983). This position owes much to Oakeshott, *On Human Conduct*, esp. part 3, 'On Civil Association'.
43. Oakeshott, op. cit., p. 326.
44. See Aquinas, *Philosophical Texts*, XV–XX (London, 2nd imp., 1952).
45. See discussion of C.W. Jenks' *The Common Law of Mankind* (London, 1958) in Chapter 4.4.
46. Bull, *Anarchical Society*, p. 30.
47. See Chapter 5.4–5.6, and B.F. Midgley, *The Natural Law Tradition and the Theory of International Relations* (London, 1975), ch. 6.

2 POLITICAL REALISM AND THE PRIMACY OF THE STATE

1. Thomas Hobbes, *Leviathan* (Harmondsworth, 1968), ch. XII, p. 185.
2. Ibid., ch. XII, p. 186.
3. Ibid., ch. XIV, p. 190.
4. Ibid., ch. XIV, p. 190.
5. A wholly prudential interpretation of obligation in respect of just behaviour under the Hobbesian contract is offered in Brian Barry, 'Warrender and His Critics', in Jack Lively and Andrew Reeve, eds, *Modern Political Theory* (London, 1989).
6. On Hobbes' account of the sovereign, and the nature of political obligation generally, see Michael Walzer, *Obligations* (Cambridge, Mass., 1970), ch. 4.
7. Hobbes, *Leviathan*, ch. XVIII, pp. 230–1.
8. Ibid., ch. XIII, pp. 187–8.
9. For a provocative discussion of 'crackpot realism', see C. Wright Mills, *The Causes of World War Three* (New York, 1958).
10. See discussion of Hobbes' state of nature in Marshall Cohen, 'Moral Skepticism and International Relations', in Charles R. Beitz, Marshall Cohen, Thomas Scanlon and A. John Simmons, eds, *International Ethics* (Princeton, 1985), pp. 23–33. For an interesting comparison of the accounts of pre-social man and of the idea of a social contract in Hobbes, Locke and Rousseau, see Andrzej Rapaczynski, *Nature and Politics* (Ithaca, 1987).
11. Cohen, 'Moral Skepticism and International Relations', p. 31.
12. See Wolfram F. Hanreider, 'Dissolving International Politics: Reflections on the Nation-State', in *The American Political Science Review*, vol. 72, no. 4, 1978.
13. G.W.F. Hegel, *Philosophy of Right* (New York, 1952), §§333–6.
14. See discussion in Chapter 4.4 below.
15. Charles R. Beitz, *Political Theory and International Relations* (Princeton, 1979), pp. 56–63.
16. On the history of the balance of power, see David Hume, 'The Balance of Power', in *Essays Moral, Political and Literary* (London, 1951). For a more recent treatment, see Herbert Butterfield, 'The Balance of Power', in *Diplomatic Investigations*, eds Herbert Butterfield and Martin Wight (London, 1966); and Hedley Bull, *Anarchical Society*, ch. 5. On collective security and world government as alternatives to the balance of power, see Inis L. Claude Jr, *Power and International Relations* (New York, 1962).
17. David Hume, *A Treatise of Human Nature* (Glasgow, 1972), bk. III, p. 290.
18. The supposed inevitability of the use of force wherever the interests of the collectivity is asserted over the global interest and reasons for the limited success with which modern attempts to curb the use of force in warfare have met form the main themes of Robert E. Osgood and Robert W. Tucker, *Force, Order, and Justice* (Baltimore, 1967).

19. 'You cannot win at the conference table anything that *it seems evident* you could not win on the battlefield, or are not resolved to win', Paul Ramsey, *The Just War* (New York, 1968), p. 41.
20. See Richard K. Betts, 'Paranoids, Pygmies, Pariahs and Non-Proliferation', in *Foreign Policy*, vol. XXVII, no. 3, Summer 1977.
21. Cohen, 'Moral Skepticism and International Relations', p. 33.
22. Cf. Hans J. Morgenthau's view that 'interest defined as power is an objective category which is universally valid', *Politics Among Nations* (New York, 1985), p. 10. On the determinants of national power, and on the role of elites in the construction of the 'national interest', see Max Weber, 'Structures of Power', in *From Max Weber: Essays in Sociology* (London, 1948), p. 172. A useful further discussion is in David Beetham, *Max Weber and the Theory of Modern Politics* (Cambridge, 1985), ch. 5.
23. This may be true of political democracies, too. The classic text on this remains C. Wright Mills, *The Power Elite* (New York, 1956).
24. Niccolò Machiavelli, *The Prince* (Harmondsworth, 1961), pp. 99–101.
25. Morgenthau, *Politics Among Nations*, p. 10.
26. Ibid., ch. 1 *passim*. See also Morgenthau, 'Another "Great Debate": The National Interest of the US', in *The American Political Science Review*, vol. 46, no. 4, 1952. A world state might ultimately replace the current state system as the form of global political organisation. But Morgenthau considers that such a state could only come into being after a world community, of the sort he considers to be absent at present, were established. The rediscovery of diplomacy as a means of conciliating and accommodating national interests, rather than as an expression of 'nationalistic universalism' and a means of appealing to domestic interests, is viewed as essential to recreating a world community. See James Speer, 'Hans Morgenthau in the World State', in *World Politics*, vol. 20, no. 2, January 1968.
27. Morgenthau, *Politics Among Nations*, p. 12. See also Robert W. Tucker, 'Professor Morgenthau's Theory of Political Realism', in *American Political Science Review*, vol. 46, no. 1, March 1952; and J.L. Vasquez, 'Colouring it Morgenthau', in *British Journal of International Studies*, vol. 5, 1979.
28. Vasquez, op. cit., p. 13. For a critical response to Morgenthau's account of the national interest by another realist writer, see Raymond Aron, *Peace and War* (London, 1966), pp. 591–600. Aron argues that the nature of ideologies and national goals, and the threats posed thereby to other states, must qualify mutual respect of national interests as a prudential and quasi-moral principle.
29. See Kenneth W. Thompson, *The Moral Issue in Statecraft* (Baton Rouge, 1966). For a general survey of realist thought and its historical origins, see also his *Political Realism and the Crisis of World Politics* (Princeton, 1960).
30. Thompson, *The Moral Issue in Statecraft*, pp. 137–8. For an interesting and more contemporary statement of a realist position, see J.D.B. Miller, *World of States* (London, 1981).
31. Hume, *A Treatise of Human Nature*, III, pt. II, esp. §§1 and 2; for a good discussion of Hume on justice, see Barry Stroud, *Hume* (London,

1977), ch. 9. Cf. the famous arguments of Thomas Paine, *Rights of Man* (Harmondsworth, 1984), pp. 163–4. For Paine, 'everything [to] which government can usefully add... has been performed by the common consent of society, without government' (p. 164). The indefeasible rights of man are more threatened by government than secured by it.

32. See Mills, *The Power Elite*, chs 7–10. For a more recent argument for the inherent class bias of the institutions of the modern state, see Ralph Miliband, *The State in Capitalist Society* (London, 1986). See also T.B. Bottomore, *Elites and Society* (Harmondsworth, 1966). Cf. the liberal-pluralist theory of politics, in which government policy reflects the outcome of the competition of societal interests within a political system allowing high degrees of representation and issue-contestation. See Robert A. Dahl, *Polyarchy: Participation and Opposition* (New Haven, 1971).

33. The classic 'New Right' statement of the dangers inherent in the collectivist-corporatist state is F.A. Hayek, *Road to Serfdom* (London, 1944). For a more recent attack on the extended state, see Hayek's *New Studies* (London, 1978), chs 7 and 8. For a critical response to New Right arguments, see Ruth Levitas, ed., *The Ideology of the New Right* (Cambridge, 1986).

34. These views are developed in, amongst many other works, George F. Kennan, *American Diplomacy 1900–50* (London, 1952).

35. Reinhold Niebuhr, *Moral Man and Immoral Society* (New York, 1932), p. 9.

36. Ibid. p. 18. See, also, Robert C. Good, 'The National Interest and Political Realism: Niebuhr's "Debate" with Morgenthau and Kennan', in *Journal of Politics*, vol. 22, no. 4, November 1960; and John H. Herz, 'Political Realism Revisited', in *International Studies Quarterly*, vol. 25, no. 2, 1981.

37. Ernst Cassirer, *The Myth of the State* (New Haven and London, 1946), part 3, *passim*.

38. For these arguments, see John H. Herz, *International Politics in the Atomic Age* (New York, 1959).

39. For Herz's later reflections, see 'The Territorial State Revisited: Reflections on the Future of the Nation-State', in James A. Rosenau, ed., *International Politics and Foreign Policy: A Reader in Research and Theory* (New York, 1969).

40. See David Luban, 'The Romance of the Nation-State', in *Philosophy and Public Affairs*, vol. 9, no. 4, Summer 1980.

41. John Locke, *Two Treatises of Government* (London, 1924), book II, V.

42. Morgenthau, *Politics Among Nations*, p. 13.

43. See Benedetto Croce, *Politics and Morals* (New York, 1945). Croce rejects the idea of a distinct realm of 'political' ethics. *Pace* Hegel, he argues that the moral apotheosis of the state must lead to chronic international disorder. A state that 'elevates' politics to the status of ethics will in the end tolerate no rivals.

44. E.H. Carr, *The Twenty Years' Crisis* (London, 1946), p. 159 and pp. 166–7. See also Whittle Johnson, 'E. H. Carr's Theory of International Relations: A Critique', in *Journal of Politics*, vol. 29, no. 4,

November 1967. For a recent realist argument in a similar vein, J.D.B. Miller, 'Morality, Interests and Rationalization', in Ralph Pettman, ed., *Moral Claims in World Affairs* (London, 1979).

45. See discussion in Morgenthau, *Politics Among Nations*, part 5, ch. 17.
46. See F.A. Hayek, 'The Atavism of Social Justice', in *New Studies* (London, 1978).
47. The blending of old nationalisms and revolutionary fervour is well illustrated in E.H. Carr, *The Russian Revolution from Lenin to Stalin*, chs 9, 10, 18 (London, 1979).
48. J.D.B. Miller, 'Morality, Interests and Rationalization', op. cit.
49. See Kenneth Waltz, *Man, the State, and War* (New York, 1959), ch. 5.
50. See the discussion of this in Niebuhr, *Moral Man and Immoral Society*, chs 9, 10.
51. A theme developed at length in Robert W. Tucker, *The Inequality of Nations* (New York, 1977), discussed further below.
52. A sympathetic treatment of these doctrines is given in David G. Green, *The New Right* (Brighton, 1987).
53. See Inis L. Claude Jr, 'Domestic Jurisdiction and Colonialism', in Martin Kilson, ed., *New States in the Modern World* (Cambridge, Mass., 1975).
54. On the cultural understanding of human rights and the problems of cross-cultural comparisons of rights observance, see R.J. Vincent, *Human Rights and International Relations* (Cambridge, 1986), ch. 3. See also Peter Berger, 'Are Human Rights Universal?', in *Commentary*, vol. 64, no. 3, September 1977.
55. See James Piscatori, 'Islam in the International Order', in Hedley Bull and Adam Watson, eds, *The Expansion of International Society* (Oxford, 1984).
56. Hedley Bull, *The Anarchical Society* (London, 1977), p. 82.
57. See Martin Wight, *Power Politics* (Harmondsworth, 1986).
58. Emerich de Vattel, *The Law of Nations* (Washington DC, 1916), pp. 7–8.
59. See discussion in Julius Stone, 'Approaches to the Notion of International Justice', in Richard A. Falk and Cyril E. Black, ed., *The Future of the International Legal Order* (Princeton, 1969), §III.
60. Louis J. Halle, 'Introduction' to Robert E. Klein, *Sovereign Equality Among States* (Toronto and Buffalo, 1974), pp. ix–x.
61. Robert E. Klein, *Sovereign Equality Among States* (Toronto and Buffalo, 1974).
62. Ibid., p. 5.
63. Ibid., p. 155.
64. On incentives for nuclear proliferation, see George Quester, *The Politics of Nuclear Proliferation* (Baltimore, 1973). See also R.K. Betts, 'Paranoids, Pygmies, Pariahs and Non-Proliferation', in *Foreign Policy*, vol. XXVII, no. 3, Summer 1977; and S. Chan, 'Incentives for Nuclear Proliferation: The Case of International Pariahs', in *Journal of Strategic Studies*, vol. 3, no. 1, May 1980. See also Louis René Beres, *Apocalypse* (Chicago, 1980). On nuclear proliferation as a problem of international interdependence, see Joseph Nye, 'Non-proliferation: A Long-term Strategy', in *Foreign Affairs*, vol. LVI, no. 1, January 1978.

65. Hobbes, *Leviathan*, ch. XIV, pp. 189–90.
66. J.J. Rousseau, 'The State of War', in M.G. Forsyth, H.M.A. Keens-Soper and P. Savigear, eds, *The Theory of International Relations*, (London, 1970), p. 175.
67. Robert W. Tucker, *Inequality of Nations* (New York, 1977). For a review of this book, Bull's *Anarchical Society* and Klein's *Sovereign Equality Among States*, see Graham Evans, 'All States are Equal but . . .', in *Review of International Studies*, vol. 7, no. 1, 1981.
68. For a much more sympathetic account of the claims put forward by the 'Group of 77' states, see R.H. Green and H.W. Singer, 'Towards a Rational and Equitable New International Economic Order', in *World Development*, vol. 3, no. 6, June 1975.
    See also Robert W. Cox, 'Ideologies and the New International Economic Order: Reflections on Some Recent Literature', in *International Organization*, vol. 33, no. 22, 1979.
69. See P.T. Bauer, *Reality and Rhetoric: Studies in the Economics of Development* (London, 1984), for a trenchant statement of the conservative position.
70. See discussion in Bull, *Anarchical Society*, ch. 4, esp. pp. 86–98.
71. Ibid., pp. 96–8.
72. See discussion of Kant's *Perpetual Peace* (New York, 1957) in Chapter 3.1.
73. Noam Chomsky, 'The Rule of Force in International Affairs', in *For Reasons of State* (London, 1973).
74. See discussion of Hans Kelsen's theory of law in Chapter 4.4.
75. This is the position taken by Bull in *The Anarchical Society*, ch. 6. See also Morgenthau, *Politics Among Nations*, pt. 6 *passim* for a similar view of the decentralised nature of the 'enforcement' of international law.
76. Joan Edelman Spero, *The Politics of International Economic Relations* (London, 1977), p. 204.
77. For a criticism of realism as a normative theory, see R.L. Rothstein, 'On the Costs of Realism', in *Political Science Quarterly*, vol. 87, 1972.

3 THE COSMOPOLITAN THEORY OF INTERNATIONAL JUSTICE

1. See Martin Wight, *Systems of States* (Leicester, 1977); and Brian Porter, 'Martin Wight's Political Theory', in Michael Donelan, ed., *The Reason of States* (London, 1978). For an account of the status of moral principles which rejects Kantian absolutism, see J.L. Mackie, *Ethics* (Harmondsworth, 1977).
2. Immanuel Kant, *Fundamental Principles of the Metaphysics of Ethics* (London, 1969), p. 67.
3. Kant, *Perpetual Peace* (Indianapolis and New York, 1957), p. 31.
4. See Kant, 'Idea for a Universal History from a Cosmo-Political Point of View', in M.G. Forsyth, H.M.A. Keens-Soper and P. Savigear, eds, *The Theory of International Relations* (London, 1970).

5. See Kant, 'On the Commonplace: That may be Correct in Theory but is Useless in Practice', in *The Theory of International Relations*, op. cit.

6. Kant, *Perpetual Peace*, p. 11.

7. Ibid., pp. 12–13. On the applicability of this thesis to liberal democratic states in the twentieth century, see Michael W. Doyle, 'Kant, Liberal Legacies and Foreign Affairs', parts I and II, in *Philosophy and Public Affairs*, vol. 12, nos 3 and 4, 1983. For two informative discussions of Kant's international theory, see Ian Clark, *Reform and Resistance in the International Order* (Cambridge, 1980), ch. 2; and F.H. Hinsley, *Power and the Pursuit of Peace* (Cambridge, 1963), ch. 4.

8. Kant, *Perpetual Peace*, p. 16.

9. Ibid., pp. 18–19.

10. Ibid., p. 20.

11. Ibid., p. 4.

12. See 'The Metaphysical Elements of Justice' pp. 247–8, in Forsyth, Keens-Soper and Savigear, eds, *The Theory of International Relations* op. cit. Kant's philosophy makes war the absolute contradiction of universal right. Nonetheless, if war is unavoidable, the problem of just action in the conduct of war from the perspective of the Categorical Imperative remains. For a recent Kantian approach, see Thomas Nagel, 'War and Massacre', in Marshall Cohen, Thomas Nagel and Thomas Scanlon eds, *War and Moral Responsibility* (Princeton, 1974). Cf. Richard Wasserstrom, 'On the Morality of War', in Richard Wasserstrom, ed., *War and Morality* (Belmont, Calif., 1970).

13. Kant, *Perpetual Peace*, p. 19.

14. Ibid., p. 19.

15. S.I. Benn and R.S. Peters, *Social Principles and the Democratic State* (London, 1959), p. 51.

16. See the discussion of Wolff in Chapter 4.4 below.

17. For this argument, see Robert E. Osgood and Robert W. Tucker, *Force, Order, and Justice* (Baltimore, 1967), esp. pt. 1, ch. 3.

18. For a more sympathetic account of the problems and benefits of the transition from Morgenthau's 'Aristocratic International' of diplomatists to the era of democratic diplomacy, see Harold Nicholson, *Diplomacy* (London, 1950), esp. chs 2–4.

19. See Martin Wight, 'Why Is There No International Theory?', in Herbert Butterfield and Martin Wight, eds, *Diplomatic Investigations* (London, 1966). See also Norman Angell, *The Great Illusion* (Cambridge, 1910).

20. Ernst B. Haas, *Beyond the Nation-State* (Stanford, 1964), p. 6. See also Haas, 'Regionalism, Functionalism and Universal International Organisation' in *World Politics*, vol. 8, 1956. For a more general survey of functionalist and regionalist theories, see James E. Dougherty and Robert L. Pfaltzgraff Jr, eds, *Contending Theories of International Relations* (New York, 1981), ch. 10.

21. David Mitrany, *A Working Peace System* (Chicago, 1966), p. 17. See also Mitrany, 'The Functional Approach to World Organisation', in *International Affairs*, vol. 24, no. 3, July 1948. Mitrany continues to argue that, whilst regional organisations have partially altered the

political 'shape' of the state, its essential nature remains unaltered. The state is currently at the limit of its possibilities; see Mitrany, 'The Functional Approach in Historical Perspective', in *International Affairs* vol. 47, no. 3, July 1971.

22. On the over-extension of the state in terms of social provision, see 'The Reintegration of the State in Western Europe', in Martin Kolinsky, ed., *Divided Loyalties* (Manchester, 1978).

23. Mitrany, *A Working Peace System*, p. 65. But cannot the state as we know it be thought to have its own purposes and interests in survival? Cf. Anthony de Jasay, *The State* (Oxford, 1985), Introduction.

24. See Wolfram F. Hanreider, 'Dissolving International Politics: Reflections on the Nation-State', in *The American Political Science Review*, vol. 72, 1978.

25. Herbert Marcuse, *One-Dimensional Man* (London, 1964).

26. John Kenneth Galbraith, *The Affluent Society* (Harmondsworth, rev. ed., 1984).

27. F.A. Hayek, *Law, Legislation and Liberty* (London, 1982), II, ch. 9 (London, 1982); Robert Nozick, *Anarchy State and Utopia* (Oxford, 1974), pt. 2, ch. 7.

28. James Burnham, *The Managerial Revolution* (New York, 1941).

29. In this context, it is worth noting that in Max Weber's account, bureaucracy, whilst viewed as a 'purely technical instrument', is nonetheless not apolitical; indeed, it tends to usurp the sphere of political action which Weber insists must remain independent. See 'Bureaucracy', in *From Max Weber: Essays in Sociology* (London, 1948). On Weber's account of the social bases of bureaucracy, see David Beetham, *Max Weber and the Theory of Modern Politics* (Cambridge, 1985), pp. 63–7.

30. For a view of international integration as something quite distinct from either federalism or functionalism, see Donald J. Puchala, 'Of Blind Men, Elephants and International Integration', in *Journal of Common Market Studies*, vol. 10, no. 3, 1972.

31. See G.W.F. Hegel, *Philosophy of Right* (New York, 1952), §324, §331.

32. On the pressures brought to bear upon the state to 'redistribute' social goods, see Anthony de Jasay, *The State* (Oxford, 1985), esp. ch. 4.

33. For arguments against the welfare state, see David G. Green, *The New Right* (Brighton, 1987), part II, esp. ch. 9. On the so-called 'overload' thesis of the modern welfare state, see Samuel Brittan, *The Economic Consequences of Democracy* (Aldershot, 1988).

34. See John Herz, 'The Territorial State Revisited: Reflections on the Future of the Nation-State', in James A. Rosenau, ed., *International Politics and Foreign Policy* (New York, 1969).

35. See discussion in Steven Lukes, *Individualism* (Oxford, 1973), ch. 20.

36. See Rajni Kothari, *Footsteps into the Future* (Amsterdam, 1974).

37. Ibid., p. 133.

38. Peter Mansfield, *The Arabs* (Harmondsworth, 1978), pp. 319–20.

39. See John Rawls, *A Theory of Justice*, ch. 1, §3; ch. 2, §§11–12.

40. See Brian Barry, 'Justice as Fairness', in Hugo A. Bedau, ed., *Justice and Equality* (Englewood Cliffs, 1971).

41. Richard Falk, *This Endangered Planet* (New York, 1971), p. 323.

42. A collection of essays representative of the main WOMP concerns is in Saul Mendlowitz, ed., *On the Creation of a Just World Order: Preferred Worlds for the 1990s* (New York, 1975).
43. Falk, *This Endangered Planet*, p. 332.
44. Ibid., p. 346.
45. Ibid., p. 347.
46. Cf. J.S. Mill, *Considerations on Representative Government* (London, 1972), ch. 16.
47. Falk, *This Endangered Planet*, p. 352.
48. Robert C. Johansen, *The National Interest and the Human Interest* (Princeton, 1980), p. 21.
49. Ibid., p. 21.
50. A note of dissent about the practicality of global implementation of 'preferred values' is introduced by Carl-Friedrich von Weizsäcker, 'A Sceptical Contribution', in Saul H. Mendlowitz, ed., *On the Creation of a Just World Order* (New York, 1975).
51. Richard Falk, *The End of World Order* (New York, 1983), p. 76.
52. Hedley Bull, *Anarchical Society* (London, 1977), p. 280.
53. Barrington Moore Jr, *Injustice: The Social Bases of Obedience and Revolt* (London, 1979), p. 46.
54. Ibid., pp. 46–7.
55. These views are developed in Frantz Fanon, *The Wretched of the Earth* (Harmondsworth, 1967).
56. See Peter Berger, 'Are Human Rights Universal?', in *Commentary*, vol. 64, no. 3, September 1977.
57. Kothari, *Footsteps into the Future*, p. 10.
58. See Johansen, *The National Interest and the Human Interest*, pp. 31–3; and Falk, *The End of World Order*, p. 76.
59. See Ian Clark, *Reform and Resistance in the International Order* (Cambridge, 1980), esp. Conclusion.
60. On the problems of applying contractarian theories of justice (such as that of John Rawls, examined in Chapter 5) globally, see Peter Danielson, 'Theories, Intuitions and the Problem of Worldwide Distributive Justice', in *Philosophy of the Social Sciences*, vol. 3, no. 4, December 1973.
61. A famous attack on contractarian theories of the state is made by David Hume, 'Of the Original Contract', in *Essays Moral, Political and Literary* (London, 1951). For a modern critique of contract theory, see Barrie Paskins, 'Obligation and the Understanding of International Relations', in Michael Donelan, ed., *Reason of States* (London, 1978). Whilst the force which the state monopolises is never socially neutral in its application, this force is not the only means by which the state maintains order and mediates between conflicting social interests. This fact also presents problems for the global projection of a central political authority as a solution to world order problems. See Inis L. Claude Jr, *Power and International Relations* (New York, 1962), ch. 6, pp. 224–42.
62. See Philip Windsor, 'The Justification of the State', in Michael Donelan, ed., *The Reason of States* (London, 1978).

63. See Jean-Jacques Rousseau, 'Judgement on Saint-Pierre's Project for Perpetual Peace', in Forsyth, Keens-Soper and Savigear, eds, *The Theory of International Relations*, op. cit.

4 JUSTICE IN A SOCIETY OF STATES

1. Walter Schiffer, *The Legal Community of Mankind*, chs. 1 and 2 (New York, 1954, 1972).
2. Hugo Grotius, *De Jure Belli ac Pacis Libri Tres* (Oxford, 1925), *passim* and later specific references.
3. Adda Bozeman, 'The International Order in a Multicultural World', in Hedley Bull and Adam Watson, eds, *The Expansion of International Society* (Oxford, 1984). On the idea of international society generally, see Martin Wight, *Power Politics* (Harmondsworth, 1986), ch. 10; Joseph Frankel, *International Relations* (London, 1964), ch. 6. For a more optimistic, Lockean view of the prospects for international society, see Bull, 'Society and Anarchy in International Relations', in Herbert Butterfield and Martin Wight, eds, *Diplomatic Investigations* (London, 1966); cf. John Locke, *Two Treatises on Government* (London, 1924); and on the possibility of the 'legal and moral climate' of international relations being able to gradually adapt itself to non-Western influences, see Bull, 'The Revolt Against the West' in Hedley Bull and Adam Watson, eds, *The Expansion of International Society* (Oxford, 1984). On differing conceptions of political legitimacy as constraints on the development of international society, see Martin Wight, *Systems of States* (Leicester, 1977), ch. 6.
4. On 'westernism' as an ideological obstacle to development, see Samir Amin, 'Universality and Cultural Spheres', in *Imperialism and Unequal Development* (Sussex, 1977); see also Ronald Dore, 'Unity and Diversity in Contemporary World Culture', in Hedley Bull and Adam Watson, eds, *The Expansion of International Society* (Oxford, 1984).
5. Wight, *Power Politics*, p. 238.
6. Kedourie berates the former metropolitan states for having 'allowed' independence to territories with limited resources and unrepresentative political systems; see 'A New International Disorder', in Hedley Bull and Adam Watson, eds, *The Expansion of International Society* (Oxford, 1984). Kedourie's views on the main sources of international disorder are similar to those of Robert W. Tucker, *Inequality of Nations* (New York, 1977), discussed in Chapter 2.5.
7. See Rupert A. Emerson, 'Self-Determination', in *American Journal of Law*, vol. 65, no. 3, July 1971.
8. Hans J. Morgenthau, *Politics Among Nations* (New York, 1985), pp. 12–13.
9. See discussion of Vattel in 4.3 below.
10. For an uncompromising account of the systemic nature of conflict, see Kenneth N. Waltz, *Theory of International Politics* (Reading, Mass., 1979).

11. When Morgenthau expresses doubt about the possibility of reducing
     international conflict through greater understanding and knowledge,
     he is really being sceptical about the capacity of mass publics to respond
     rationally to information. It is the forces of propaganda and the 'moral
     crusade' for the mind of the common man that he sees as the most
     destructive influence on international relations. See Hans J. Mor-
     genthau, *Politics Among Nations* (New York, 1985), pp. 347–59. Others
     have lamented the intrusion of popular expectations in the rational
     conduct of foreign policy; see Coral Bell, *The Diplomacy of Détente*
     (London, 1977), *passim*. Cf. Noam Chomsky's account of the role of
     intellectuals both in misinforming mass publics and in legitimising the
     actions of the ruling elites into whose service they are co-opted, in his
     Towards a New Cold War (London, 1982), esp. chs 1 and 2. In his view, it
     is the function of ideology to hide the real nature of their actions from
     ruling elites themselves as much as from the attention of their publics.
     Evidently, cultural, racial and ideological stereotypes lead to images and
     interpretations of states' actions and intentions become self-reinforcing,
     and are themselves often sufficient to generate conflict. See Robert
     Jervis, *Perception and Misperception in International Politics* (Princeton,
     1976). On the consequences of misperception of adversaries in a military
     context, see Ken Booth, *Strategy and Ethnocentrism* (London, 1979).
     The relative lack of development of mutual understanding of the na-
     tional, cultural and political context of states' behaviour is seen by some
     writers as a reason for the retarded development of international society.
     See Kenneth Boulding, 'National Images and International Systems', in
     Journal of Conflict Resolution, vol. III, 1959, and John W. Burton, *World
     Society* (Cambridge, 1972).
12. See Morgenthau, *Politics Among Nations*, pp. 384–94.
13. See Robert E. Klein, *Sovereign Equality Among States* (Toronto and
     Buffalo, 1974), pp. 143–55.
14. Ibid., p. 153. The fear of intervention by more powerful states and the
     threat of escalation of violence may, however, discourage new states
     from taking their grievances to the UN Security Council. See Peter
     Lyon, 'The Emergence of the Third World', in Hedley Bull and Adam
     Watson, eds, *The Expansion of International Society* (Oxford, 1984),
     pp. 236–7.
15. See James Mayall, 'International Society and International Theory', in
     Michael Donelan, ed., *The Reason of States* (London, 1978).
16. Wight, *Power Politics*, p. 105.
17. Hedley Bull and Adam Watson, 'Conclusion', in Bull and Watson, eds,
     The Expansion of International Society (Oxford, 1984), pp. 433–4.
18. The most comprehensive modern treatment of the natural law tradition
     is found in E.B.F. Midgley, *The Natural Law Tradition and the Theory
     of International Relations* (London, 1975). See also Leo Strauss' excel-
     lent *Natural Right and History* (Chicago, 1950).
19. Grotius, *De Jure Belli ac Pacis Libri Tres*, pp. 14–15.
20. Grotius follows Aquinas in this view: '[The] communication of the
     eternal law to rational creatures is called the natural law. The natural
     light of the reason, by which we discern what is right and wrong, is

naught else but the impression on us of divine light.' Thomas Aquinas, Thomas Gilby, ed., *Philosophical Texts* (London, 1952), §1047, p. 358.

21. James Brown Scott, 'Introduction' to Grotius, *De Jure Belli ac Pacis Libri Tres*, pp. xxxi.

22. Hedley Bull, 'The Grotian Conception of International Society', in Butterfield and Wight, eds, *Diplomatic Investigations*, op. cit.

23. Grotius, *De Jure Belli ac Pacis Libri Tres*, p. 17.

24. Ibid., p. 16.

25. Christian Wolff, *Jus Gentium Methodo Scientifica Pertractatum* (Oxford, 1934).

26. Ibid., p. 84.

27. Ibid., p. 85.

28. Emerich de Vattel, *The Law of Nations or the Principles of Natural Law* (Washington DC, 1916). For a thorough discussion of Vattel and the earlier natural law influences upon his work, see Francis Stephen Ruddy, *International Law in the Enlightenment* (New York, 1975).

29. Vattel, *Law of Nations*, introduction, §2.

30. For a general discussion, see Peter F. Butler, 'Legitimacy in a States System: Vattel's Law of Nations', in Michael Donelan, ed., *The Reason of States* (London, 1978).

31. Hersch Lauterpacht, 'The Grotian Tradition in International Law', in *British Yearbook of International Law*, vol. XXIII, 1946.

32. Ibid., p. 27.

33. See discussion of Vattel in Julius Stone, 'Approaches to the Notion of International Justice', §III, in Richard A. Falk and Cyril E. Black, eds, *The Future of the International Legal Order* (Princeton, 1969).

34. Wolff, *Jus Gentium Methodo Scientifica Pertractatum*, pp. 24-34. See Lauterpacht's discussion of this in 'The Grotian Tradition in International Law', §4.

35. See A.L. Burns, 'Injustice and Evil in the Politics of the Powers', in Ralph Pettman, ed., *Moral Claims in World Affairs* (London, 1979).

36. L. Oppenheim, *International Law* (London, 1905), vol. I, pp. 19-20.

37. See Shlomo Avineri, *Hegel's Theory of the Modern State* (Cambridge, 1972).

38. Hegel, *Philosophy of Right* (New York, 1952), §331.

39. Ibid., §§330-40. For John Austin, law is defined as the command of the sovereign. Since there is no sovereign in the international sphere, there can be no international law in the true sense. See Austin, *The Province of Jurisprudence Determined* (London, 1954), Lecture VI.

40. H.L.A. Hart, *The Concept of Law* (Oxford, 1961), p. 209.

41. Ibid., p. 229.

42. Ibid., p. 231.

43. Rousseau, *The Social Contract* (Harmondsworth, 1968), pp. 50-1.

44. Hans Kelsen, *The General Theory of Law and the State* (Cambridge, Mass., 1946).

45. Austin, quoted in Hedley Bull, *Anarchical Society*, pp. 129-30.

46. Kelsen, op. cit., pp. 367-8.

47. Ibid., pp. 368-9.

48. Ibid., p. 366.

49. Jean Bodin, *Six Books of the Commonwealth* ([1640] Oxford, 1967), Book I.
50. John Plamenatz, *Man and Society* (London, 1963), vol. 1, p. 101.
51. Hegel, *Philosophy of Right*, §330.
52. Oppenheim, *International Law*, p. 117.
53. Ibid. p. 18.
54. S.I. Benn and R.S. Peters, *Social Principles and the Democratic State* (London, 1959), p. 366.
55. Hart, *Concept of Law*, pp. 217–18.
56. See Alan James, 'Sovereignty: Ground Rule or Gibberish?', in *Review of International Studies*, vol. 10, no. 1, January 1984, for the view that 'sovereignty' is not reducible to a single set of definitions. It is in large part a question of what is regarded by other actors as a sovereign entity. On the relationship between power, authority and sovereignty, see D.D. Raphael, *Problems of Political Philosophy* (London, 1976), ch. 3. For a comprehensive history of the doctrine of state sovereignty, see F.H. Hinsley, *Sovereignty* (London, 1966).
57. See Hersch Lauterpacht, *The Function of Law in the International Community* (Oxford, 1933).
58. Ibid., ch. 1, §2.
59. Ibid., p. 3.
60. Ibid., p. 44. For a general discussion of the 'monist' legal theory common to both Lauterpacht and Kelsen (i.e. the position that international law is in principle supreme even in the domestic sphere), and for a further discussion of the identification of the subjects of international law, see Ian Brownlie, *Principles of Public International Law* (Oxford, 1966), ch. 2.
61. See C. Wilfred Jenks, *The Common Law of Mankind* (London, 1958).
62. Ibid., p. 8.
63. For an excellent account of the principal ideas of the natural law theorists, including modern proponents, see Walter Schiffer, *The Legal Community of Mankind* (New York, 1954), part 1, chs 1–4, and *passim*. Schiffer's is a more sceptical account of the translation of natural law principles into contemporary international legal practice than that offered by Lauterpacht or Jenks.
64. Jenks, *Common Law of Mankind*, p. 20.
65. Ibid., p. 46.
66. See Julius Stone, 'Approaches to the Notion of International Justice', §4.
67. Ibid., p. 434.
68. Ibid., pp. 434–35.
69. Ian Brownlie, 'The Expansion of International Society: Consequences for the Law of Nations', in Hedley Bull and Adam Watson, eds, *The Expansion of International Society* (Oxford, 1984), pp. 364–5.
70. Ibid., pp. 366–9.
71. Leo Gross, 'The Right of Self-Determination in International Law', in Martin Kilson, ed., *New States in the Modern World* (Cambridge, Mass., 1975). On the international legal shift towards territorial contiguity as the basis for statehood, see Inis L. Claude Jr, 'Domestic

Jurisdiction and Colonialism', in Martin Kilson, ed., *New States in the Modern World* (Cambridge, Mass., 1975).

72. Gross, 'The Right of Self-Determination in International Law', p. 144.
73. See Aian James, 'Sovereignty: Ground Rule Or Gibberish?'.
74. See Rosalyn Higgins, 'Intervention and International Law' in Hedley Bull, ed., *Intervention in World Politics* (Oxford, 1984).
75. Ibid., p. 42. The limits of the capability, both past and present, of international law in the prevention or even regulation of intervention, given the facts of power politics, are discussed in Anthony Carty, *The Decay of International Law?* (Manchester, 1986), ch. 6.
76. Michael Akehurst, 'Humanitarian Intervention', in Hedley Bull, ed., *Intervention in World Politics* (Oxford, 1984).
77. Georg Schwarzenberger, *Economic World Order?* (Manchester, 1970).
78. Ibid., p. 5.
79. Ibid., p. 63.
80. Ibid., pp. 63–4.
81. See Richard Rosecrance, 'International Theory Revisited', in *International Organization*, vol. 35, vol. 4, 1981.
82. Max Weber, 'Structures of Power', §1 in *From Max Weber: Essays in Sociology*, eds Hans Gerth and C. Wright Mills (London, 1948).
83. R.J. Vincent, *Human Rights and International Relations* (Cambridge, 1986), p. 143.

5 HUMAN RIGHTS, THE STATE AND GLOBAL JUSTICE

1. Most especially, on self-determination see Alfred Cobban, *The Nation-State and National Self-Determination* (London, rev. ed., 1969), and for a more contemporary discussion, Peter Breuilly, *Nationalism and the State* (Manchester, 1985). On intervention, the classic, though difficult, text remains R. J. Vincent, *Nonintervention and International Order* (Princeton, 1974). See, too, the recent selection of essays in Ian Forbes and Mark Hoffman, eds, *Political Theory, International Relations and the Ethics of Intervention* (Basingstoke and New York, 1993).
2. Jeremy Bentham, 'Declaration of Rights', in *Bentham's Political Thought*, ed. Bikkhu Parekh (London, 1973), p. 268.
3. Ibid., p. 272.
4. Ibid., p. 273.
5. Ibid., p. 274.
6. T.H. Green, *Lectures on the Principle of Political Obligation and Other Writings* (Cambridge, 1986), pp. 107–8.
7. Ibid., pp. 109–10.
8. Alan Gewirth, *Human Rights* (Chicago, 1982); see also his 'The Epistemology of Human Rights', in Ellen Frankel Paul, Fred D. Miller, Jr and Jeffrey Paul, eds, *Human Rights* (Oxford, 1984).
9. Gewirth, 'The Epistemology of Human Rights', p. 16.
10. Ibid., p. 18.
11. Ibid., p. 19.

12. For this argument, see Hedley Bull, 'Human Rights and World Politics', in Ralph Pettman, ed., *Moral Claims in World Affairs* (London, 1979). For a strident defence of the Western approach, and supposed Western success, in the area of human rights, see Daniel P. Moynihan, 'The Politics of Human Rights' in *Commentary*, vol. 64, no. 2, August 1977. See also Peter Berger, 'Are Human Rights Universal?' in *Commentary*, vol. 64, no. 3, September 1977.
13. Bull, 'Human Rights in World Politics', p. 88.
14. Ibid., p. 90.
15. Amnesty International, *Political Imprisonment in the People's Republic of China* (London, 1978).
16. Maurice Cranston, *What Are Human Rights?* (London, 1973), pp. 68–9. For a general attack on the idea of economic and social rights, see ch. 8. Cf. L.J. MacFarlane's strong affirmation of the complementarity of the principal sorts of human rights, *The Theory and Practice of Human Rights* (London, 1985); and also John Gray, *Beyond the New Right* (London, 1993), pp. 99–110.
17. F.A. Hayek, *Law, Legislation and Liberty* (London, 1982), vol. II, p. 103.
18. See Robert Nozick, *Anarchy, State and Utopia* (Oxford, 1974), pp. 167–74.
19. Hayek, *op. cit.*, p. 105.
20. Gewirth, 'The Epistemology of Human Rights', op. cit., pp. 8–9.
21. Bernard Williams, 'The Idea of Equality', in Peter Laslett and W.G. Runciman, eds, *Philosophy, Politics and Society* (Oxford, 1962), p. 163; see also Christopher Ake, 'Justice as Equality', in *Philosophy and Public Affairs*, vol. 5, no. 1, Fall 1975.
22. Nozick, *Anarchy, State and Utopia*, p. 233.
23. Williams, 'The Idea of Equality', p. 164.
24. Ibid., pp. 163–9.
25. See Kenneth Waltz, 'The Myth of National Interdependence', in Charles P. Kindleberger, ed., *The International Corporation* (Cambridge, Mass., 1960), for the contrary view that international inequalities of power, and a low (in absolute terms) degree of functional specialisation, strictly limit the degree of international interdependence, and therefore the necessity of principles to regulate international cooperation. Against Waltz's view, see Richard Rosecrance and Arthur Stein, 'Interdependence: Myth or Reality?', in *World Politics*, vol. 26, no. 1, October 1973. For a general view of interdependence theory, see James A. Rosenau, *The Study of Global Interdependence* (London, 1980).
26. See Richard Little, 'Power and Interdependence: A Realist Critique', in R.J. Barry Jones and Peter Willetts, eds, *Interdependence on Trial* (London, 1984).
27. See Robert O. Keohane and Joseph S. Nye, *Power and Interdependence* (Boston, 1977).
28. Many interdependence theorists see transnational relations as a challenge to the primacy of the state. But to take the paradigm case of multinational corporations, writers of both left and right have pointed

262   *Notes*

to the essential role of state policy in determining the context of global corporate operations, and the use of economic policy to fulfil states' political goals. See Robin Murray, 'The Internationalization of Capital and the Nation State', in *New Left Review*, no. 67, May–June 1971; and Bill Warren, 'How International is Capital?', in Hugo Radice, ed., *International Firms and Modern Imperialism* (Harmondsworth, 1975). For a conservative argument for the continuing centrality of the state in international relations, see Robert Gilpin, 'The Politics of Transnational Economic Relations', in Robert O. Keohane and Joseph S. Nye, eds, *Transnationalism and World Politics* (Cambridge, Mass., 1972).

29. See discussion in Willy Brandt et al., *North–South: A Programme for Survival* (London, 1980), ch. 3.

30. On the different meanings and ideological uses of the concept of interdependence, see R.J. Barry Jones, 'The Definition and Identification of Interdependence', in R. J. Barry Jones and Peter Willetts, eds, *Interdependence on Trial* (London, 1984). On interdependence theory as an obscuration of international inequalities, see Kal J. Holsti, 'A New International Politics: Diplomacy in Complex Interdependence', in *International Organization*, vol. 32, no. 2, Spring 1978. David A. Baldwin argues, against Keohane and Nye, that interdependence need not imply any mutuality of benefit, however unequally shared; see his 'Interdependence and Power: A Conceptual Analysis', in *International Organization*, vol. 34, no. 4, Autumn 1980.

31. Orlando Letelier and Michael Moffit, *The International Economic Order* (Washington D.C., 1977), p. 29.

32. On different approaches to reform of the international economic system, see Richard Falk, *The End of World Order* (New York, 1983), pp. 46–55.

33. Ankie Hoogvelt, *The Third World in Global Development* (London, 1982), p. 69 and ch. 1 *passim*. For the view that self-reliance and disengagement are the only ultimate hope for economic development for the poorest countries, see Samir Amin, 'UNCTAD IV and the New International Economic Order', in Harry Goulbourne, ed., *Politics and State in the Third World* (London, 1979). Cf. R.H. Green and H.W. Singer, 'Towards a Rational and Equitable New International Economic Order', in *World Development*, vol. 3, no. 6, June 1975.

34. Hoogvelt, *Third World in Global Development*, p. 23.

35. See Thomas E. Weisskopf, 'Capitalism, Underdevelopment and the Future of the Poor Countries', in J.N. Bhagwati, ed., *Economics and World Order* (London, 1972).

36. Hoogvelt, *Third World in Global Development*, p. 45.

37. Gunnar Myrdal, *The Challenge of World Poverty* (Harmondsworth, 1970), amongst many other works.

38. Johann Galtung, 'A Structural Theory of Imperialism', in *Journal of Peace Research*, vol. 13, no. 2, 1971.

39. Rajni Kothari, *Footsteps into the Future* (Amsterdam, 1974), p. 50.

40. See Peter B. Evans, 'National Autonomy and Economic Development', in Robert O. Keohane and Joseph S. Nye, eds, *Transnationalism and World Politics* (Cambridge, Mass., 1972).

41. See J.A. Hobson, *Imperialism: A Study* (London, 1938), and V.I. Lenin, 'Imperialism, the Highest Stage of Capitalism', in *Selected Works* (Moscow, 1968).

42. On 'classical' Marxist and modern dependency theories, see Anthony Brewer, *Marxist Theories of Imperialism* (London, 1980). For a comparative discussion of liberal, structuralist and Marxist approaches, see Joan Edelman Spero, *The Politics of International Economic Relations* (London, 1982), pp. 138–41, and pt. 3 *passim*. See also James O'Connor, 'The Meaning of Economic Imperialism', in R.J. Rhodes, ed., *Imperialism and Underdevelopment* (New York, 1970).

43. Letelier and Moffit, *The International Economic Order*, p. 52.

44. André Gunder Frank, 'The Development of Underdevelopment', in Michael Smith, Richard Little and Michael Shackleton, eds, *Perspectives on World Politics* (London, 1981). See also, Immanuel Wallerstein, 'The Rise and Future Demise of the World Capitalist System: Concepts for Comparative Analysis', in *Perspectives on World Politics*, op. cit., p. 377.

45. This view is developed in Theresa Hayter, *Aid as Imperialism* (Harmondsworth, 1971), pp. 157–61 and *passim*. Aid becomes most politically sensitive when it is seen as a form of intervention. see David A. Baldwin, 'Foreign Aid, Intervention, and Influence', in *World Politics*, vol. 21, no. 3, April 1969. For a realist perspective on aid as a means of furthering the national interest of the donor, see Samuel P. Huntington, 'Foreign Aid For What and For Whom?', in *Foreign Policy*, vol. 4, Winter 1970–1. Cf. Howard Wriggins, 'Political Outcomes of Foreign Assistance: Influence, Involvement of Intervention?', in *Journal of International Affairs*, vol. 22, no. 2, 1968.

46. P.T. Bauer's critique of the 'orthodox' approach to development is expounded in his *Dissent on Development* (London, 1974) and *Reality and Rhetoric: Studies in the Economics of Development* (London, 1984).

47. Bauer, *Reality and Rhetoric*, p. 51.

48. Paul Streeten, *First Things First* (New York, 1981).

49. Ibid., p. 17.

50. John Rawls, *A Theory of Justice* (Oxford, 1972), ch. 2, §§11–12.

51. Streeten, *First Things First*, p. 22.

52. Hoogvelt, *The Third World in Global Development*, p. 9.

53. Henry Shue, *Basic Rights: Subsistence, Affluence and US Foreign Policy* (Princeton, 1980).

54. See Maurice Cranston, *What Are Human Rights?*, ch.8.

55. Shue, *Basic Rights*, p. 9.

56. Ibid., p. 19.

57. Ibid., p. 18.

58. Ibid., p. 40.

59. It would also include the prohibition of the use of military force against states to prevent their pursuing alternative routes to development. The experience of the Cold War era has been that economic dependence may be reinforced by the imposed hegemony of the political and ideological system of a superpower upon its client states. Noam Chomsky has argued persuasively that it was the desire to prevent

any alternative paths to economic development in the countries of Latin America and Indochina, rather than any genuine communist threat to 'geo-political' security, that led to intervention by the United States in those areas. See *The Chomsky Reader* (London, 1987), part IV, 'The United States and the World'.

60. Rawls, *A Theory of Justice*, p. 4. For a general critique of Rawls' position, especially the derivation of the 'maximin' difference principle, see Brian Barry, *The Liberal Theory of Justice* (Oxford, 1973). See also R.M. Hare, 'Rawls' Theory of Justice', in Norman Daniels, ed., *Reading Rawls* (Oxford, 1975); Thomas Nagel, 'Rawls on Justice', in *Philosophical Review*, vol. LXXXII, no. 2, April 1973; and T.M. Scanlon, 'Rawls' Theory of Justice', in *Reading Rawls*, op. cit. Richard Miller has argued that Rawls' hypothetical persons in the Original Position are forced to exclude from their decision-making possible knowledge about the nature of class in the society-to-be, and that they could not rationally adopt distributive principles in the absence of such vital knowledge. See 'Rawls and Marxism', in *Reading Rawls*, op. cit.

61. Rawls, *A Theory of Justice*, pp. 61–2.
62. Ibid., p. 62.
63. Ibid., p. 8.
64. Ibid., p. 457.
65. Ibid., p. 378.
66. For the extension of a modified version of Rawls' difference principle to international relations, see Charles R. Beitz, 'Justice and International Relations', in *Philosophy and Public Affairs*, vol. 4, no. 4, Summer 1975.
67. Robert Amdur, 'Rawls' Theory of Justice: Domestic and International Perspectives', in *World Politics*, vol. 29, no. 3, April 1977.
68. Beitz, *Political Theory and International Relations*, pt. 3, §§1–4.
69. Peter Singer, 'Famine, Affluence and Morality', in Charles R. Beitz, Marshall Cohen, Thomas Scanlon and A. John Simmons, eds, *International Ethics* (Princeton, 1985), pp. 252–3. See also Singer, 'The Right to be Rich or Poor' in *The New York Review of Books*, March 6th, 1975; and Hugo A. Bedau, 'Radical Egalitarianism', in Hugo A. Bedau, ed., *Justice and Equality* (Englewood Cliffs, 1971). For a more plausible, though still radical, view of the relationship between the consumption of the rich and the poverty of the poor, and of what this entails in terms of moral responsibility, see Onora O'Neill, 'Lifeboat Earth', in *Philosophy and Public Affairs*, vol. 4, no. 3, Spring 1975. For a much fuller statement of her position, see *Faces of Hunger* (London, 1985).
70. Singer, 'Famine, Affluence and Morality', p. 252.
71. Bauer, *Dissent on Development*, p. 126.
72. See Peter A. French, 'Morally Blaming Whole Populations', in Virginia Held, Sidney Morgenbesser and Thomas Nagel, eds, *Philosophy, Morality and International Affairs* (New York, 1974). For two interesting account of intergenerational responsibilities, see Clayton D. Hubin, 'Justice and Future Generations', in *Philosophy and Public Affairs*, vol. 6, no. 1, Fall 1976, and Rawls, *A Theory of Justice*, ch. 5, §44.

73. See Gewirth, 'Are There Any Absolute Rights?', in *Human Rights,* op. cit.
74. Nozick, *Anarchy, State and Utopia,* pp. 178–82.
75. See John Locke, *Two Treatises of Government* (London, 1924), book II, ch. 5.
76. See Hayek's essay, 'The Atavism of Social Justice', in *New Studies* (London, 1978).
77. Barrington Moore Jr, *Injustice: The Social Bases of Obedience and Revolt* (London, 1979) ch. 1. For a powerful argument against exclusively individualistic conceptions of rights and welfare, see Steven Lukes, *Individualism* (Oxford, 1973), chs 17, 18 and 20.
78. See Max Weber, 'Politics as a Vocation', in H.H. Gerth and C. Wright Mills, eds *'From Max Weber: Essays in Sociology'* (London, 1948), pp. 117–28.

Bibliography

Ake, Christopher. 'Justice as Equality'. *Philosophy and Public Affairs*, vol. 5, no. 1, Fall 1975, pp. 69–89.

Akehurst, Michael. *A Modern Introduction to International Law*. Unwin Hyman, London, 6th ed., 1987.

Amdur, Robert. 'Rawls' Theory of Justice: Domestic and International Perspectives'. *World Politics*, vol. 29, no. 3, April 1977, pp. 438–61.

Amin, Samir. *Imperialism and Unequal Development*. Harvester Press, Sussex, 1977.

Amnesty International. *Political Imprisonment in the People's Republic of China*. Amnesty International Publications, London, 1978.

Angell, Norman. *The Great Illusion*. University Press, Cambridge, 1910.

Aquinas, St. Thomas. *Philosophical Texts*. Trans. and intro. Thomas Gilby. Oxford University Press, London, 2nd imp., 1952.

Aristotle. *The Ethics*. Trans. J.A.K. Thomson. Penguin, Harmondsworth, rev. ed., 1976.

Aron, Raymond. *Peace and War*. Weidenfeld and Nicolson, London, 1966.

Austin, John. *The Province of Jurisprudence Determined*. Weidenfeld and Nicolson, London, 1954.

Avineri, Shlomo. *Hegel's Theory of the Modern State*. Cambridge University Press, Cambridge, 1972.

Baldwin, David A. 'Foreign Aid, Intervention, and Influence'. *World Politics*, vol. 21, no. 3, April 1969, pp. 425–47.

Barry, Brian. 'Reflections on Justice as Fairness'. *Justice and Equality*. Ed. Hugo A. Bedau. Prentice-Hall, Englewood Cliffs, New Jersey, 1971.

—— *The Liberal Theory of Justice*. Oxford University Press, Oxford, 1973.

Bauer, P.T. *Dissent on Development*. Weidenfeld and Nicolson, London, 1974.

—— *Reality and Rhetoric: Studies in the Economics of Development*. Weidenfeld and Nicolson, London, 1984.

Bedau, Hugo A. 'Why Do We Have The Rights We Do?'. *Human Rights*. Eds Ellen Frankel Paul, Fred D. Miller Jr and Jeffrey Paul. Basil Blackwell, Oxford, 1984.

Beitz, Charles R. 'Justice and International Relations'. *Philosophy and Public Affairs*, vol. 4, no. 4, Summer 1975, pp. 360–89.

—— *Political Theory and International Relations*. Princeton University Press, Princeton, New Jersey, 1979.

Benn, S.I. and Peters, R.S. *Social Principles and the Democratic State*. George Allen & Unwin, London, 1959.

Bentham, Jeremy. *Bentham's Political Thought*. Ed. Bikkhu Parekh. Croom Helm, London, 1973.

Beres, Louis René. *Apocalypse*. University of Chicago Press, Chicago, 1980.

Berger, Peter. 'Are Human Rights Universal?'. *Commentary*, vol. 64, no. 3, September 1977, pp. 60–3.

Berki, R.N. 'On Marxian Thought and the Problem of International Relations'. *World Politics*, vol. 24, no. 1, October 1971, pp. 80–105.

Berlin, Isaiah. *Four Essays on Liberty*. Oxford University Press, Oxford, 1969.

Betts, R.K. 'Paranoids, Pygmies, Pariahs and Non-Proliferation'. *Foreign Policy*, vol. XXVII, no. 3, pp. 157–83, Summer 1977.

Bodin, Jean. *Six Books of the Commonwealth*. Trans. and abridged M.J. Tooley. Basil Blackwell, Oxford, 1967.

Bottomore, T.B. *Elites and Society*. Penguin, Harmondsworth, 1966.

Boulding, Kenneth. 'The Concept of a World Interest'. *Economics and the Idea of Mankind*. Ed. Bert F. Hoselitz. Columbia University Press, New York, 1965.

Brandt, Willy (et al.). *North–South: A Programme for Survival*. Pan, London, 1980.

Brewer, Anthony. *Marxist Theories of Imperialism*. Routledge and Kegan Paul, London, 1980.

Brewin, Christopher. 'Justice in International Relations'. *The Reason of States*. Ed. Michael Donelan. George Allen & Unwin London, 1978.

Brownlie, Ian. *Principles of Public International Law*. Clarendon, Oxford, 1966.

Bull, Hedley. 'The Grotian Conception of International Society'. *Diplomatic Investigations*. Eds Herbert Butterfield and Martin Wight. George Allen & Unwin, London, 1966.

—— 'Society and Anarchy in International Relations'. *Diplomatic Investigations*. Eds Herbert Butterfield and Martin Wight. George Allen & Unwin, London, 1966.

—— *The Anarchical Society*. Macmillan, London, 1977.

—— *Intervention in World Politics*. Clarendon, Oxford, 1984.

Bull, Hedley and Watson, Adam, eds. *The Expansion of International Society*. Clarendon Press, Oxford, 1984.

Burnham, James. *The Managerial Revolution*. John Day, New York, 1941.

Burton, John W. *World Society*. Cambridge University Press, Cambridge, 1972.

Butler, Peter F. 'Legitimacy in a States System: Vattel's Law of Nations'. *The Reason of States*. Ed. Michael Donelan. George Allen & Unwin, London, 1978.

Butterfield, Herbert and Wight, Martin, eds. *Diplomatic Investigations*. George Allen & Unwin, London, 1966.

Campbell, Tom. *The Left and Rights*. Routledge and Kegan Paul, London, 1983.

Carr, E.H. *The Twenty Years' Crisis*. Macmillan, London, 2nd ed., 1946.

—— *The Russian Revolution from Lenin to Stalin 1917–1929*. Macmillan, London, 1979.

Carty, Anthony. *The Decay of International Law?* Manchester University Press, Manchester, 1986.

Chomsky, Noam. 'The Rule of Force in International Affairs'. *For Reasons of State*. Fontana, London, 1973.

—— *The Chomsky Reader*. Serpent's Tail, London, 1987.

Clark, Ian. *Reform and Resistance in the International Order*. Cambridge University Press, Cambridge, 1980.

Claude, Inis L., Jr. *Power and International Relations.* Random House, New York, 1962.

—— 'Domestic Jurisdiction and Colonialism'. *New States in the Modern World.* Ed. Martin Kilson. Harvard University Press, Cambridge, Mass., 1975.

Cobban, Alfred. *The Nation-State and National Self-Determination.* Collins, London, rev. ed., 1969.

Cohen, Marshall. 'Moral Skepticism and International Relations'. *International Ethics.* Eds Charles R. Beitz, Marshall Cohen, Thomas Scanlon and A. John Simmons. Princeton University Press, Princeton, New Jersey, 1985.

Cranston, Maurice. *What Are Human Rights?* The Bodley Head, London, 1973.

Croce, Benedetto. *Politics and Morals.* Philosophical Library, New York, 1945.

Dahl, Robert. *Polyarchy: Participation and Opposition.* Yale University Press, New Haven, 1971.

Danielson, Peter. 'Theories, Intuitions and the Problem of Worldwide Distributive Justice'. *Philosophy of the Social Sciences,* vol. 3, no. 4, December 1973, pp. 331–8.

De Jasay, Anthony. *The State.* Basil Blackwell, Oxford, 1985.

Donelan, Michael. *Elements of International Political Theory.* Clarendon, Oxford, 1990.

Doyle, Michael W. 'Kant, Liberal Legacies and Foreign Affairs', parts I and II. *Philosophy and Public Affairs,* vol. 12, nos 3 and 4, 1983.

Durkheim, Emile. *The Division of Labor in Society.* Free Press, New York, 1933.

Dworkin, Ronald. *Taking Rights Seriously.* Duckworth, London, 2nd ed., 1978.

Emerson, R. 'Self-Determination'. *American Journal of Law,* vol. 65, no. 3, July 1971, pp. 459–75.

Falk, Richard. *This Endangered Planet.* Random House, New York, 1971.

—— *Human Rights and State Sovereignty.* Holmes and Meier, New York, 1981.

—— *The End of World Order.* Holmes and Meier, New York, 1983.

Fanon, Frantz. *The Wretched of the Earth.* Trans. Constance Farrington. Penguin, Harmondsworth, 1967.

Forbes, Ian and Hoffman, Mark, eds. *Political Theory, International Relations and the Ethics of Intervention.* Macmillan and St. Martin's Press, Basingstoke and New York, 1993.

Forsyth, M.G., Keens-Soper, H.M.A. and Savigear, P., eds. *The Theory of International Relations.* George Allen & Unwin, London, 1970.

Frank, André Gunder. 'The Development of Underdevelopment'. *Perspectives on World Politics.* Eds Michael Smith, Richard Little and Michael Shackleton. Croom Helm, London, 1981.

French, Peter A. 'Morally Blaming Whole Populations'. *Philosophy, Morality and International Affairs.* Eds Virginia Held, Sidney Morgenbesser and Thomas Nagel. Oxford University Press, New York, 1974.

Frost, Mervyn. *Towards a Normative Theory of International Relations* Cambridge University Press, Cambridge, 1986.

Galbraith, John Kenneth. *Economics and the Public Purpose*. André Deutsch, London, 1974.
—— *The Affluent Society*. Penguin, Harmondsworth, 4th ed., 1984.
Galtung, Johann. 'A Structural Theory of Imperialism'. *Journal of Peace Research*, vol. 13, no. 2, 1971, pp. 81–94.
Gewirth, Alan. 'Are There Any Absolute Rights?' *Philosophical Quarterly*, vol. 31, no. 122, January 1981, pp. 1–16.
—— *Human Rights*. Chicago University Press, Chicago and London, 1982.
Gilpin, Robert. *War and Change in World Politics*. Cambridge University Press, Cambridge, 1981.
Gray, John. *Liberalism*. Open University Press, Milton Keynes, 1986.
—— *Beyond the New Right*. Routledge, London, 1993.
Green, David G. *The New Right*. Harvester Wheatsheaf, Brighton, Sussex, 1987.
Green, Philip. *The Pursuit of Inequality*. Martin Robertson, Oxford, 1981.
Green, R.H. and Singer, H.W. 'Towards a Rational and Equitable New International Economic Order'. *World Development*, vol. 3, no. 6, June 1975, pp. 427–44.
Green, T.H. *Lectures on the Principle of Political Obligation and Other Writings*. Eds Paul Harris and John Morrow. Cambridge University Press, Cambridge, 1986.
Groom, A.J.R. 'The Functionalist Approach and East–West Co-operation in Europe'. *Journal of Common Market Studies*, vol. 13, 1975, pp. 21–60.
Gross, Leo. 'The Right of Self-Determination in International Law'. *New States in the Modern World*. Ed. Martin Kilson. Harvard University Press, Cambridge, Mass., 1975.
Grotius, Hugo. *De Jure Belli ac Pacis Libri Tres*. Trans. Francis W. Kelsey. The Classics of International Law. Clarendon, Oxford, 1925.
Haas, Ernst B. 'Regionalism, Functionalism and Universal International Organisation'. *World Politics*, vol. 8, 1956, pp. 238–63.
—— *Beyond the Nation-State*. Stanford University Press, Stanford, Calif., 1964.
Hanreider, Wolfram F. 'Dissolving International Politics: Reflections on the Nation-State'. *The American Political Science Review*, vol. 72, no. 4, 1978, pp. 1276–87.
Hart, H.L.A. *The Concept of Law*. Oxford University Press, Oxford, 1961.
—— 'Are There Any Natural Rights?' *Theories of Rights*. Ed. Jeremy Waldron. Oxford University Press, Oxford, 1984.
Hayek, F.A. 'The Atavism of Social Justice'. *New Studies*. Routledge and Kegan Paul, London, 1978.
—— *Law, Legislation and Liberty*, vols. I–III. Routledge and Kegan Paul, London, rev. ed., 1982.
Hayter, Theresa. *Aid as Imperialism*. Penguin, Harmondsworth, 1971.
Hegel, G.W.F. *Philosophy of Right*. Trans. T.M. Knox. Oxford University Press, New York, 1952.
Herz, John H. *International Politics in the Atomic Age*. Columbia University Press, New York, 1959.
—— 'The Territorial State Revisited: Reflections on the Future of the Nation-State'. *International Politics and Foreign Policy: A Reader in*

Research and Theory. Ed. James A. Rosenau. Free Press, New York, rev. ed., 1969.

Hinsley, F.H. *Power and the Pursuit of Peace.* Cambridge University Press, Cambridge, 1963.

—— *Sovereignty.* C.A. Watts & Co., London, 1966.

Hobbes, Thomas. *Leviathan.* Ed. and intro. C.B. Macpherson. Penguin, Harmondsworth, 1968.

Hobson, J.A. *Imperialism: A Study.* Allen & Unwin, London, rev. ed., 1938.

Hoogvelt, Ankie. *The Third World in Global Development.* Macmillan, London, 1982.

Hubin, D. Clayton. 'Justice and Future Generations'. *Philosophy and Public Affairs*, vol. 6, no. 1, Fall 1976, pp. 70–83.

Hume, David. *Essays Moral, Political and Literary.* Ed. F. Watkins. Nelson and Sons, London, 1951.

—— *A Treatise of Human Nature*, 2 vols. Fontana/Collins, Glasgow, 1962, 1972.

James, Alan. 'Sovereignty: Ground Rule or Gibberish?'. *Review of International Studies*, vol. 10, no. 1, January 1984, pp. 1–18.

Jenks, C. Wilfred. *The Common Law of Mankind.* Stevens, London, 1958.

Jervis, Robert. *Perception and Misperception in International Politics.* Princeton University Press, Princeton, New Jersey, 1976.

Johansen, Robert C. *The National Interest and the Human Interest.* Princeton University Press, Princeton, New Jersey, 1980.

Johnson, James Turner. *Just War Tradition and the Restraint of War.* Princeton University Press, Princeton, New Jersey, 1981.

Kant, Immanuel. *Perpetual Peace.* Bobbs-Merrill, Indianapolis and New York, 1957.

—— *Fundamental Principles of the Metaphysics of Ethics.* Trans. Thomas Kingsmill Abbott. Longmans, London, 10th ed., 1969.

—— *Political Writings.* Ed. H. Reiss. Cambridge University Press, Cambridge, 2nd ed., 1991.

Kelsen, Hans. *The General Theory of Law and the State.* Trans. A. Wedberg. Harvard University Press, Cambridge, Mass., 1946.

—— *What Is Justice?* University of California Press, 1967.

Kennan, George F. *American Diplomacy 1900–50.* Secker and Warburg, London, 1952.

Keohane, Robert O. and Nye, Joseph S. *Power and Interdependence.* Little, Brown, Boston, 1977.

Klein, Robert E. *Sovereign Equality Among States.* Foreword by Louis J. Halle. University of Toronto Press, Toronto and Buffalo, 1974.

Knorr, Klaus and Rosenau, James N., eds. *Contending Approaches to International Politics.* Princeton University Press, Princeton, New Jersey, 1969.

Kothari, Rajni. *Footsteps into the Future.* North-Holland, Amsterdam, 1974.

Lauterpacht, Hersch. *The Function of Law in the International Community.* Clarendon, Oxford, 1933.

—— 'The Grotian Tradition in International Law'. *British Yearbook of International Law*, vol. XXIII, 1946, pp. 1–53.

Lenin, V.I. *Selected Works.* Progress, Moscow, 1968.

Letelier, Orlando and Moffit, Michael. *The International Economic Order.* Transnational Institute, Washington D.C., 1977.

Levi, Werner. 'The Relative Irrelevance of Moral Norms in International Politics'. *Foreign Policy Decision-Making.* Eds Richard C. Snyder, H.W. Bruck and Burton Sapin. Free Press, New York, 1963.

Linklater, Andrew. *Men and Citizens in the Theory of International Relations.* Macmillan, London, 2nd ed., 1990.

Locke, John. *Two Treatises on Government.* J.M. Dent, London, 1924.

Luban, David. 'The Romance of the Nation-State'. *Philosophy and Public Affairs*, vol. 9, no. 4, Summer 1980, pp. 392–7.

Lucas, J.R. *On Justice.* Clarendon, Oxford, 1980.

Lukes, Steven. *Marxism and Morality.* Oxford University Press, Oxford, 1985.

MacFarlane, L.J. *The Theory and Practice of Human Rights.* Maurice Temple Smith, London, 1985.

Machiavelli, Niccolò. *The Prince.* Trans. and intro. George Bull. Penguin, Harmondsworth, 1961.

Mansfield, Peter. *The Arabs.* Penguin, Harmondsworth, rev. ed., 1978.

Marcuse, Herbert. *One-Dimensional Man.* Routledge and Kegan Paul, London, 1964.

Marx, Karl. *Selected Writings.* Ed. David McLellan. Oxford University Press, Oxford, 1977.

Mayall, James. 'International Society and International Theory'. *The Reason of States.* Ed. Michael Donelan. George Allen & Unwin, London, 1978.

Mazrui, Ali. *Towards a Pax Africana.* Weidenfeld and Nicolson, London, 1967.

Mendlowitz, Saul, ed. *On the Creation of a Just World Order: Preferred Worlds for the 1990s.* Free Press, New York, 1975.

Midgley, E.B.F. *The Natural Law Tradition and the Theory of International Relations.* Paul Elek, London, 1975.

Miliband, Ralph. *The State in Capitalist Society.* Quartet, London, 1986.

Mill, John Stuart. *Utilitarianism, On Liberty and Considerations on Representative Government.* J.M. Dent, London, new. ed., 1972.

—— 'A Few Words on Non-Intervention'. *Dissertations and Discussions*, vol. III. Longmans, Green, Reader and Dyer, London, 2nd ed., 1875.

Miller, David. *Social Justice.* Clarendon, Oxford, 1976.

Miller, J.D.B. 'Morality, Interests and Rationalization'. *Moral Claims in World Affairs.* Ed. Ralph Pettman. Croom Helm, London, 1979.

—— *World of States.* Croom Helm, London, 1981.

Mills, C. Wright. *The Power Elite.* Oxford University Press (Galaxy), New York, 1956.

—— *The Causes of World War Three.* Simon & Schuster, New York, 1958.

Mitrany, David. 'The Functional Approach to World Organization'. *International Affairs*, vol. 24, no. 3, July 1948, pp. 350–63.

—— *A Working Peace System.* Intro. Hans J. Morgenthau. Quadrangle, Chicago, 1966.

—— 'The Functional Approach in Historical Perspective'. *International Affairs* vol. 47, no. 3, July 1971, pp. 532–43.

Moore, Barrington, Jr. *Injustice: The Social Bases of Obedience and Revolt.* Macmillan, London, 1979.

Morgenthau, Hans J. *Politics Among Nations.* Alfred A. Knopf, New York, 6th ed., 1985.

Moynihan, Daniel P. 'The Politics of Human Rights'. *Commentary*, vol. 64, no. 2, August 1977, pp. 19–26.

Myrdal, Gunnar. *The Challenge of World Poverty.* Penguin, Harmondsworth, 1970.

Nagel, Thomas. 'Rawls on Justice'. *Philosophical Review*, vol. LXXXII, no. 2, April 1973, pp. 220–34.

—— 'War and Massacre'. *War and Moral Responsibility.* Eds. Marshall Cohen, Thomas Nagel and Thomas Scanlon. Princeton University Press, Princeton, New Jersey, 1974.

Nardin, Terry. *Law, Morality and the Relations of States.* Princeton University Press, Princeton, New Jersey, 1983.

Nelson, W.N. 'Special Rights, General Rights and Social Justice'. *Philosophy and Public Affairs*, vol. 3, no. 4, Summer 1974, pp. 410–30.

Niebuhr, Reinhold. *Moral Man and Immoral Society.* Charles Scribner's, New York, 1932.

Nozick, Robert. *Anarchy, State and Utopia.* Basil Blackwell, Oxford, 1974.

Oakeshott, Michael. *On Human Conduct.* Clarendon, Oxford, 1975.

O'Connor, James. 'The Meaning of Economic Imperialism'. *Imperialism and Underdevelopment.* Ed. R.J. Rhodes. Monthly Review Press, New York, 1970.

O'Neill, Onora. 'Lifeboat Earth'. *Philosophy and Public Affairs*, vol. 4, no. 3, Spring 1975, pp. 273–92.

—— *Faces of Hunger.* Allen and Unwin, London, 1986.

Oppenheim, L. *International Law*, vol. I. Longmans, London, 1905.

Osgood, Robert E. and Tucker, Robert W. *Force, Order, and Justice.* Johns Hopkins Press, Baltimore, 1967.

Paine, Thomas. *Rights of Man.* Penguin, Harmondsworth, 1984.

Pettman, Ralph ed. *Moral Claims in World Affairs.* Croom Helm, London, 1979.

Plamenatz, John. *Man and Society*, 2 vols. Longman, London, 1963.

Porter, Brian. 'Martin Wight's Political Theory'. *The Reason of States.* Ed. Michael Donelan. George Allen & Unwin, London, 1978.

Pufendorf, Samuel. *De Jure Naturae et Gentium, Libri Octo.* Trans. C.H. and W.A. Oldfather. The Classics of International Law. Clarendon, Oxford, 1934.

—— *On the Duty of Man and Citizen.* Ed. James Tully. Cambridge University Press, Cambridge, 1991.

Quester, George. *The Politics of Nuclear Proliferation.* Johns Hopkins University Press, Baltimore, 1973.

Radice, Hugo, ed. *International Firms and Modern Imperialism.* Penguin, Harmondsworth, 1975.

Rawls, John. *A Theory of Justice.* Oxford University Press, Oxford, 1972.

Rescher, Nicholas. *Distributive Justice.* Bobbs-Merrill, Indianapolis, 1966.

Rousseau, Jean-Jacques. *The Social Contract.* Trans. and intro. Maurice Cranston. Penguin, Harmondsworth, 1968.

—— *A Discourse on Inequality.* Penguin, Harmondsworth, 1984.

Ruddy, Francis Stephen. *International Law in the Enlightenment.* Oceana, Dobbs Ferry, New York, 1975.

Scanlon, T.M. 'Rawls' Theory of Justice'. *Reading Rawls*. Ed. Norman Daniels. Basil Blackwell, Oxford, 1975.
—— 'Rights, Goals and Fairness'. *Public and Private Morality*. Ed. Stuart Hampshire. Cambridge University Press, Cambridge, 1978.
Schiffer, Walter. *The Legal Community of Mankind*. Columbia University Press, New York, 1954.
Schwarzenberger, Georg. *Economic World Order?* Manchester University Press, Manchester, 1970.
Shue, Henry. *Basic Rights: Subsistence, Affluence and US Foreign Policy*. Princeton University Press, Princeton, New Jersey, 1980.
Sidgwick, Henry. *Elements of Politics*. Macmillan, London, 1897.
Singer, Peter. 'The Right To Be Rich or Poor'. *The New York Review of Books*, March 6th, 1975.
—— 'Famine, Affluence and Morality'. *International Ethics*. Eds Charles R. Beitz, Marshall Cohen, Thomas Scanlon and A. John Simmons. Princeton University Press, Princeton, New Jersey, 1985.
Smith, Michael, Little, Richard and Shackleton, Michael. *Perspectives on World Politics*. Croom Helm, London, 1981.
Smith, W.H. 'Justice: National, International or Global?' *Moral Claims in World Affairs*. Ed. Ralph Pettman. Croom Helm, London, 1979.
Spero, Joan Edelman. *The Politics of International Economic Relations*. George Allen & Unwin, London, 2nd ed., 1982.
Stone, Julius. 'Approaches to the Notion of International Justice'. *The Future of the International Legal Order*. Eds Richard A. Falk and Cyril E. Black. Princeton University Press, Princeton, New Jersey, 1969.
Streeten, Paul. *First Things First*. World Bank/Oxford University Press, New York, 1981.
Thompson, Kenneth W. *Political Realism and the Crisis of World Politics*. Princeton University Press, Princeton, New Jersey, 1960.
—— *The Moral Issue in Statecraft*. Louisiana University Press, Baton Rouge, 1966.
Tucker, Robert C. 'Marx and Distributive Justice'. *Nomos VI: Justice*. Eds Carl J. Friedrich and John W. Chapman. Prentice-Hall, Atherton Press, New York, 1963.
Tucker, Robert W. 'Professor Morgenthau's Theory of Political Realism'. *American Political Science Review*, vol. 46, no. 1, March 1952, pp. 214–24.
—— *The Inequality of Nations*. Basic Books, New York, 1977.
Vattel, Emerich de. *The Law of Nations or the Principles of Natural Law*. Trans. Charles G. Fenwick. The Classics of International Law, no. 4, vol. 3. Carnegie Institution, Washington DC, 1916.
Vincent, R.J. *Nonintervention and International Order*. Princeton University Press, Princeton, New Jersey, 1974.
—— 'Western Conceptions of a Universal Moral Order'. *British Journal of International Studies*, vol. 4, no. 1, April 1978, pp. 20–46.
—— *Human Rights and International Relations*. Cambridge University Press, Cambridge, 1986.
Vitoria, Francisco de. *Political Writings*. Cambridge University Press, Cambridge, 1991.

Waltz, Kenneth. *Man, the State, and War*. Columbia University Press, New York, 1959.

—— *Theory of International Politics*. Addison-Wesley, Reading, Mass., 1979.

Walzer, Michael. *Just and Unjust Wars*. Penguin, Harmondsworth, 1980.

—— *Spheres of Justice*. Basil Blackwell, Oxford, 1983.

Weber, Max. *From Max Weber: Essays in Sociology*. Trans., ed. and intro. H.H. Gerth and C. Wright Mills. Routledge and Kegan Paul, London, 1948.

Weisskopf, Thomas E. 'Capitalism, Underdevelopment and the Future of the Poor Countries'. *Economics and World Order*. Ed. J.N. Bhagwati. Collier–Macmillan, London, 1972.

Wight, Martin. 'Western Values in International Relations'. *Diplomatic Investigations*. Eds Herbert Butterfield and Martin Wight. George Allen & Unwin, London, 1966.

—— 'Why Is There No International Theory?' *Diplomatic Investigations*. Eds Herbert Butterfield and Martin Wight. George Allen & Unwin, London, 1966.

—— *Systems of States*. Leicester University Press, Leicester, 1977.

—— *Power Politics*. Penguin, Harmondsworth, 2nd ed., 1986.

Williams, Bernard. 'The Idea of Equality'. *Philosophy, Politics and Society*. Eds Peter Laslett and W.G. Runciman. Basil Blackwell, Oxford, 1962.

Windsor, Philip. 'The Justification of the State'. *The Reason of States*. Ed. Michael Donelan. George Allen & Unwin, London, 1978.

Wolff, Christian. *Jus Gentium Methodo Scientifica Pertractatum*. Trans. Joseph H. Drake. Classics of International Law. Clarendon, Oxford, 1934.

Wood, Alan W. 'The Marxian Critique of Justice'. *Philosophy and Public Affairs*, vol. 1, no. 3, Spring 1972, pp. 244–82.

Wriggins, Howard. 'Political Outcomes of Foreign Assistance: Influence, Involvement or Intervention?' *Journal of International Affairs*, vol. 22, no. 2, 1968, pp. 220–5.

Index